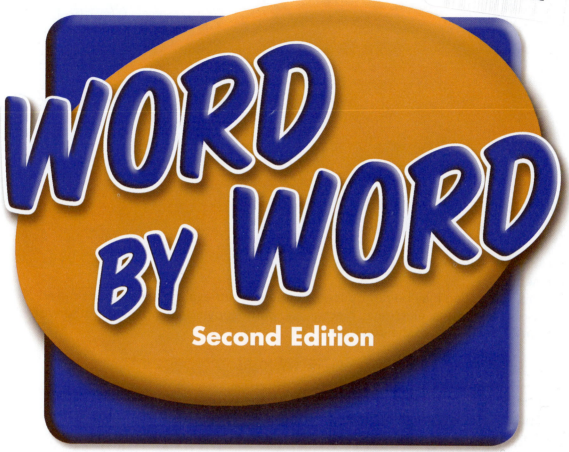

WORD BY WORD

Second Edition

Steven J. Molinsky • Bill Bliss

Contributing Authors
Elizabeth Handley
Lisa Varandani
with
Sharon Carlson
Jill Goodsell

PEARSON
Longman

Word by Word Beginning Lifeskills Workbook

Pearson Education, 10 Bank Street, White Plains, NY 10606

Editorial director: Pam Fishman
Vice president, director of design and production: Rhea Banker
Director of electronic production: Aliza Greenblatt
Director of manufacturing: Patrice Fraccio
Senior manufacturing manager: Edith Pullman
Marketing director—adult and higher education: Oliva Fernandez
Digital layout specialist: Lisa Ghiozzi
Text design: Wendy Wolf
Cover design: Tracey Munz Cataldo/Warren Fischbach
Realia creation: Warren Fischbach
Illustrations: Richard E. Hill

ISBN 0-13-193545-3
Longman on the Web
Longman.com offers online resources for teachers and students. Access our Companion Websites,
our online catalog, and our local offices around the world.

Visit us at longman.com.

Printed in the United States of America
4 5 6 7 8 9 10 – QWD – 09 08

CONTENTS

A SENDING A LETTER

What's on the envelope?

Richard M. Turner
76 Sunset Street, Apt. 4F
Miami, FL 33140

US

1. What's his first name?   *Richard* _____
2. What's his last name? _____
3. What's his middle initial? _____
4. What's his zip code? _____
5. What's his apartment number? _____
6. What's his address? _____

B ADDRESSING AN ENVELOPE

Interview a classmate. Then fill out the envelope below with the classmate's name and address. (Don't forget the city, state, and zip code.)

US

_____

_____

_____

C WHAT'S MISSING?

This envelope isn't complete.

Susan R.
    Maple Street, Apt.
Dallas,

US

Check the five things that are missing.

☑ apartment number   ☐ city   ☐ first name   ☐ last name
☐ state   ☐ street   ☐ street number   ☐ zip code

Fill out the form with the following personal information.

| (323) 524–9612 | Simpson | 3D | 90036 | 4/26/81 | fsimpson@ail.com |
| 26 Main Street | Los Angeles | T. | Fred | CA | 914–33–6237 |

REGISTRATION FORM

NAME | FIRST | | MIDDLE INITIAL

LAST

MAILING ADDRESS
STREET | APT. #

CITY | STATE | ZIP CODE

TELEPHONE NUMBER | E-MAIL ADDRESS
(323) 524-9612

DATE OF BIRTH | SEX | SOCIAL SECURITY NUMBER
☐ Male ☐ Female

Month/Day/Year

Now fill out the form with your personal information.

REGISTRATION FORM

NAME | FIRST | | MIDDLE INITIAL

LAST

MAILING ADDRESS
STREET | APT. #

CITY | STATE | ZIP CODE

TELEPHONE NUMBER | E-MAIL ADDRESS

DATE OF BIRTH | SEX | SOCIAL SECURITY NUMBER
☐ Male ☐ Female

Month/Day/Year

Fill in the missing words.

| DATE | E-MAIL | FIRST | LAST | PLACE | SOCIAL SECURITY |

LAST NAME: C O L L I N S | | | | **NAME:** E L L E N

NUMBER: 2 0 9 – 5 7 – 3 5 0 2

OF BIRTH: 1 2 – 1 5 – 7 1

OF BIRTH: N E W Y O R K N Y

ADDRESS: E C O L L I N S 9 @ A I L . C O M

A MALE OR FEMALE?

Look at page 2 of the Picture Dictionary. Which words are male? Which are female? Which are both?

Male	Female	Male and Female
husband	wife	parents

B FAMILY ALBUMS

Brian's Family Album

Brian Charlie Tina

Helen George

Walter Louise

brother	grandmother	siblings
father	grandparents	sister
grandfather	mother	

My name is Brian, and these are the people in my family. Charlie is my _____**brother**_____ [1], and Tina is my _____ [2]. I'm lucky because they're great _____ [3]. Helen is my _____ [4], and George is my _____ [5]. They're both wonderful parents. Walter and Louise are my _____ [6]. Walter is my _____ [7], and Louise is my _____ [8].

Jane's Family Album

Peter

Jane John

Caroline

children	daughter	son
wife	husband	

My name is Jane, and these are the people in my family. John is my _____ [9]. He always tells me he's happy I'm his _____ [10]. We have two wonderful _____ [11]—a _____ [12], Peter, and a _____ [13], Caroline. I love my family very much.

Who are the people in your family? Draw or bring to class pictures of the people in your family and label the pictures. Then tell a classmate about your pictures.

Reaching Out!

Your Family Album

__g__ 1. Your mother and father are your

_____ 2. Your sister and brother are your

_____ 3. Your daughter and son are your

_____ 4. Your children's children are your

_____ 5. Your parents' parents are your

_____ 6. Your mother's father is your

_____ 7. Your father's mother is your

_____ 8. Your son's daughter is your

a. children.

b. grandchildren.

c. granddaughter.

d. grandfather.

e. grandmother.

f. grandparents.

g. parents.

h. siblings.

D A FAMILY TREE

Who are they?

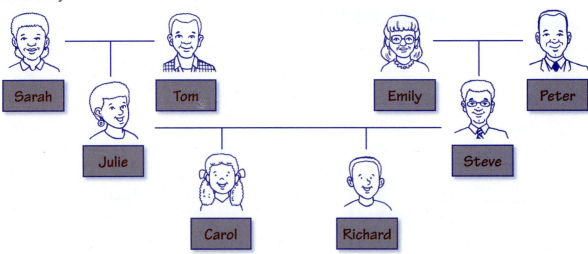

__n__ 1. Julie is Steve's

_____ 2. Julie is Carol and Richard's

_____ 3. Steve is Julie's

_____ 4. Steve is Carol and Richard's

_____ 5. Carol is Richard's

_____ 6. Carol is Julie and Steve's

_____ 7. Carol is Sarah and Tom's

_____ 8. Emily and Peter are Carol's

_____ 9. Peter is Carol's

_____ 10. Richard is Sarah and Tom's

_____ 11. Richard is Carol's

_____ 12. Julie and Steve are Richard's

_____ 13. Richard is Steve and Julie's

_____ 14. Carol and Richard are Julie and Steve's

a. brother.

b. children.

c. daughter.

d. father.

e. grandfather.

f. granddaughter.

g. grandparents.

h. grandson.

i. husband.

j. mother.

k. parents.

l. sister.

m. son.

n. wife.

Reaching Out!

Your Family Tree

Draw a family tree diagram of your family and label the people's names. Then write about some of the people in your family. Where do they live? What do they do? Show your family tree to a classmate and tell about it.

A WHO ARE THEY GOING TO INVITE?

Carla is getting married, and her relatives are planning a party for her—a wedding shower. The party is only for females. Who are they going to invite? Check all of Carla's female relatives.

- ☑ her aunt
- ☐ her brother
- ☐ her niece
- ☐ her uncle
- ☐ her mother
- ☐ her father
- ☐ her nephew
- ☐ her sister-in-law
- ☐ her new father-in-law
- ☐ her new mother-in-law
- ☐ her new brother-in-law

B ANN'S NEW FAMILY

Alice   Ronald

Karen   Tom   Dan   Janet   Peter   Ann

Jerry   Suzy

| daughter-in-law | sisters-in-law | cousins | niece | mother-in-law |
| brothers-in-law | father-in-law | uncle | aunt | nephew |

My name is Ann. I just married Peter today, and I like my new family very much. My __mother-in-law __¹, Alice, and my _____², Ronald, are very nice. I'm happy that I'm their _____³. I have two new _____⁴, Janet and Karen, and two new _____⁵, Dan and Tom. They're great! Peter always talks about his _____⁶, Jerry, and his _____⁷, Suzy. The two _____⁸ are good friends. I think Peter is their favorite _____⁹. And now I'm Jerry and Suzy's _____¹⁰. I'm very happy with my new family.

C WHO ARE THEY?

1. I'd like to introduce you to my _____aunt_____. She's my mother's sister.
2. This is my _____. He's my sister's son.
3. I'd like you to meet my _____. He's my daughter's husband.
4. This is my _____. She's my brother's daughter.
5. I'd like to introduce you to my _____. He's my mother's brother.
6. I'd like you to meet my _____. He's my aunt and uncle's son.

Bring in pictures of some of your relatives and write about them. Where do they live? What do they do? Who is your favorite relative? Share your pictures and descriptions with your classmates.

Reaching Out!

Your Relatives

5

A Wonderful Job and a Wonderful Family

Emma Romero has a very important job. Emma works at the Mission Adult School. She works in the office there. Every day people come to the school to register for English classes. These people come from many different countries, and they speak many different languages.

To register for classes, new students fill out a registration form. The form asks for the person's first name, middle initial, and surname. The form also asks for the person's address. This includes the person's street number, street name, city, state, and zip code. In addition, the form asks for the person's area code and telephone number and also for the person's social security number. The form also asks for the person's date of birth and place of birth. The form is very difficult for many people, but Emma can help them because she speaks four languages! She speaks English and Spanish, and she also knows some Chinese and Arabic.

Emma has a large family. She and her husband, Manuel, have three children. They have two sons, David and Luis, and they have one daughter, Paula. Emma's mother and father also live with them in their home. Emma's sister and brother-in-law and their children live in a different home on the same street. David, Luis, and Paula are happy because they can see their aunt, uncle, and cousins every day. Emma is happy because her parents take care of the children every day when she and her husband go to work.

Emma always says, "I'm very lucky. I have a wonderful job, and I have a wonderful family!"

1. New students at the Mission Adult School fill out _____.
   a. an English class
   b. a job
   c. a large family
   d. a registration form

2. An address includes _____.
   a. an area code
   b. a telephone number
   c. a street number
   d. a social security number

3. 238–44–8271 is _____.
   a. an apartment number
   b. a social security number
   c. a date of birth
   d. a street number

4. The word *surname* means _____.
   a. first name
   b. middle name
   c. middle initial
   d. last name

5. Emma is Manuel's _____.
   a. wife
   b. husband
   c. daughter
   d. son

6. The Romeros have _____ children.
   a. two
   b. three
   c. four
   d. five

7. According to the story, David is Paula's _____.
   a. cousin
   b. sister
   c. brother
   d. son

8. The _____ take care of the children while the parents are working.
   a. aunt and uncle
   b. parents
   c. grandparents
   d. cousins

A WHERE ARE THEY?

Look at the classroom on page 4 of the Picture Dictionary. Where is everything? Which objects are on the wall? Which are on the floor? Which are on the table? Which are on the bookcase? Write the words where they belong.

bookcase	chalkboard	desks	map	overhead projector
screen	wastebasket	bulletin board	computer	globe
monitor	P.A. system	teacher's desk	whiteboard	chairs
clock	keyboard	mouse	pencil sharpener	tables

On the Wall	On the Floor	On the Table	On the Bookcase
bulletin board	bookcase		

B THE SUPPLY CLOSET

What's in the supply closet? Look in the supply closet and check what's there.

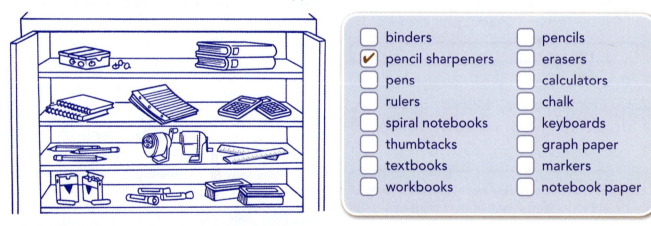

- [ ] binders
- [✓] pencil sharpeners
- [ ] pens
- [ ] rulers
- [ ] spiral notebooks
- [ ] thumbtacks
- [ ] textbooks
- [ ] workbooks
- [ ] pencils
- [ ] erasers
- [ ] calculators
- [ ] chalk
- [ ] keyboards
- [ ] graph paper
- [ ] markers
- [ ] notebook paper

C WHICH IS DIFFERENT?

1. a. pen   (b.) mouse   c. chalk   d. marker
2. a. student   b. teacher   c. teacher's aide   d. teacher's desk
3. a. keyboard   b. P.A. system   c. monitor   d. printer
4. a. wastebasket   b. bulletin board   c. screen   d. chalkboard
5. a. binder   b. spiral notebook c. printer   d. workbook
6. a. desk   b. bookcase   c. bulletin board   d. table

Write about your classroom. What's on the wall? What's on the floor? What other things are in your classroom? Where are they? Compare your classroom description with a classmate's.

Reaching Out!

Your Classroom

COMPLETE THE TEST

Look at the test below. The instructions for each section are missing. Fill in the blanks with the instructions in the box. Then take the test.

> Circle the correct answer.
> Cross out the words.
> Match the words.
>
> Put the actions in order.
> Put the words in order.
>
> Underline the correct answer.
> Unscramble the words.

CLASSROOM ACTION TEST

A) Match the words.

1. Open ⟍   your name.
2. Sign   your hand.
3. Turn off ⟋   your book.
4. Help   the lights.
5. Raise   each other.

B) _____

6. Erase (your seat   the class   (the board)).
7. (Stand   Say   Share) your name.
8. (Take   Put   Do) notes.
9. Look in (page 10   the word   the dictionary).
10. (Collect   Lower   Check) your answers.

C) _____

11. Close your (lights   <u>book</u>   question).
12. Go over the (group   answers   partner).
13. Do your (mistakes   shades   homework).
14. Pronounce the (word   class   tests).

D) _____

15. Spell (your name   the word   ~~your seat~~).
16. Work (your dictionary   alone   as a class).
17. (Turn on   Bring in   Hand in) your homework.
18. Listen to the (question   answer   blanks).
19. (Copy   Read   Ask) the word.

E) _____

20. sheet. / the / answer / Mark
   <u>Mark the answer sheet.</u>
21. work. / your / Do / own
   _____
22. out / paper. / Take / of / piece / a
   _____
23. groups. / Break / into / up / small
   _____
24. separate / paper. / sheet / of / on / Write / a /
   _____

F) _____

25. (___partner___) Work with a **nprtear**.
26. (_____) Correct your **kitesams**.
27. (_____) **Raptee** your name.
28. (_____) **Dsssuic** the question.
29. (_____) Put **wyaa** your book.

G) _____

____ Go to the board.
____ Take your seat.
__1__ Stand up.
____ Write on the board.

Reaching Out!
Correcting Your Test

Check your answers to this test with a classmate. Work together. Help each other. Correct your mistakes.

Reaching Out!
Class Survey

Take a class survey. How do students in your class like to work? Alone? With a partner? In small groups? As a class?

A A PICTURE

behind	between	in front of
next to	to the left of	to the right of

1. Al is _____**next to**_____ Ron.

2. Ron is _____ Al and Tim.

3. Ann is _____ Ron.

4. Tim is _____ Pam.

5. Pam is _____ Ann.

6. Sue is _____ Ann.

Draw a picture of your friends, your family, or your class. Label the people. Where is everyone in the picture? Tell a classmate about your picture.

Reaching Out!

Your Picture

B LABEL THE BOXES

Read about the supply closet and label the boxes.

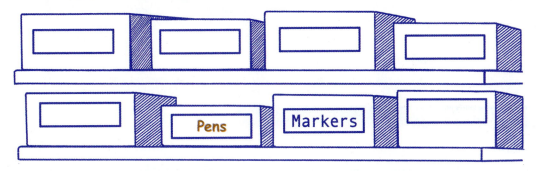

The pens are to the left of the markers. The workbooks are above the markers. The erasers are to the right of the workbooks. The workbooks are between the notebooks and the erasers. The pencils are next to the markers. The rulers are below the calculators.

C WHERE IS IT?

Look at the classroom on page 4 of the Picture Dictionary. Where is everything?

_e_ **1.** The whiteboard is	**a.** in front of the chalkboard.
____ **2.** The clock is	**b.** under the computer.
____ **3.** The books are	**c.** above the chalkboard.
____ **4.** The pencil sharpener is	**d.** in the bookcase.
____ **5.** The teacher is	**e.** below the loudspeaker.
____ **6.** The table is	**f.** on the bookcase.

Write about your classroom. Where is everything? Compare your description with a classmate's.

Reaching Out!

Your Classroom

A CHECKLIST: What Do You Do Every Day?

Check the things you do every day.

- ☐ brush my hair
- ☐ brush my teeth
- ☐ comb my hair
- ☐ cook dinner
- ☐ eat breakfast

- ☐ eat dinner
- ☐ get dressed
- ☐ get undressed
- ☐ get up
- ☐ go to bed

- ☐ have lunch
- ☐ make breakfast
- ☐ make lunch
- ☐ make the bed
- ☐ put on makeup

- ☐ shave
- ☐ sleep
- ☐ take a bath
- ☐ take a shower
- ☐ wash my face

B WHEN DO YOU DO IT?

Look at your checklist. When do you do each activity? Write each activity where it belongs.

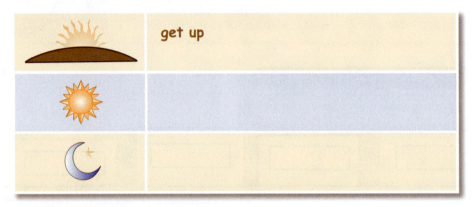

get up

C WHICH COMES FIRST?

1. a. I eat dinner.   (b.) I eat breakfast.
2. a. I get up.   b. I take a shower.
3. a. I have lunch.   b. I make lunch.

4. a. I take a bath.   b. I get undressed.
5. a. I put on makeup.   b. I wash my face.
6. a. I go to bed.   b. I sleep.

D FILL OUT THE QUESTIONNAIRE

YOUR EATING HABITS

1. Do you eat breakfast every day?
   ☐ Yes. I eat a big breakfast.   ☐ Yes. I eat a small breakfast.   ☐ No. I don't eat breakfast.

2. Do you eat lunch every day?
   ☐ Yes. I eat a big lunch.   ☐ Yes. I eat a small lunch.   ☐ No. I don't eat lunch.

3. Do you eat dinner every day?
   ☐ Yes. I eat a big dinner.   ☐ Yes. I eat a small dinner.   ☐ No. I don't eat dinner.

4. When do you eat dinner?
   ☐ I eat before 7:00.   ☐ I eat between 7:00 and 8:00.   ☐ I eat after 8:00.

Reaching Out!

Eating Habits

Interview students and teachers in your school. Ask about their eating habits. Do people in different countries have different eating habits? Discuss as a class.

A COMPLETE THE NOTES

Mrs. Smith wrote these notes to her children. Fill in the missing words.

clean	come	go	do	feed	iron	Study	take	walk	wash

Susie,

The car is in the repair shop. You need to
_____take_____ ¹ the bus to school. And please
_____ ² home from school on time!
You need to _____ ³ the dishes and
_____ ⁴ the laundry.

Thanks.

Charlie,

After school, please _____ ⁵ to the
store. We need food for dinner. Also, don't
forget to _____ ⁶ the dog and
_____ ⁷ the cat. And remember, you
have a test tomorrow. _____ ⁸ !

Mom

Susie and Charlie,

Thanks for your help. When I get home
from work, I'm going to _____ ⁹ the
house and _____ ¹⁰ .

B YOUR DAY

What are you going to do tomorrow? Check
everything you're going to do.

- [ ] clean the apartment
- [ ] do the laundry
- [ ] feed the baby
- [ ] feed the cat
- [ ] feed the dog
- [ ] go to school
- [ ] go to work
- [ ] go to the store
- [ ] iron
- [ ] study
- [ ] walk the dog
- [ ] wash the dishes

C PLAN YOUR DAY

When are you going to do each activity? Put
the activities you're going to do in order.

MY DAY

1. _____
2. _____
3. _____
4. _____
5. _____
6. _____
7. _____
8. _____

Take a class survey. What are the students in your class going to do tomorrow?
How many students are going to clean? How many students are going to do
the laundry? Ask about all the chores and report back.

Reaching Out!

Class Survey

11

A WHEN DO YOU DO THESE ACTIVITIES?

Look at the activities on page 11 of the Picture Dictionary. What do you like to do on a rainy day? What do you like to do on a sunny day? What do you like to do on both types of days? Write the activities on the lines where they belong.

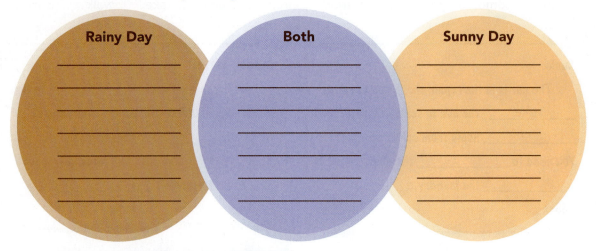

Rainy Day

_____
_____
_____
_____
_____
_____

Both

_____
_____
_____
_____
_____
_____

Sunny Day

_____
_____
_____
_____
_____
_____

B PERSONAL ADS

The following people are looking for friends. Read their personal ads.

A

I like to swim and play basketball. I exercise every day.

B

I like to read and listen to music. I play the guitar and the piano.

C

I like to watch television and play cards.

D

I like computers. I use the computer every day.

Who are you going to choose for a friend: A, B, C, or D? Why?

_____.
_____.

C YOUR PERSONAL AD

Write your own personal ad. Tell about yourself. What do you like to do?

Reaching Out!

A Vacation Day

Tomorrow is a vacation day. There isn't any school. It's a day to relax. Interview a classmate. What is your classmate going to do tomorrow?

MARIO'S FREE TIME

Look at all the things in Mario's room. What does Mario do in his free time?

1. _____He watches TV._____   4. _____   7. _____
2. _____   5. _____   8. _____
3. _____   6. _____   9. _____

E **FILL OUT THE QUESTIONNAIRE**

Indicate your answers with a check mark.

	Y O U R L E I S U R E A C T I V I T I E S				
	0 = I don't like to. 1 = I like to a little. 2 = I like to. 3 = I like to very much.				
		0	1	2	3
1.	Do you like to play cards?	[ ]	[ ]	[ ]	[ ]
2.	Do you like to watch TV?	[ ]	[ ]	[ ]	[ ]
3.	Do you like to listen to music?	[ ]	[ ]	[ ]	[ ]
4.	Do you like to read?	[ ]	[ ]	[ ]	[ ]
5.	Do you like to swim?	[ ]	[ ]	[ ]	[ ]
6.	Do you like to exercise?	[ ]	[ ]	[ ]	[ ]
7.	Do you like to play basketball?	[ ]	[ ]	[ ]	[ ]
8.	Do you like to write letters?	[ ]	[ ]	[ ]	[ ]
9.	Do you like to use a computer?	[ ]	[ ]	[ ]	[ ]
10.	Do you like to plant flowers?	[ ]	[ ]	[ ]	[ ]

Take a class survey. What do the students in your class like to do? What *don't* they like to do? Talk with the class about the results of the survey.

Reaching Out!

Class Survey

A WHAT'S THE ANSWER?

_c_ 1. Hello.
____ 2. May I please speak to Julie?
____ 3. I'd like to introduce my brother, Paul.
____ 4. What's new?
____ 5. Thanks.
____ 6. How are you doing?
____ 7. Bye.

a. Nice to meet you.
b. See you later.
c. Hi.
d. Fine, thanks.
e. Yes. Hold on a moment.
f. You're welcome.
g. Not much.

B A TELEPHONE CALL

See you soon	Fine	Can you please say that again	What's new
Hold on a moment	Hi	May I ask you a question	
You're welcome	Thanks	May I please speak to Rose	

A. Hello. This is Mary.
   _____**May I please speak to Rose**_____ [1]?
B. Yes. _____ [2].
C. _____[3], Mary. _____ [4]?
A. Not too much. How are you?
C. _____[5].
A. _____ [6]?
C. Sure. What is it?
A. What's Ellen's telephone number? I need to speak to her.

C. 661–567–2491.
A. _____ [7]?
C. Yes. 661–567–2491.
A. _____[8].
C. _____[9].
A. Bye.
C. _____[10].

C CORRECT THE MISTAKES!

1. Nice meet you.   _____**Nice to meet you.**_____
2. Hi. I'm name is Susan.   _____
3. Sorry. I no understand.   _____
4. May I speak a question?   _____
5. What's now with you?   _____
6. Can please you repeat that?   _____
7. Robert not here right now.   _____
8. May you please say that again?   _____
9. I like to introduce my sister.   _____
10. Hi. How are you going?   _____

Reaching Out!

Your Everyday Conversation

Make a list of the everyday conversation expressions on pages 12 and 13 of the Picture Dictionary. Check how many times you use each expression in one day. Then compare with a classmate.

A TODAY'S WEATHER

Look at the chart and complete the information about today's weather.

City	Weather	Temp.
Chicago		30°F
Denver		50°F
Houston		70°F
Los Angeles		90°F
Miami		94°F
New York		52°F

__d__ 1. It's sunny   a. in Chicago.

____ 2. It's snowing   b. in Miami.

____ 3. It's cloudy   c. in Houston.

____ 4. It's windy   d. in Los Angeles.

____ 5. It's raining   e. in Denver.

____ 6. It's drizzling   f. in New York.

| cool | cold | hot | warm |

7. It's _____ in Chicago.

8. It's _____ in Los Angeles and Miami.

9. It's _____ in Denver and New York.

10. It's _____ in Houston.

B HOW DO YOU LIKE THE WEATHER?

What do you think of the weather in the cities below? Check your answers in the chart and then compare your answers with a classmate's.

City	W	Hi/Lo
Athens	s	85/75
London	f	72/60
Miami	h	92/80
Moscow	t	53/42
Sydney	w	74/63
Toronto	sn	30/19

Very Bad	Bad	Okay	Good	Very Good
❑	❑	❑	❑	❑
❑	❑	❑	❑	❑
❑	❑	❑	❑	❑
❑	❑	❑	❑	❑
❑	❑	❑	❑	❑
❑	❑	❑	❑	❑

f=foggy, h=hazy, s=sunny, sn=snow, t=thunderstorms, w=windy

C WHICH IS DIFFERENT?

1. a. Fahrenheit   b. thermometer   c. Celsius   d. Centigrade

2. a. sleeting   b. snowing   c. lightning   d. hailing

3. a. muggy   b. hazy   c. foggy   d. smoggy

4. a. thunderstorm   b. raining   c. lightning   d. heat wave

5. a. cool   b. drizzling   c. freezing   d. warm

6. a. humid   b. muggy   c. windy   d. hot

Reaching Out!

What's today's weather in five different cities? Look in the newspaper or watch a weather report on TV. Then compare with a classmate.

Today's Weather

A Teacher and Her Students

Every morning, Linda gets up, takes a shower, brushes her teeth, and gets dressed. Sometimes she makes breakfast, and sometimes her husband, Jim, makes breakfast. After they eat breakfast, Linda walks the dog, and Jim feeds the cat. Then Linda and Jim drive to work. Linda works in a school. Jim works in a store. The school is next to the store, so they drive to work together.

Every morning, Juan gets up, takes a shower, brushes his teeth, and gets dressed. He makes breakfast while his wife, Diana, feeds the baby. After they have breakfast, Diana's parents come to their apartment. They watch the baby while Juan and Diana go to school. When it's sunny, Juan and Diana walk to school. When it's raining, they take the bus. They get to school, walk into their classroom, sit down at their desks, and take out their pens, paper, and textbooks.

When Linda walks into her classroom every morning, she always says, "Good morning, class!"

Juan and Diana and the other students always answer, "Good morning, Linda! How are you today?"

You see, Linda works at the Central Adult Education School. She's an English teacher there. Juan and Diana are her students. They study English at the school every morning.

All the students say that Linda is an excellent teacher. When they have questions, she always answers them. When they make mistakes in their homework, she always corrects them. Linda's classes are always interesting. Sometimes the students work with a partner or in small groups, sometimes they work as a class, and sometimes they work at computers.

Linda likes her job at the Central Adult Education School. She's very glad she works there, and her students are glad, too.

1. Linda works in _____.
   a. a store
   b. a school
   c. an apartment
   d. a house

2. Linda is Jim's _____.
   a. student
   b. teacher
   c. wife
   d. husband

3. It's raining this morning. Juan and Diana are _____.
   a. taking the bus to school
   b. driving to school
   c. walking to school
   d. not going to school

4. When her students have questions, Linda always _____.
   a. corrects them
   b. says, "Good morning, class!"
   c. answers them
   d. works with a partner

5. From the story, you know that _____.
   a. Juan and Diana have a dog
   b. Juan and Diana have a cat
   c. Juan and Diana are parents
   d. Juan and Diana don't have a car

6. In the last paragraph of the story, the word *job* means _____.
   a. school
   b. students
   c. family
   d. work

A NUMBERS AND NUMBER WORDS

Fill in the missing numbers.

Cardinal Numbers	
12	**twelve**
	eighty
19	
27	
	thirty-eight
290	

Ordinal Numbers	
5th	**fifth**
10th	
	fortieth
30th	
	seventy-first
11th	

B NUMBERS IN MY LIFE

These are important numbers for Carlos Montero. Look at his identification card and complete the sentences below. Write the numbers in words.

IDENTIFICATION CARD

Name: Carlos Montero

Social Security Number: 749-26-1895

Telephone Number: 305-478-2931

Address: 17 Maple Ave., Apt. 14

Miami, FL

Zip Code: 33156

1. His apartment number is ____**fourteen**____.
2. His street number is _____.
3. His zip code is _____ _____ _____ _____ _____.
4. His telephone number is _____ _____ _____-_____

_____ _____-_____ _____ _____.

5. His social security number is _____ _____ _____-

_____ _____-_____ _____ _____ _____.

C WHICH FLOOR?

Look at the directory of the Central Medical Building and complete the sentences.

Central Medical Building	
	Floor
Alan Anderson, MD	9
Carol Chang, MD	1
Olivia Fernandez, MD	3
Robert Harris, MD	14
Charles Lee, MD	16
Nancy O'Brian, MD	2
Paula Peterson, MD	4

1. Dr. Anderson is on the _____**ninth**_____ floor.
2. Dr. Chang is on the _____ floor.
3. Dr. Fernandez is on the _____ floor.
4. Dr. Harris is on the _____ floor.
5. Dr. Lee is on the _____ floor.
6. Dr. O'Brian is on the _____ floor.
7. Dr. Peterson is on the _____ floor.

Reaching Out!

How many students are there in your English class? How many are male? How many are female? In your classroom, who sits in the first row? the second row? the third row? Where do the students come from? How many are from each different country?

My Class

TIME

A WHAT'S THE TIME?

Complete the clocks.

1. nine o'clock   2. six fifteen   3. one twenty   4. eleven thirty

   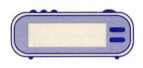

5. two forty-five   6. three thirty   7. four fifty   8. ten to nine

B WHICH TIME IS CORRECT?

Choose the correct time.

1. a. It's three thirty.
   b. It's three thirteen.

2. a. It's a quarter to two.
   b. It's two forty-five.

3. a. It's ten to ten.
   b. It's ten after ten.

4. a. It's a quarter to seven.
   b. It's a quarter after six.

5. a. It's midnight.
   b. It's noon.

6. a. It's four oh five.
   b. It's five oh four.

7. a. It's five fifty.
   b. It's a quarter after five.

8. a. It's 3 A.M.
   b. It's 3 P.M.

C MATCH THE TIMES

Look at the train schedule and match the times.

City	Train 1	Train 2
Easton	1:10	2:10
Weston	1:15	2:15
Greenville	1:30	2:30
Centerville	1:40	2:40
Lakewood	1:45	2:45
Hampton	1:55	2:55
Kingston	2:05	3:05

1. Train 1 leaves Easton at   half past two.
2. Train 2 leaves Weston at   five to two.
3. Train 2 leaves Greenville at   a quarter to three.
4. Train 1 leaves Centerville at   one ten.
5. Train 2 leaves Lakewood at   one forty.
6. Train 1 leaves Hampton at   two fifteen.
7. Train 1 leaves Kingston at   two oh five.

Reaching Out!

Every Day

Write about times in your everyday life. For example: I get up at six o'clock. I go to school/work at . . . . Then interview a classmate and write about your classmate's daily schedule.

A WHAT'S THE AMOUNT?

| $6.30 | $25.42 | $2.50 | $10.71 | $1.76 | $2.05 |

1. ___$2.50___

2. _____

3. _____

4. _____

5. _____

6. _____

B HOW MUCH?

1. 2 nickels   4 quarters $10.00
2. $1.00   5 pennies   a dime
3. 5 twenty-dollar bills   10¢ $ .25
4. a quarter $100   one dollar
5. $ .05   2 five-dollar bills   5¢
6. a ten-dollar bill   2 dimes and a nickel   a hundred-dollar bill

C BACK-TO-SCHOOL SALE

Write the prices on the coupons.

1. A pencil costs ten cents.
2. A spiral notebook costs a dollar seventy-five.
3. A binder costs two sixty-seven.
4. A calculator costs fifteen dollars.
5. Notebook paper costs eighty-nine cents.
6. A ruler costs fifty-five cents.
7. A printer costs one hundred twenty-five dollars.
8. A pencil sharpener costs four thirty-three.
9. A monitor costs seven hundred dollars.

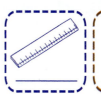

10¢

What are your ten favorite things? How much did they cost? Write the prices. Tell a classmate what the objects are. Have your classmate guess how much you paid for them.

Reaching Out!

How Much?

A WHICH DAY?

Look at the calendar on page 18 of the Picture Dictionary and complete the sentences below.

1/31/12	Friday	Monday	Wednesday	Thursday	weekend

1. January 20, 2012 is on a _____Friday_____.
2. January 2, 2012 is on a _____.
3. January 21 and 22 is a _____.

4. The last day of the month is _____.
5. 1/25/2012 is on a _____.
6. January 26, 2012 is on a _____.

B MONTHS OF THE YEAR

Complete the chart.

Month	Abbreviation	Number
October	OCT	10
		2
	AUG	
December		
May		
	JUL	
		4
	MAR	
	SEP	
January		

C DATES

Complete the chart.

Month/Day/Year	Month/Day/Year
August 25, 2007	8/25/07
	2/29/04
June 11, 1994	
	3/1/00
April 21, 2009	
February 3, 2001	
	7/7/77
	1/5/05
May 31, 2006	
October 8, 2008	

D TODAY

Write about today.

1. The year is _____.
2. The month is _____.

3. The day of the week is _____.
4. Today's date is _____.

E U.S. HOLIDAYS

Look at a calendar for this year. Write the date of the holidays.

Example: My birthday is on _____May 2_____. This year it's on a _____Wednesday_____.

1. Independence Day is on _____. This year it's on a _____.
2. New Year's Day is on _____. This year it's on a _____.
3. Halloween is on _____. This year it's on a _____.
4. Veterans Day is on _____. This year it's on a _____.

Reaching Out!
Holidays

What are some holidays in your country? What are the dates? Compare with a classmate. Then tell the class about holidays in your countries.

A TIME LINE

Complete the time line using time expressions.

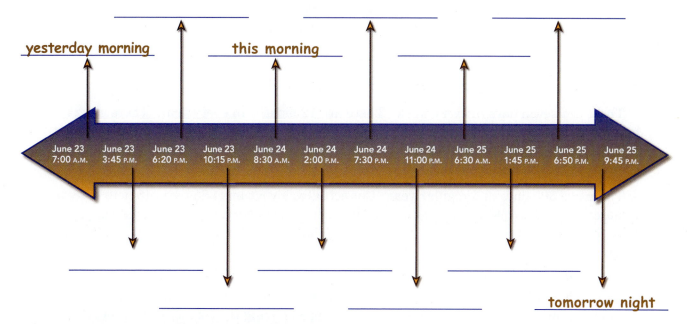

yesterday morning   this morning

tomorrow night

B SEASONS

Match the months and seasons.

February   Summer   May

October   Spring   January

July   Winter   November

April   Fall   August

C MARIA'S CALENDAR

Look at Maria's calendar. Finish the sentences about her schedule.

Sunday	Monday	Tuesday	Wednesday	Thursday	Friday	Saturday
1	2	3	4	5	6	7
walk the dog	walk the dog	walk the dog	walk the dog	walk the dog	walk the dog	walk the dog
do the laundry	go to school	go to work	go to school	go to school	go to work	clean the house
wash the dishes	go to the store	wash the dishes	iron	wash the dishes	go to the store	iron

1. She goes to work _____twice a week_____.
2. She washes the dishes _____.
3. She cleans the house _____.
4. She walks the dog _____.

5. She goes to the store _____.
6. She goes to school _____.
7. She does the laundry _____.
8. She irons _____.

What activities do you do every week? How many times a week do you do them? Interview a classmate about what he or she does every week.

Reaching Out!

Every Week

21

Leap Year

Thirty days has September,
April, June, and November.
All the rest have thirty-one,
Except February,
And it has twenty-eight days time.
But in leap years, February has twenty-nine.

There are seven days in every week. There are 12 months in every year. There are 24 hours in every day. But there isn't the same number of days in every month. This popular children's rhyme helps us answer the question, "How many days are there in each month of the year?" It also teaches us about leap years.

There are 365 days in a regular year. But actually, a year has 365 days, 15 hours, 48 minutes, and 46 seconds. What do we do with these extra hours, minutes, and seconds? Every four years, we add an extra day to the year, and we call it a leap year. The extra day is always at the end of February.

Leap years are very important. They keep the calendar correct. Each day can have the same number of hours. Each week can have the same number of days. Each year can have the same number of months. Each season can happen during the correct months of the year. This is all possible thanks to an extra day in February during each leap year.

1. The number of hours in a day is _____.
   a. 7
   b. 12
   c. 24
   d. 30

2. There are 31 days in _____.
   a. June
   b. July
   c. April
   d. February

3. A leap year has _____.
   a. 364 days
   b. 365 days
   c. 366 days
   d. 369 days

4. The extra day in a leap year is _____.
   a. December 31st
   b. March 1st
   c. February 28th
   d. February 29th

5. According to the children's rhyme, four months of the year have _____.
   a. 30 days
   b. 31 days
   c. 32 days
   d. 24 hours

6. In the third line of the children's rhyme, *all the rest* refers to _____.
   a. the other days
   b. the other months
   c. the other weeks
   d. the other years

7. According to the story, a leap year happens _____.
   a. every year
   b. every February
   c. every four months
   d. every four years

8. The year 2008 is a leap year. Therefore, the leap year after that will be _____.
   a. 2009
   b. 2010
   c. 2012
   d. 2014

A JOE'S TAXI

Joe drives a taxi. Look at the pictures and check where he went today.

9:00 A.M.

10:15 A.M.

11:00 A.M.

12:45 P.M.

2:10 P.M.

3:30 P.M.

```
___ duplex
___ house
___ farm
___ dormitory
___ shelter
___ ranch
 ✓  townhouse
___ mobile home
___ houseboat
___ nursing home
___ condo
___ apartment building
```

B WHERE DO THEY LIVE?

Complete the sentences.

__d__ 1. The Carter family lives in   a. suburbs.

____ 2. The Browns live in the   b. duplex.

____ 3. Bill and Tammy live in a   c. farm.

____ 4. Dave and Greg live in an   d. a shelter.

____ 5. Julie lives on a   e. apartment building.

C HOUSING IN COMMUNITIES

The graph below shows the number of houses and condominiums in four different communities. Look at the graph and complete the chart.

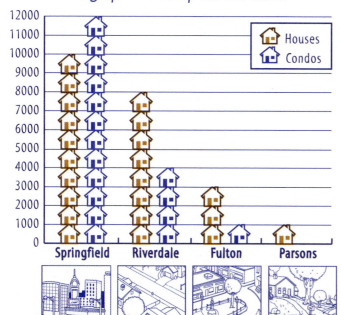

Name of Community	Type of Community	Number of Houses	Number of Condominiums
Fulton	town	3,000	
Parsons			
Riverdale			
Springfield			

Where do your classmates live? Interview them about their types of housing and communities. Then write sentences about them.

Reaching Out!

My House

23

A TRUE OR NOT TRUE?

Look at the living room on page 21 of the Picture Dictionary. Check True or Not True.

	True	Not True
1. The fireplace screen is behind the fireplace.	____	✔
2. The photograph is above the bookcase.	✔	____
3. The painting is below the mantel.	____	____
4. The floor lamp is next to the armchair.	____	____
5. The coffee table is to the left of the rug.	____	____
6. The stereo system is in the wall unit.	____	____
7. The window is below the loveseat.	____	____
8. The TV is between the DVD player and the VCR.	____	____
9. The throw pillow is under the couch.	____	____

B WHICH IS DIFFERENT?

1. a. sofa   b. magazine holder   c. loveseat   d. armchair
2. a. wall   b. ceiling   c. floor   d. plant
3. a. end table   b. bookcase   c. pillow   d. coffee table
4. a. floor lamp b. window   c. lamp   d. wall unit
5. a. picture   b. DVD player   c. stereo system   d. VCR

C GOING SHOPPING!

Read the store directory. Then check the floor where you can find each of the following items.

House & Home Store

Floor	
1	Couches Loveseats Armchairs
2	Lamps Floor Lamps Plants
3	Wall Units Bookcases End Tables
4	Televisions DVD Players Stereo Systems

	1st Floor	2nd Floor	3rd Floor	4th Floor
1.	____	____	✔	____
2.	____	____	____	____
3.	____	____	____	____
4.	____	____	____	____
5.	____	____	____	____

Reaching Out!

Things to Buy

Make a list of five living room items you want to buy. Go to a furniture or department store, look at the directory to see where these items are, find out how much they cost, and then report back to the class.

A IN THE DINING ROOM

Look at the dining room on page 22 of the Picture Dictionary. Circle the correct answer in each sentence.

1. The candle is in the ((candlestick)   vase).
2. The knife is to the left of the (spoon   fork).
3. The coffee pot is on the (table   tray).
4. The (serving bowl   salad bowl) is on the table.
5. The (saucer   plate) is under the cup.
6. The (china   teapot) is in the china cabinet.
7. The tablecloth is on the (table   buffet).
8. The (mug   cup) is between the bowl and the glass.

B THE YARD SALE

You're at the Johnsons' yard sale. Check the items on your list that the Johnsons are selling today.

To Buy 🛒

✓ teapot
  sugar bowl
  butter dish
  chandelier
  pitcher
  buffet
  dining room chairs
  salt shaker
  pepper shaker
  napkins

C HOW MUCH IS IT?

Look at the prices in the scene above and complete the chart.

glass	$1
	$7
	$1.50
china cabinet	
	50¢
	$5
	$40
sugar bowl	

D FROM MOST TO LEAST

Write the items in Exercise C in order of price.

MOST MONEY

buffet
_____
_____
_____
_____
_____
_____
_____
_____

LEAST MONEY

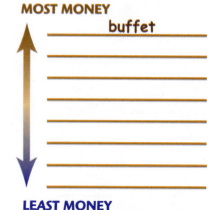

You're going to have a yard sale! Make a list of all the dining room items you want to sell and the price for each. Then ask a classmate if your prices are too high or too low.

Reaching Out!

Yard Sale

A YOUR BED

Do you have these items on your bed? Check Yes or No.

Item	Yes	No
bedspread		
dust ruffle		
box spring		
electric blanket		
flat sheet		
blanket		
fitted sheet		
bed frame		
comforter		
mattress		

B WHERE ARE THEY?

Look at the bedroom on page 23 of the Picture Dictionary and check where you see the items.

	On the Nightstand	On the Dresser	On the Bed	On the Window
blinds				✔
pillow				
alarm clock				
jewelry box				
curtains				
bed frame				
headboard				
lamp				

C TWO FURNISHED APARTMENTS

There are two furnished apartments for rent in your area. Compare the bedrooms in these apartments, and write the items you see in the correct places below.

Bedroom 1

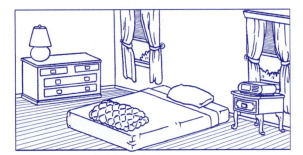

Bedroom 2

Bedroom 1

curtains
_____
_____
_____
_____

Bedrooms 1 & 2

_____
_____
_____
_____

Bedroom 2

_____
_____
_____
_____

Reaching Out!

My Bedroom

On a separate sheet of paper, draw a picture of your bedroom and write sentences to describe it. Compare with a classmate.

A WHERE IN THE KITCHEN?

Look at the kitchen on page 24 of the Picture Dictionary and find the following items. Then write them in the correct column.

cabinet	cookbook	dish rack	dishwasher detergent	garbage pail	microwave
potholder	spice rack	canister	cutting board	dishwasher	
food processor	kitchen chair	placemat	refrigerator	toaster oven	

Floor	Counter	Wall	Kitchen Table
kitchen chair			

B BARGAIN HUNTING

Compare the following advertisements for The Kitchen Store and Home-Mart, and circle the lower price for each item. Then put these "bargain items" on your shopping list.

C IN MY KITCHEN

What do you have in your kitchen? Check the items you have on the following list.

- ☐ freezer
- ☐ stove
- ☐ kitchen sink
- ☐ dishwasher
- ☐ garbage disposal
- ☐ burners
- ☐ paper towel holder
- ☐ oven
- ☐ trash compactor
- ☐ faucet
- ☐ refrigerator
- ☐ toaster oven

Make a list of ten kitchen items you use most often. Then compare lists with a classmate.

Reaching Out!

Kitchen Items

A WHICH IS DIFFERENT?

1. a. crib   b. cradle   c. night light   d. changing table
2. a. stuffed animal b. doll   c. teddy bear   d. chest of drawers
3. a. baby backpack   b. changing pad   c. baby carriage   d. stroller
4. a. high chair   b. swing   c. crib bumper   d. booster seat
5. a. stretch suit   b. car seat   c. baby carrier   d. baby seat

B THE BABY REGISTRY

Pamela Chen is going to have a baby. She's at The Baby Store today, and she's looking at her "baby registry"—the list of baby items her friends and family can buy for her at the store. Look at the baby registry and decide if each sentence is True or False.

The Baby Store

Mother: *Pamela Chen*

Item	Wants	Received
	2	0
	3	3
	1	0
	3	2
	2	1
	1	1
	1	1
	1	0

1. Pamela wants one car seat.   True   False
2. She received two rattles.   True   False
3. She wants one baby monitor.   True   False
4. She wants three potties.   True   False
5. She didn't receive any mobiles.   True   False
6. She wants a crib.   True   False
7. She received two strollers.   True   False
8. She wants one food warmer, and she received it. True   False

C BABIES IN YOUR COUNTRY

What do people use for babies in your country? Check the items below.

☐ toy chest   ☐ diaper pail   ☐ playpen   ☐ walker   ☐ baby monitor
☐ swing   ☐ night light   ☐ car seat   ☐ baby backpack   ☐ stroller
☐ mobile   ☐ crib bumper   ☐ food warmer ☐ potty   ☐ cradle

Reaching Out!

What to Buy

Make a list of the ten most important things to buy a baby. Then compare your list with a classmate's list.

A YOUR NEW BATHROOM

You just moved into a new apartment. This is your bathroom. Make a list of all the things you're going to buy for your bathroom. Where are you going to put them? Look at page 26 of the Picture Dictionary to make sure you don't forget anything important.

Item	Location
shower curtain	above the bathtub

Item	Location

B WHAT IS IT?

__k__ 1. You brush your teeth with

____ 2. You wash your face with

____ 3. You dry your hands and face with

____ 4. You dry your hair with

____ 5. You turn the water on and off with

____ 6. You let the water out of the bathtub with

____ 7. You fix the toilet with

____ 8. You clean the bathtub and sink with

____ 9. You stand in the bathtub on

____ 10. You weigh yourself on

____ 11. You put dirty clothes in

____ 12. You put soap in

a. a hand towel.

b. a plunger.

c. a faucet.

d. a scale.

e. a rubber mat.

f. a hair dryer.

g. a hamper.

h. a washcloth.

i. a drain.

j. a soap dish.

k. a toothbrush.

l. a sponge.

Draw a picture of your bathroom. What's in it? Where is everything? Show your picture to a classmate. Then have your classmate use the picture to describe your bathroom.

Reaching Out!

Your Bathroom

Ⓐ REPAIR TIME!

Check the six things that someone needs to repair.

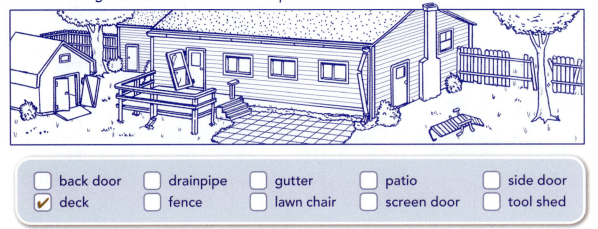

☐ back door	☐ drainpipe	☐ gutter	☐ patio	☐ side door
☑ deck	☐ fence	☐ lawn chair	☐ screen door	☐ tool shed

Ⓑ WHICH HOUSE IS FOR SALE?

Read the following Internet advertisement. Then look at the houses below and put a check under the house that's in the ad.

17 Willow Drive, Glendale, Florida $350,000

4 Bedrooms, 2 Bathrooms

This beautiful house has a large front porch, a 2-car garage, a new roof, new shutters and a satellite dish. It's near schools and shopping.

_____   _____   _____   _____

Ⓒ YOUR AD FOR A HOUSE

Write an advertisement for a house you would like to buy.

_____   _____

_____

_____

Reaching Out!

Your Dream House

Draw a picture of the house you would love to own someday. Write about it. Compare your picture and description with a classmate's.

A HOW MANY?

Look at pages 28 and 29 of the Picture Dictionary. How many of these do you see?

mailboxes	15
vacancy signs	
intercoms	
sprinklers in the sprinkler system	
buzzers	
balconies	

B A NEW APARTMENT

Lisa is looking for a new apartment. Number the following 1–6 in the correct order.

- [ ] Give a security deposit.
- [ ] Meet the landlord.
- [ ] Open the lock with the key.
- [1] See a vacancy sign.
- [ ] Sign a lease.
- [ ] Rent a moving truck.

C PEOPLE, PLACES, AND THINGS

Put these words into the correct groups.

balcony	door chain	fire escape	lobby	storage room
basement	doorman	fire exit	neighbor	superintendent
building manager	fire alarm	hallway	smoke detector	tenant

People	Places	Safety Items
building manager		

D THE BEST APARTMENT

These four people are looking for apartments. Look at the chart to see what each person needs. Look at the ads and find the best apartment for each person. Write the ad number in the chart.

	Ellen	Tom	Jerry	Ann
Has a car	✔			✔
Needs air conditioning			✔	
1st floor is okay	✔	✔		
Needs storage	✔	✔		
Wants a swimming pool		✔		
Needs laundry room in building		✔	✔	
Needs an elevator			✔	
BEST APARTMENT (#)				

#1 Apartment for Rent: Laundry, swimming pool, and whirlpool, first floor. Storage room in basement, elevator to roof. A nice place!

#3 Apartment for Rent: Laundry, elevator, air conditioning, garbage chute, fourth floor, no parking.

#2 Apartment for Rent: Parking lot, third floor, stairs only, nice neighbors.

#4 Apartment for Rent: First floor off of courtyard. Security gate, storage locker, one parking space in parking garage.

What are apartment buildings like in your country? How are they different from apartment buildings in the U.S.? Write a paragraph about it. Then compare with a classmate.

Reaching Out!

Apartment Buildings

A THIS HOUSE HAS PROBLEMS!

This house has a lot of problems! Check the problems you see.

- [ ] The door doesn't open.
- [ ] The doorbell doesn't ring.
- [✔] The roof is leaking.
- [ ] There are mice.
- [ ] A sink is clogged.
- [ ] There are fleas.
- [ ] The hot water heater is broken.
- [ ] A wall is cracked.
- [ ] The bathroom tiles are loose.
- [ ] There are rats.
- [ ] The front steps are broken.
- [ ] The heating system is broken.
- [ ] There are cockroaches.

B THESE PEOPLE REPAIR THINGS

Match the repairperson with what that person fixes and the reason why.

1. chimneysweep	roof	dirty
2. plumber	paint	isn't working
3. roofer	sink	broken
4. painter	chimney	leaking
5. locksmith	cable TV	peeling
6. cable TV company	lock	clogged

C LOOK IN THE YELLOW PAGES!

These people need help! Look in the Yellow Pages to find the phone numbers of repairpeople who can fix their problems.

Temperature Zone
- Heating
- Air conditioning

555-257-6983
Call today!

 **Janet Lowe Carpenter**
New building & repairs
555-258-8836
Free estimate

Shaw's Appliance Repair
We fix small & large appliances
Low prices
555-254-8278

Bug Be Gone!
Exterminator Service
✓ Termites
✓ Rats
✓ Ants
555-254-4963

FIX IT NOW!
Joe Lombard
Handyman
Over 25 years experience
555-258-3176

Jerry Wong
Electrician
555-258-1879

1. Timothy has ants in his kitchen! What number should he call? **555-254-4963**
2. Amy's air conditioning isn't working! What number should she call? _____
3. Kevin's front light doesn't go on! What number should he call? _____
4. The tiles in Anna's kitchen are loose! What number should she call? _____
5. The Bakers' refrigerator is broken! What number should they call? _____
6. Robert's bedroom door doesn't open! What number should he call? _____

Reaching Out!
Repairpeople

Make a list of the best repairpeople you know. Share your list with the class.

A MATCHING SUPPLIES

Match the items that go together.

__d__ 1. garbage can
____ 2. broom
____ 3. window cleaner
____ 4. vacuum cleaner
____ 5. mop
____ 6. cleanser

a. bucket
b. paper towels
c. sponge
d. recycling bin
e. dustpan
f. vacuum cleaner bag

B CLEANING IN YOUR HOUSEHOLD

Who cleans your house or apartment? Write the name of the person next to each chore.

1. polish the furniture _____
2. clean the bathroom _____
3. take out the garbage _____
4. wash the windows _____
5. vacuum _____

C YOUR CLEANING SUPPLIES

Check the cleaning supplies you have in your home right now. Then make a shopping list of other cleaning supplies you need to buy.

☐ ammonia   ☐ furniture polish   ☐ window cleaner
☐ dust cloth   ☐ floor wax   ☐ paper towels
☐ scrub brush   ☐ broom   ☐ feather duster

Cleaning Supplies to Buy
_____
_____
_____
_____
_____

D TIME SPENT ON CHORES

What information do you see? Which chore does each person spend the most time doing? the least time doing? Fill in the table with numbers 1–4. (1 = most time spent, 4 = least time spent)

Time spent cleaning each week

☐ sweeping   ☐ vacuuming
☐ dusting   ☐ mopping

Carl   Jane
Lily   Ron

CHORES	Carl	Jane	Lily	Ron
	4			
	2			
	1			
	3			

Which chores do you spend the most time on every week? Make a list of the chores and how much time you spend on each of them every week. Then make a pie chart to show this information. Compare with a classmate.

Reaching Out!

Weekly Chores

A THE SUPPLY CABINET

Look at the supply cabinet on page 33 of the Picture Dictionary and circle the correct answer.

1. The yardstick is next to the ((fly swatter)   paint thinner).
2. The paint roller is in the (sandpaper   paint pan).
3. The work gloves are in front of the (glue   bug spray).
4. The batteries are next to the (fuses   extension cord).
5. The flashlight is above the (spray gun   step ladder).
6. The electrical tape is to the right of the (duct tape   masking tape).

B WHO USES THEM?

What home supply item does each household repairperson use?

1. An electrician uses _____lightbulbs_____.
2. An exterminator uses _____ and _____.
3. A plumber uses _____.
4. A carpenter uses _____.
5. The heating and air conditioning service uses _____.
6. A painter uses _____ and _____.

duct tape
lightbulbs
a mousetrap
paint
a plunger
roach killer
a spray gun
a tape measure

C THIS WEEK'S SPECIALS!

Look at the items on sale this week at Harry's Hardware Store. Then check True or Not True for each sentence.

Harry's Hardware Store

This Week's Specials!

$5.49 $2.99 $7.95

$2.25 $8.25

$3.95 $1.50 $1.20

	True	Not True
1. The masking tape costs $2.99.	✔	____
2. The glue costs $3.95.	____	____
3. The flashlights cost $1.50.	____	____
4. Electrical tape is on sale.	____	____
5. The tape measure costs $5.49.	____	____
6. Paint brushes are on sale.	____	____
7. The lightbulbs cost $1.50.	____	____
8. The oil costs $1.20.	____	____
9. Yardsticks are on sale.	____	____
10. The work gloves cost $7.95.	____	____

Reaching Out!

Household Problems

When was the last time you had to fix something in your home? Describe the problem, and make a list of the supplies you used to fix the problem. Compare your experience with a classmate's.

A **GREG'S TOOLBOX**

Greg is cleaning his toolbox. Help him take inventory.
Put a check next to each item he has and tell how many.

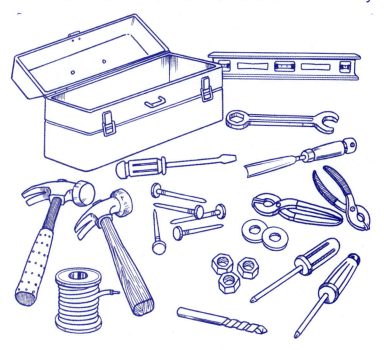

Tool/Hardware	✔	How Many?
bolt		
chisel		
drill bit		
hammer	✔	2
hand drill		
level		
machine screw		
mallet		
nail		
nut		
Phillips screwdriver		
pliers		
scraper		
screwdriver		
washer		
wire		
wire stripper		
wood screw		
wrench		

B **YOUR TOOLBOX**

Do you have any tools? Check the ones you have.

- ☐ hammer
- ☐ screwdriver
- ☐ hand drill
- ☐ saw
- ☐ chisel
- ☐ pliers
- ☐ level
- ☐ scraper
- ☐ wire stripper
- ☐ Phillips screwdriver
- ☐ plane
- ☐ power saw

C **TOOLS IN THEIR TOOLBOXES**

The chart on the left shows the tools each person has. Complete the bar graph on the right to
show the total number of tools they have.

	Carla	Frank	Sofia	Robert	Teresa
hammer			X		X
saw	X	X	X		X
hacksaw	X	X	X		
pliers	X		X	X	
screwdriver	X	X	X	X	X
wrench			X		

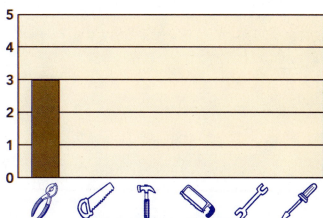

Make a list of the five most important tools to have and tell why.
Then compare your list with a classmate's list.

Reaching Out!

Important Tools

A THREE KINDS OF TOOLS

clippers	hoe	lawnmower	nozzle	shovel	trowel	weeder
hedge trimmer	hose	line trimmer	pruning shears	sprinkler	watering can	

Tools for Digging	Tools for Cutting	Tools for Watering
hoe		

B WHAT ARE THEY USING?

Circle the correct word.

1. Dorothy's leaf blower is broken. She's using a (nozzle (rake)).
2. Jeffrey is planting vegetables. He's using a (shovel   weeder).
3. Alice is pruning the bushes. She's using pruning (shears   seeds).
4. Larry's sprinkler is broken. He's using a (gas can   watering can).
5. Arthur is watering his garden. He's using a (hoe   hose).
6. Ellen is planting flowers. She's using (fertilizer   yard waste bags).
7. Rita is trimming the hedges. She's using (a line trimmer   clippers).
8. Ed is mowing his lawn. He's using a lawnmower and a (hoe   line trimmer).

C GARDEN TOOLS FOR SALE

Look at the ad below and complete the chart.

$15 $19 $14 $33 $12

$27 $25 $60 $150 $30

Item	Price
shovel	$25.00
	$15.00
wheelbarrow	
	$150.00
weeder	
	$19.00
pruning shears	
	$33.00
line trimmer	
	$12.00

Reaching Out!

Useful Tools

In your opinion, what are the five most useful gardening tools? How much do these tools cost? Make a list of these tools and their prices. Then compare with a classmate.

Maria's Successful Business

When Maria came to the United States five years ago, she spoke only Spanish. She cleaned houses during the day, and she studied English at school in the evening. Now, Maria speaks English very well, and she is very successful. Last year she started her own cleaning company. She and her employees clean many houses, apartments, townhomes, and condominiums. The people who use Maria's company are very happy because Maria and her employees work very hard.

In each home, they clean the living room, the dining room, the bedroom, the kitchen, and the bathroom. There are many things to clean. They dust the coffee table, the lamps, the lampshades, and the wall unit in the living room. They also change the vacuum cleaner bag and vacuum the rug. They use a broom and a dustpan to sweep the dining room floor, and they use furniture polish to polish the dining room table and the buffet. They wash the windows and dust the furniture in the bedroom. They use a sponge mop to mop the kitchen floor. They use cleanser, a scrub brush, and a sponge to clean the bathroom.

Maria also has a small catering business. She prepares meals for families, and she also prepares food for big parties. She usually cooks the food in the oven in her apartment, and then she uses the microwave at a family's home to reheat the food. Everybody agrees that her food is delicious.

Maria's companies are growing! She now has five employees in her cleaning company and two employees in her catering business. Maria is taking adult education courses in business and accounting during the evening. She hopes this will help her companies grow even more in the future.

1. In the living room, Maria and her employees _____.
   a. cook food
   b. sweep the floor
   c. vacuum the rug
   d. use a sponge mop

2. A dining room has a _____.
   a. coffee table
   b. dressing table
   c. changing table
   d. buffet

3. People use a microwave to _____.
   a. clean
   b. cook
   c. mop
   d. sweep

4. People use a catering company to _____.
   a. prepare food
   b. take a class
   c. clean the house
   d. start a business

5. The word *employees* means _____.
   a. courses
   b. workers
   c. companies
   d. businesses

6. According to the story, Maria and her employees don't clean _____.
   a. townhomes
   b. apartments
   c. offices
   d. condominiums

7. Maria has _____.
   a. two companies
   b. five companies
   c. two employees
   d. three employees

8. Maria is now studying _____.
   a. catering
   b. cooking
   c. cleaning
   d. accounting

A WHERE CAN HE GO?

Alex is planning an anniversary party for his parents. Look at the list of things he has to do to get ready for the party. Where can he go to get everything he needs on the list? Look at pages 36 and 37 of the Picture Dictionary to help you decide. Sometimes he can go to more than one place.

TO DO

1 buy an anniversary card
2 buy a cake
3 buy food for the party
4 buy flowers
5 get a haircut
6 get my suit cleaned
7 buy a new shirt and tie
8 buy a gift for Mom and Dad
   (DVD player? computer? TV?)

1. ____card store, drug store, book store____
2. _____
3. _____
4. _____
5. _____
6. _____
7. _____
8. _____

B SHOPPING IN GLENDALE

| Star's Coffee Shop | | Main Street Clinic | Blake's Pharmacy | | Classy Copy Center | Central Opticians | | Glendale Bus Station |

| Busy Bee Day-Care Center | | Midtown Bank | Bill's Book Store | Phil's Furniture Store | | Sam's Service Station |

Look at the map of downtown Glendale. Where can you do the following things?

1. cash a check?   ____Midtown Bank____
2. buy a sofa?   _____
3. get gas?   _____
4. have breakfast?   _____
5. see a doctor?   _____
6. buy a ticket to Chicago?   _____
7. get a new pair of glasses?   _____
8. buy an English dictionary?   _____
9. buy aspirin and cold medicine?   _____
10. make copies of important documents?   _____
11. leave your child when you're at work?   _____

Reaching Out!

Places You Like

Which places on pages 36 and 37 of the Picture Dictionary do you recommend in your community? Compare with a classmate.

A WHERE IS IT?

Here is a map of the Glendale Mall.

Look at the map and find the building.

1. It's between the jewelry store and the hardware store.   *shoe store*
2. It's across from the shoe store. _____
3. It's between the travel agency and the photo shop. _____
4. It's next to the toy store. _____
5. It's between the pizza shop and the restaurant. _____
6. It's across from the restaurant and next to the music store. _____

B SHOPPING AT THE MALL

Where can you do the following things at the Glendale Mall? Write the number of the place.

1. get a new hairstyle? __4__
2. buy a pair of sandals or sneakers? ____
3. rent a movie? ____
4. buy a dog or a cat? ____
5. buy a CD? ____
6. eat a quick lunch? ____
7. buy a bracelet, necklace, and earrings? ____
8. have a quick dessert? ____
9. buy a hammer? ____
10. get a manicure? ____
11. exercise? ____
12. see a science fiction film? ____
13. buy a game, a doll, or a teddy bear? ____
14. eat a very nice dinner? ____
15. buy clothes for a pregnant woman? ____
16. buy film for your camera? ____
17. plan a trip? ____

(continued)

Tell about your favorite shopping mall. Which of the places on pages 38 and 39 of the Picture Dictionary are in the mall? What are your favorite places in the mall? Compare with a classmate.

Reaching Out!

A Shopping Mall

WHAT DO YOU RECOMMEND?

What stores and other places around town do you recommend in your community? Where are they? Choose five places from the list below and complete the chart.

hair salon	jewelry store	photo shop	shoe store	toy store
hardware store	laundromat	pizza shop	shopping mall	travel agency
health club	music store	restaurant	supermarket	video store
ice cream shop	pet shop			

Places Around Town	Name of Place You Recommend	Where Is It?
shoe store	Elegant Shoes	on Fifth Avenue next to the jewelry store

D **YOUR SHOPPING HABITS**

Fill out the questionnaire and compare your answers with a classmate's.

How often do you go to the...?

very often = once a week or more   often = 1 to 3 times a month   sometimes = 4 to 11 times a year   rarely = 1 to 3 times a year

	very often	often	sometimes	rarely	never
hair salon	❑	❑	❑	❑	❑
hardware store	❑	❑	❑	❑	❑
health club	❑	❑	❑	❑	❑
ice cream shop	❑	❑	❑	❑	❑
laundromat	❑	❑	❑	❑	❑
library	❑	❑	❑	❑	❑
movie theater	❑	❑	❑	❑	❑
music store	❑	❑	❑	❑	❑
park	❑	❑	❑	❑	❑
pizza shop	❑	❑	❑	❑	❑
post office	❑	❑	❑	❑	❑
restaurant	❑	❑	❑	❑	❑
shoe store	❑	❑	❑	❑	❑
shopping mall	❑	❑	❑	❑	❑
supermarket	❑	❑	❑	❑	❑
video store	❑	❑	❑	❑	❑

Reaching Out!

This Month

Which of the places on pages 38 and 39 of the Picture Dictionary did you go to this month? What did you do there? Compare with a classmate.

A CAN YOU FIND THEM?

Look at pages 40 and 41 of the Picture Dictionary. What people, vehicles, and buildings do you see?

People	Vehicles	Buildings
bus driver		

B WHERE IS IT?

Look at the scene on pages 40 and 41 of the Picture Dictionary. Where is everything?

1. The city hall is between the courthouse and the ((police station)   subway station).
2. There's a (parking lot   parking garage) next to the subway station.
3. There's a (fire alarm box   fire hydrant) next to the mailbox.
4. The (motorcycle   bus) is next to the curb.
5. There's a (parking meter   public telephone) in front of the office building.

C SPRINGFIELD'S BUDGET

The graph below shows how the city of Springfield spent money in 2005 and 2006. Use the graph to complete the list on the right. Number the items from 1 (the least money) to 7 (the most money).

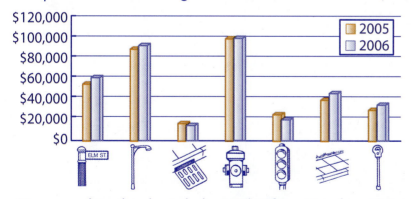

```
___ fire hydrants
___ parking meters
___ traffic lights
 1  sewers
___ sidewalks
___ street lights
___ street signs
```

Now complete the charts below with information from the graph.

Money Spent in 2005	
sidewalks	$40,000
	$100,000
	$30,000
	$25,000
	$15,000
	$90,000
	$55,000

Money Spent in 2006	
parking meters	$34,000
	$13,000
	$45,000
	$100,000
	$20,000
	$60,000
	$93,000

(continued)

1. a. fire hydrant   b. trash container   (c.) manhole   d. mailbox
2. a. bus stop   b. crosswalk   c. taxi stand   d. subway station
3. a. street vendor   b. cab driver   c. bus driver   d. sewer
4. a. pedestrian   b. police officer   c. taxi driver   d. meter maid
5. a. garbage truck   b. taxicab   c. motorcycle   d. bus
6. a. police station   b. fire station   c. courthouse   d. jail
7. a. ice cream truck   b. drive-through window   c. motorcycle   d. subway
8. a. office building   b. parking garage   c. parking lot   d. city hall
9. a. manhole   b. subway station   c. sewer   d. traffic light

E TWO INTERSECTIONS

Go to two busy intersections in your city or town. Check everything you see at each intersection.

(1 = first intersection; 2 = second intersection)

	1	2		1	2		1	2
bus	__	__	mailbox	__	__	police station	__	__
bus stop	__	__	manhole	__	__	sewer	__	__
cab	__	__	meter maid	__	__	sidewalk	__	__
city hall	__	__	motorcycle	__	__	street	__	__
courthouse	__	__	newsstand	__	__	street light	__	__
crosswalk	__	__	office building	__	__	street vendor	__	__
fire alarm box	__	__	parking garage	__	__	subway station	__	__
fire hydrant	__	__	parking lot	__	__	taxi stand	__	__
fire station	__	__	parking meter	__	__	traffic light	__	__
garbage truck	__	__	pedestrian	__	__	trash container	__	__
ice cream truck	__	__	police officer	__	__			

What did you see? Write each word in the correct place in the diagram.

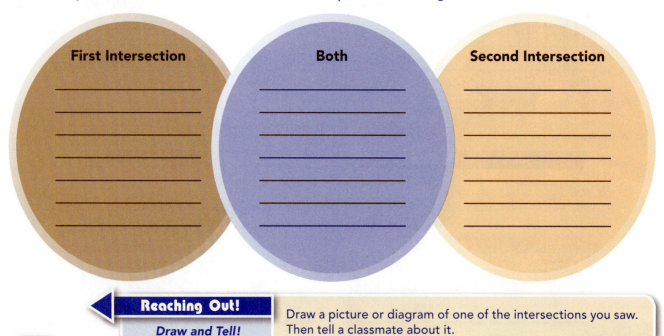

First Intersection

_____

_____

_____

_____

_____

_____

Both

_____

_____

_____

_____

_____

Second Intersection

_____

_____

_____

_____

_____

_____

Reaching Out!

Draw and Tell!

Draw a picture or diagram of one of the intersections you saw.
Then tell a classmate about it.

New Downtown Center Opens
by David Wong

JACKSON, June 4—The new Downtown Center opened yesterday evening. This group of buildings includes a shopping mall, a hotel, a movie theater, and an apartment building. People who live and work in the center of Jackson think that the new complex will solve many of the city's problems.

Downtown Center is at the intersection of Commerce Avenue and Main Street. This part of town had many problems. The intersection had a parking lot, a park, an office building with cracked walls, and a motel with peeling paint. Both buildings closed many years ago. There weren't any stores or restaurants in the area, so there weren't any pedestrians on the street.

"The place was terrible!" said Oscar Loyola, a taxi driver. "The street lights were all broken. The park had weeds, garbage, and rats. People just didn't want to come to this part of town."

But that all changed at 7:00 P.M. yesterday when Mayor Brenda Wilson officially opened the new Downtown Center. "Look at these beautiful buildings!" she said to a crowd of men, women, and children. "We can be proud of our city again!"

All four buildings in the new Downtown Center are at the intersection of Commerce and Main. Pedestrians can use crosswalks to go across the street to get from one building to another. The intersection has new traffic lights and a police officer. People can also walk under the street to get to any building. "All four buildings have one basement. When it's raining, I can go from my building directly to the shopping mall or the movie theater, and I don't need to go out on the street!" said Shirley Hunt, who lives in the 125-unit apartment building.

The mall has 40 stores, including two department stores, a book store, a card store, and many others. It has eight restaurants and a parking garage. The hotel has 150 rooms, and there are six movies playing in the movie theater. "It's fantastic!" said Loyola as he sat in his cab at the hotel's taxi stand. "It's a great day for the city of Jackson!"

1. The new Downtown Center includes _____.
   a. one building
   b. two buildings
   c. three buildings
   d. four buildings

2. The new Downtown Center DOESN'T include _____.
   a. a movie theater
   b. a shopping mall
   c. a motel
   d. an apartment building

3. The cab driver's last name is _____.
   a. Jackson
   b. Loyola
   c. Hunt
   d. Wilson

4. The hotel has _____.
   a. 40 stores
   b. 125 units
   c. four buildings
   d. 150 rooms

5. There's a parking garage in _____.
   a. the mall
   b. the hotel
   c. the movie theater
   d. the office building

6. In the first paragraph, the word *complex* means _____.
   a. intersection
   b. group of buildings
   c. problems
   d. people

7. This article is probably from _____.
   a. a book
   b. a dictionary
   c. a newspaper
   d. a notebook

8. From the article, you DON'T know about the work of _____.
   a. Shirley Hunt
   b. Brenda Wilson
   c. Oscar Loyola
   d. the police officer

A FROM YOUNG TO OLD

Number the words from young to old.

☐ teenager   ☐ girl   ☐ senior citizen   **1** infant   ☐ woman   ☐ toddler

B WHAT DO THEY LOOK LIKE?

Look at page 42 of the Picture Dictionary. Circle the correct answers.

1. The hearing-impaired person is a woman.	True	**(Not True)**
2. The pregnant woman has shoulder length hair.	True	Not True
3. The teenager is middle-aged.	True	Not True
4. The elderly man is bald.	True	Not True
5. The toddler has blond hair.	True	Not True
6. The vision-impaired person has brown wavy hair.	True	Not True

C A MISSING PERSON

Look at the picture and circle the answers.

MISSING
MARY SMITH

18 yrs. old / 5 ft. 2 in. /100 lbs.

Mary Smith is a (toddler   (teenager)).[1]
She's (short   tall)[2] and (heavy   thin)[3]
with (short   long)[4] (straight   curly)[5]
(blond   black)[6] hair.

D FATHER AND SON

George and Paul are father and son. How are they different? How are they the same? Complete the diagram.

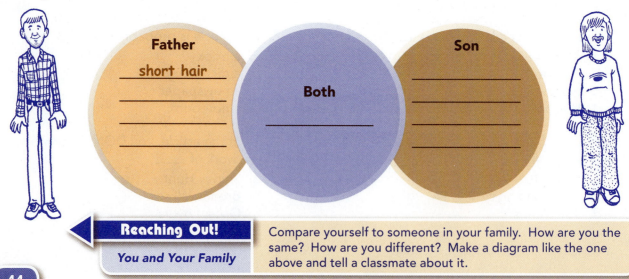

Father

short hair
_____
_____
_____

Both

_____

Son

_____
_____
_____

Reaching Out!

You and Your Family

Compare yourself to someone in your family. How are you the same? How are you different? Make a diagram like the one above and tell a classmate about it.

A SYNONYMS

1. rich	hard
2. noisy	skinny
3. thin	wealthy
4. difficult	little
5. small	loud

B OPPOSITES

1. heavy	dull
2. sharp	ugly
3. curly	short
4. tall	light
5. beautiful	straight

C WHICH WORD DOESN'T BELONG?

1. hair   a. curly   b. straight   (c.) slow   d. short
2. clothes   a. plain   b. loose   c. fancy   d. single
3. room   a. soft   b. dark   c. messy   d. wide
4. neighbor   a. honest   b. married   c. expensive   d. skinny
5. skin   a. rough   b. smooth   c. dry   d. full
6. tie   a. high   b. wide   c. plain   d. inexpensive

D PEOPLE AND THINGS YOU KNOW

Look at pages 44 and 45 of the Picture Dictionary. Find as many words as you can to describe the following.

1. your house or apartment _____

2. your street _____

3. a good friend _____

> **Reaching Out!**
>
> Write about one of these people or things you know. Read your description to a classmate.
>
> *Write About It*

E ANGELA'S ENGLISH CLASS

Angela is a good student, but she's having some problems in her English class. There are many students in her class, and they talk all the time. Sometimes she can't hear the teacher, and sometimes she can't understand him because he speaks very fast. When she doesn't know the answers, she feels uncomfortable. Also, the air conditioning isn't working, and the classroom is dirty. Angela doesn't like the class schedule. The class is only two hours a day, and Angela wants more. She likes to do homework, but she thinks it's easy.

Fill out this evaluation form for Angela.

Class Evaluation

	YES	NO
1. The class is very large.	[ ]	[ ]
2. The teacher speaks very fast.	[ ]	[ ]
3. I feel comfortable in class.	[ ]	[ ]
4. The class is very noisy.	[ ]	[ ]
5. The classroom is neat and clean.	[ ]	[ ]
6. The classroom is very hot.	[ ]	[ ]
7. The homework is very difficult.	[ ]	[ ]
8. The class is very long.	[ ]	[ ]

> **Reaching Out!**
>
> Make up an evaluation form for your English class and fill it out. Compare your evaluation with a classmate's.
>
> *Your Class Evaluation*

A DEAR JANE

Jane writes for a newspaper. She helps people with their problems. Here are some letters she received. Complete each letter with the correct name.

> Bored   Confused   Embarrassed   Exhausted   Homesick   Hungry   Jealous   Lonely   Worried

Dear Jane,
    The food at my school is terrible. There isn't anything I like to eat. All the restaurants nearby are very expensive. What can I do?
                        Hungry

Dear Jane,
    My 16-year-old daughter wants to go to school in New York next year. My husband and I don't think a large city is a safe place for a young girl. What can I do?
    _____

Dear Jane,
    I'm from Brazil, but I'm living in the United States now. I think about my country all the time. I miss my family and my friends. What can I do? _____

Dear Jane,
    I don't know anybody in my neighborhood, and I don't have any friends at work. What can I do?
    _____

Dear Jane,
    I go to school every day, and I work at night. When I'm home, I have to clean the house and do homework. I never have time to sleep. What can I do?
    _____

Dear Jane,
    I think my boyfriend likes another girl in our class. They sit together in class and help each other. What can I do?
    _____

Dear Jane,
    I'm 18 years old, and I don't know what to do. My mother says, "Find a job," but my father says, "Go to college." What do you think?
    _____

Dear Jane,
    I make big mistakes when I speak English, and my classmates think it's funny. They sometimes laugh at me. What can I do?
    _____

Dear Jane,
    Every day is the same as the day before. I get up, go to school, do my homework, and watch TV. I need a change. What can I do?
    _____

Reaching Out!
A Letter to Jane

When do you feel nervous, worried, frustrated, jealous, confused, or mad? Write a letter to Jane about it. Read your letter to a classmate.

B HOW DO YOU FEEL?

Complete the sentences with words from pages 46 and 47 of the Picture Dictionary that tell how you feel. Use more than one word for each answer.

1. I often feel _____.

2. I rarely feel _____.

3. When I first came to this country, I felt _____.

4. On the first day at this school, I felt _____.

5. When I get a good grade on a test, I feel _____.

6. When I listen to the news, I feel _____.

A Family Reunion

All the members of the Johnson family are very happy today. They are at their annual family reunion. On the first weekend in August every year, they all come together on a Sunday afternoon at the home of Grandma and Grandpa Johnson. The grandparents' home is small, but they have a large backyard. It's a very good place for the family reunion.

Grandma Johnson is a beautiful woman. She's average height, and she has long wavy gray hair. Grandpa Johnson is very handsome. He's very tall and thin, and he has short curly gray hair and a thin gray mustache. Grandma and Grandpa are very proud of their four middle-aged children and their ten young grandchildren. They are all at the reunion. All four children live in different cities, so it's very difficult for the entire family to come together. That's why they're always very excited to be at the reunion.

Carl Johnson is tired, but he's happy. Carl is Grandpa Johnson's brother, and right now he's cooking dinner on the outdoor grill. He's nervous because everybody is getting hungry, and dinner isn't ready yet. Carl looks very different from his brother. He's short and heavy, and he's bald. His wife, Betty, is putting pitchers of water on all the tables. It's a hot day, and everybody is going to be very thirsty. Carl and Betty's three children and six grandchildren are also at the reunion. All sixteen grandchildren are sitting under a big old tree in the backyard and listening to music.

It's a noisy and happy afternoon in the Johnsons' backyard. It's a beautiful day, and all the members of the Johnson family are happy to see each other again.

1. The Johnsons' home is a very good place for the family reunion because _____.
   a. the house is large
   b. the house is small
   c. the backyard is large
   d. it's a beautiful day

2. In the first paragraph, *annual* means _____.
   a. every day
   b. every weekend
   c. every year
   d. every family member

3. From the story, you know that the grandmother _____.
   a. is tall and thin
   b. has gray hair
   c. has short hair
   d. is very handsome

4. From the story, you know that Grandpa's brother _____.
   a. doesn't like to cook
   b. isn't short
   c. isn't heavy
   d. doesn't have hair

5. Everybody is going to be thirsty because _____.
   a. the weather is hot
   b. the food is hot
   c. the backyard is large
   d. Betty is putting pitchers of water on the tables

6. From the story, you DON'T know _____.
   a. the day of the week
   b. the month of the year
   c. the name of the family
   d. the name of the city or town

A ERIC'S SHOPPING LIST

Eric is going to buy fruit at the supermarket. What is he going to buy? How much is he going to spend? Look at the supermarket ad and complete the chart.

Number	Fruit	Unit Price	Total Price
3	apples	$ .40	**$1.20**
2	pears		
3		$ .60	
2	oranges		
2		$4.00	
	lemons		$1.40
1	grapefruit		
2			$7.00

B THEY GO TOGETHER

__c__ 1. strawberries   a. tangerines

_____ 2. oranges   b. limes

_____ 3. lemons   c. raspberries

_____ 4. bananas   d. honeydew melons

_____ 5. peaches   e. plantains

_____ 6. cantaloupes   f. nectarines

C LINDA'S FRUIT SALAD

This is Linda's favorite fruit salad.

Look in her refrigerator to see what ingredients she has.

What does she need to buy? Make a shopping list.

Tropical Fruit Salad

3 bananas	1 pineapple
1 papaya	6 apricots
1 coconut	1 honeydew melon
1/2 watermelon	2 mangoes
3 pears	2 apples

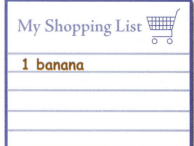

My Shopping List

1 banana

Reaching Out!

Your Fruit Salad

What fruits do you like to eat in a fruit salad? What fruits *don't* you like? Ask your classmates what they like and don't like, and compare.

A HOW LONG CAN YOU KEEP THEM?

Look at the chart and circle the correct answers.

Vegetable	On Shelf	In Refrigerator
mushrooms	1 day	2–3 days
eggplants	1 day	3–4 days
asparagus	----------	3–4 days
green beans	----------	3–4 days
broccoli	----------	3–5 days
parsley	----------	1 week

Vegetable	On Shelf	In Refrigerator
artichokes	1–2 days	1–2 weeks
beets	1 day	7–10 days
celery	----------	1–2 weeks
garlic	1 month	1–2 weeks
potatoes	1–2 months	1–2 weeks
carrots	----------	3 weeks

1. You can keep green beans in the refrigerator for 3 or 4 days. (True) Not True
2. You can keep mushrooms in the refrigerator for 3 to 5 days. True Not True
3. You can keep eggplants and beets on a kitchen shelf for a day. True Not True
4. You can keep parsley in the refrigerator for 7 days. True Not True
5. You can keep garlic in the refrigerator for one month. True Not True
6. You can keep broccoli and asparagus on a kitchen shelf. True Not True
7. You can keep celery and carrots in the refrigerator for more than a week. True Not True
8. You can keep artichokes in the refrigerator for 1 or 2 months. True Not True
9. You can keep potatoes on a kitchen shelf for more than 30 days. True Not True

B FIND THE RECEIPT

Look at the vegetables this person is buying. Put a check under the correct receipt.

John's Market

cabbage	$1.69
beets	$1.99
sweet potatoes	$1.80
onions	$2.79
jalapeños	$0.39
cucumber	$0.67
corn	$1.29
string beans	$0.99
Total	$11.61

John's Market

lima beans	$1.39
radishes	$1.69
butternut squash	$1.19
brussels sprouts	$2.39
green peppers	$1.38
potatoes	$2.00
lettuce	$1.49
spinach	$2.69
Total	$14.22

John's Market

acorn squash	$1.19
zucchini	$1.09
peas	$2.39
chili peppers	$0.39
yams	$1.98
green onions	$0.99
turnips	$1.69
bok choy	$2.69
Total	$12.41

What vegetables do you usually buy when you go shopping? Bring a shopping receipt to class and circle the vegetables on it. Compare with a classmate's receipt.

Reaching Out!

What Do You Buy?

A WHICH IS DIFFERENT?

1. a. chicken	b. turkey	c. shrimp	d. duck
2. a. drumsticks	b. tripe	c. breasts	d. thighs
3. a. pork chops	b. ribs	c. lamb chops	d. duck
4. a. flounder	b. liver	c. haddock	d. halibut
5. a. catfish	b. mussels	c. oysters	d. clams
6. a. bacon	b. ham	c. sausage	d. scallops
7. a. leg of lamb	b. roast beef	c. ground beef	d. stewing beef
8. a. trout	b. lobster	c. salmon	d. filet of sole

B LOOK AT THE RECEIPTS

Look at the four receipts and answer the questions.

Super Shopper

steak	$ 6.00
duck	$12.00
ribs	$ 5.00
bacon	$ 3.00
leg of lamb	$16.00
chicken legs	$ 4.00
ground beef	$ 5.00
Total	$51.00

Save More

scallops	$10.00
trout	$ 7.00
ham	$ 4.00
shrimp	$13.00
clams	$ 5.00
lamb chops	$ 9.00
lobster	$15.00
Total	$63.00

Price Cutter

filet of sole	$ 8.00
roast beef	$11.00
chicken thighs	$ 6.00
haddock	$ 7.00
turkey	$14.00
liver	$ 5.00
chicken wings	$ 4.00
Total	$55.00

Grocery Basket

flounder	$7.00
pork chops	$ 6.00
halibut	$ 8.00
sausages	$ 4.00
ground beef	$ 5.00
salmon	$ 7.00
chicken	$ 6.00
Total	$43.00

1. Alan likes seafood. He sometimes eats meat, but he doesn't like poultry. Find his receipt.
   Which store did he shop at? __Save More__ How much did he spend on meat? _____
   How much did he spend on seafood? _____ What kind of fish did he buy? _____

2. Mohammed doesn't eat any kind of pork or shellfish. Find his receipt.
   Which store did he shop at? _____ How much did he spend on meat? _____
   How much did he spend on fish? _____ How much did he spend on poultry? _____

3. Olga is a teenager who eats a lot of meat. She doesn't like seafood. Find her receipt.
   Which store did she shop at? _____ How much did she spend on meat? _____
   How much did she spend on poultry? _____

4. Arnold can't eat shellfish, but he likes fish, poultry, and meat. Find his receipt.
   Which store did he shop at? _____ How much did he spend on meat? _____
   How much did he spend on fish? _____ How much did he spend on poultry? _____

Reaching Out!
Food for a Week

Make a list of all the poultry, seafood, and meat you eat every week. Compare your list with a classmate's list.

A WHAT DO YOU EAT?

Look at page 51 of the Picture Dictionary. Which of these foods do you have for breakfast? for lunch? for dinner? Fill out the chart and compare your answers with a classmate's.

	Breakfast	Lunch	Dinner
I eat			
I drink			

B DAIRY PRODUCTS AND FAT

Which of these dairy products do you think has the most fat? Number the foods from 1 (highest in fat) to 10 (lowest in fat).

☐ cheese   ☐ cream cheese   ☐ milk   ☐ skim milk   ☐ sour cream
☐ cottage cheese ☐ butter   ☐ low-fat milk ☐ chocolate milk ☐ yogurt

The following charts tell how many calories from fat there are in a cup of each of these foods. Look at the charts and compare your answers. How many did you get right? Now go back and number the foods again according to the information in the charts.

cheese	394	milk	71		
cottage cheese	90	low-fat milk	21	sour cream	434
cream cheese	728	skim milk	4	yogurt	72
butter	1,628	chocolate milk	76		

C BEVERAGES AND CALORIES

Which of these beverages do you think has the most calories? Number the beverages from 1 (the most calories) to 10 (the least calories).

☐ apple juice   ☐ grapefruit juice   ☐ diet soda   ☐ herbal tea   ☐ coffee
☐ grape juice   ☐ soda   ☐ orange juice   ☐ tomato juice   ☐ cocoa

These charts tell how many calories there are in a cup of each of the beverages. Go back and number the beverages again according to the information in the charts.

apple juice	117	soda	150	orange juice	112	coffee	4
grape juice	154	diet soda	0	herbal tea	2	cocoa	218
grapefruit juice	94			tomato juice	40		

Make a list of dairy products, juices, and beverages in your refrigerator. Look at the food labels. Which of these foods are "high in calories"? Which are "low in calories"? Compare with a classmate.

Reaching Out!

Food Labels

A HOW MUCH DO YOU LIKE THEM?

For each group below, number each food (1, 2, 3, . . .) to show which ones you like the most and which ones you like the least. (Use number 1 for the one you like the most.)

Meats	Cheeses	Salads	Snack Foods
—— bologna	—— American cheese	—— cole slaw	—— nuts
—— corned beef	—— cheddar cheese	—— macaroni salad	—— popcorn
—— ham	—— mozzarella cheese	—— pasta salad	—— potato chips
—— pastrami	—— provolone	—— potato salad	—— pretzels
—— roast beef	—— Swiss cheese	—— seafood salad	—— tortilla chips
—— salami			
—— turkey			

B A CLASS SURVEY

Which are the most popular foods in your class? Add up the numbers from everybody in your class for each food item in Exercise A. The foods with the lowest totals in each group are the most popular. Write the class totals in the blanks.

Meats	Totals	Cheeses	Totals	Salads	Totals	Snack Foods	Totals
bologna	——	American cheese	——	cole slaw	——	nuts	——
corned beef	——	cheddar cheese	——	macaroni salad	——	popcorn	——
ham	——	mozzarella cheese	——	pasta salad	——	potato chips	——
pastrami	——	provolone	——	potato salad	——	pretzels	——
roast beef	——	Swiss cheese	——	seafood salad	——	tortilla chips	——
salami	——						
turkey	——						

C A CLASS PARTY

Your class is having a party. What are you going to serve? Choose the most popular foods from the class survey and plan a menu.

Our Party Menu

D WHAT DO YOU EAT?

Complete these sentences with words from page 52 of the Picture Dictionary.

1. I sometimes eat/drink _____ when I watch television.

2. I sometimes eat/drink _____ at a party.

3. I sometimes eat/drink _____ on a picnic.

4. I never eat/drink _____.

Reaching Out!

Two Interviews

Interview two classmates about the foods on page 52 of the Picture Dictionary. Which of these foods are popular in their countries? Which foods *don't* people eat? How is this different from what people eat in other countries you know?

A FIX THE SIGNS!

Look at the signs in a supermarket. Cross out the food that doesn't belong in each aisle.

Packaged Goods	Baking Products	Canned Goods	Condiments	Baked Goods
noodles	flour	soup	cookies	bread
~~mayonnaise~~	cake mix	tuna fish	salad dressing	salt
spaghetti	sugar	mustard	vinegar	rolls
rice	pickles	canned pears	olive oil	cake

B SAM'S SUPERMARKET

Fill in the missing numbers to complete the floor plan. Put the foods on the list in the correct aisles.

1 bread	17 noodles
2 cake	18 olive oil
3 cake mix	19 olives
4 canned fruit	20 peanut butter
5 canned vegetables	21 pepper
6 cereal	22 relish
7 cookies	23 rolls
8 crackers	24 rice
9 English muffins	25 salad dressing
10 flour	26 salt
11 jam	27 soup
12 jelly	28 spaghetti
13 ketchup	29 spices
14 macaroni	30 sugar
15 mayonnaise	31 tuna fish
16 mustard	32 vinegar

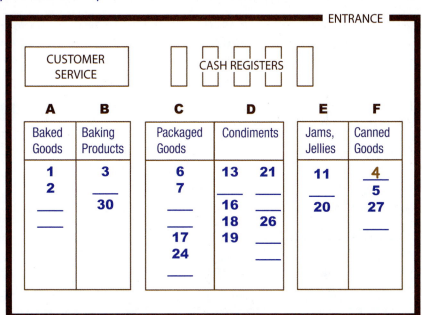

ENTRANCE

CUSTOMER SERVICE · CASH REGISTERS

A Baked Goods: 1, 2, __, __
B Baking Products: 3, __, 30
C Packaged Goods: 6, 7, __, __, 17, 24, __
D Condiments: 13, 21, 16, __, 18, 26, 19, __
E Jams, Jellies: 11, __, 20
F Canned Goods: 4, 5, 27, __

C SHOPPING WITH COUPONS

Stacy is shopping for groceries at Sam's Supermarket. She's using the coupons below. What's she going to buy? In what aisle is she going to find it? How much is she going to save? Fill out the chart.

25¢ Off · 50¢ Off · 40¢ Off · 30¢ Off · 75¢ Off · 35¢ Off

Food	Aisle	Save
cereal	C	25¢

You just moved into a new apartment! Your refrigerator and kitchen cabinets are empty. Which of the groceries on page 53 of the Picture Dictionary are you going to buy? Make a list and compare with a classmate's list.

Reaching Out!

Your Shopping List

A WHICH IS DIFFERENT?

1. a. paper cups   b. napkins   c. diapers   d. paper plates
2. a. tissues   b. soap   c. toilet paper   d. napkins
3. a. baby food   b. formula   c. wipes   d. straws
4. a. liquid soap   b. plastic wrap   c. wax paper   d. aluminum foil
5. a. cat food   b. formula   c. paper plates   d. dog food

B JUDY CHEN'S PANTRY

Judy Chen likes to keep the following things in her pantry (a tall storage cabinet in her kitchen).

baby cereal	diapers	liquid soap	paper towels	straws
baby food	dog food	napkins	sandwich bags	tissues
cat food	formula	paper cups	soap	trash bags

This is Judy's pantry. What items does she have? What does she need to buy?

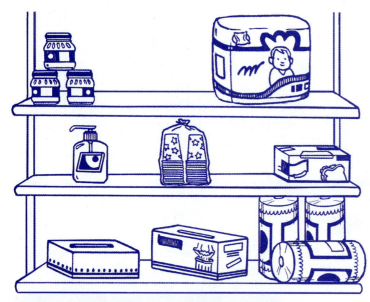

Item	Has	Needs
baby cereal		✔
baby food	✔	
cat food		
diapers		
dog food		
formula		
liquid soap		
napkins		
paper cups		
paper towels		
sandwich bags		
soap		
straws		
tissues		
trash bags		

C I USE . . . /I DON'T USE . . .

Which items in this lesson do you use in your home? Which items don't you use? Make a list.

I use . . .

I don't use . . .

Reaching Out!
Household Products

Which of the items from Picture Dictionary page 54 do you use most often? Make a list. Compare your list with a classmate's list.

A HOW MANY?

Look at the supermarket on page 55 of the Picture Dictionary. How many of the following do you see?

- ☐ shopping baskets
- ☐ cash registers
- ☐ shopping carts
- ☐ scanners
- ☐ checkout counters
- ☐ shoppers

B GROUPING WORDS

Put the words below in the correct group.

aisle	can-return machine	clerk	manager	shopper
bagger	candy	gum	produce	tabloid newspaper
cashier	checkout line	magazine	scale	

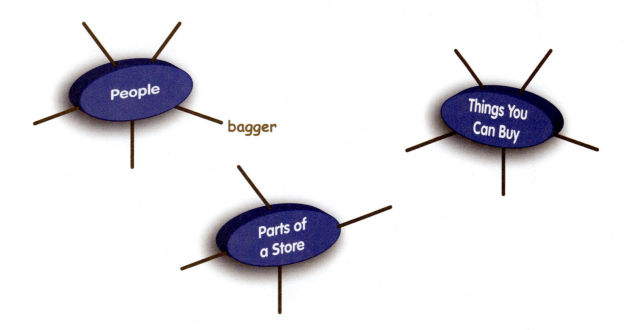

People

bagger

Things You Can Buy

Parts of a Store

C SUPERMARKETS IN YOUR COUNTRY

Check the items below that are common in supermarkets in your country.

- ☐ conveyor belts
- ☐ express checkout lines
- ☐ paper bags
- ☐ shopping carts
- ☐ plastic bags
- ☐ shopping baskets
- ☐ scanners
- ☐ bottle and can machines

Write a description of your favorite supermarket. Tell why it's your favorite. Compare your description with a classmate's.

Reaching Out!

My Favorite Supermarket

A WHAT'S THE CONTAINER?

Write each item under the correct container or quantity.

baby food	coffee	ice cream	pickles	soup	tuna fish
bananas	cookies	mayonnaise	pita bread	sour cream	yogurt
carrots	cottage cheese	milk	plastic wrap	tissues	
cereal	grapes	orange juice	potato salad	toilet paper	
cheese	ground beef	paper towels	rolls	tortillas	

Can
coffee

Box

Jar

Roll

Bunch

Half-Gallon

Package

Pound

Container

B RECYCLING IN EASTON

Read the Easton Recycling Guide and then, under each item, write P for Paper, C for Container, or X for Can't Recycle.

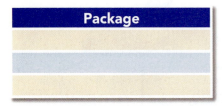

Easton Recycling Guide

PAPER
- ✓ Newspapers
- ✓ Paper bags
- ✓ Milk cartons
- ✓ Boxes
- ✓ Paper egg cartons
- Ø No dirty paper
- Ø Do not put paper in plastic bags

CONTAINERS
- ✓ Bottles
- ✓ Jars
- ✓ Food cans
- ✓ Soda cans
- ✓ Aluminum foil
- Ø No dirty containers
- Ø No plastic bags

C

Reaching Out!
Recycling

Get a recycling guide from your town. What types of containers can you recycle? When and where can you recycle? Discuss with the class.

A ABBREVIATIONS

_c_ 1. pt.   a. teaspoon

____ 2. tsp.   b. ounce

____ 3. Tbsp.   c. pint

____ 4. lb.   d. tablespoon

____ 5. oz.   e. pound

B MATCHING MEASUREMENTS

_c_ 1. 1 qt.   a. 1 fl. oz.

____ 2. 2 Tbsps.   b. 4 qts.

____ 3. 1 cup   c. 2 pints

____ 4. 8 ozs.   d. 2 cups

____ 5. 1 gallon   e. 1/2 lb.

____ 6. 16 fl. ozs. f. 8 fl. ozs.

C ADD IT UP!

| 1 ounce | 1 tsp. | 1 pint | 2 fl. ozs. | 1 quart | 1/2 gallon | 1 gal. | 3/4 lb. |

1. 1 cup + 1 cup   = ____**1 pint**____

2. 1 Tbsp. + 1 Tbsp. = _____

3. 2 qts. + 2 qts.   = _____

4. 4 ozs. + 1/2 lb. = _____

5. 2 cups + 1 pint = _____

6. 2 pts. + 1 qt.   = _____

7. 14 fl. ozs. + _____ = 1 pint

8. 1 tsp. + 1 tsp. + _____ = 1 Tbsp.

D COMPARE THE RECIPES

Amy and Rick use the same ingredients in their chili recipes, but they use different amounts. Look at the ingredients and check who uses more of each.

Amy's Homemade Chili

1 lb. ground beef	1 1/4 lbs. tomatoes
7 ozs. kidney beans	2 Tbsp. garlic
10 ozs. black beans	1 teaspoon salt
2 Tbsp. jalapeño peppers	3 Tbsp. spices
1/4 lb. onions	2 tsp. pepper
8 ozs. carrots	1/4 lb. cheese
2 fl. ozs. olive oil	1 1/2 tsp. vinegar

Rick's Delicious Chili

12 ozs. ground beef	16 ozs. tomatoes
1/2 lb. kidney beans	2 teaspoons garlic
3/4 lb. black beans	2 tsp. salt
3 tsp. jalapeño peppers	6 tsp. spices
6 ozs. onions	1 teaspoon pepper
3/4 lb. carrots	6 ozs. cheese
2 Tbsp. olive oil	1 fl. oz. vinegar

Who Uses More?	Amy	Rick
black beans		✔
carrots		
cheese		
garlic		
ground beef		
jalapeño peppers		
kidney beans		
olive oil		
onions		
pepper		
salt		
spices		
tomatoes		
vinegar		

What are the ingredients in your favorite recipe? Write the measurements for each ingredient in two different ways (for example: *1 cup of milk = 8 fl. ozs. milk*). Compare with a classmate.

Reaching Out!

Ingredients

A PREPARING THE CHILI

This is how Amy prepares her chili. What does she do first? Number the recipe steps 1–9.

> **Amy's Homemade Chili**
>
> 1. Chop up the onions, garlic, jalapeño peppers, and carrots.
> 2. Saute in olive oil over medium heat, then add the ground beef.
> 3. In a large pot, combine the ground beef and beans and cook over low heat.
> 4. Cut up the tomatoes and add to the mixture.
> 5. Add the salt, pepper, and spices.
> 6. Pour in the vinegar.
> 7. Stir.
> 8. Let the chili simmer for 20 minutes.
> 9. Grate the cheese in a separate bowl and serve the chili with cheese on top.

B IN YOUR KITCHEN

Write the names of foods you prepare in the following ways. You can write more than one answer.

1. slice ___bread, tomatoes, cheese___

2. microwave _____

3. peel _____

4. stir-fry _____

5. break _____

6. steam _____

7. beat _____

8. boil _____

C PREPARING CHICKEN

Ms. Gonzalez took a survey of her students' favorite ways to prepare chicken. Do they prefer to bake, roast, fry, grill, or broil? Look at the results on the bar graph. Then list the different ways from most popular to least popular.

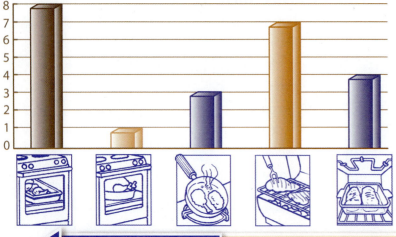

MOST POPULAR

___bake___

_____

_____

_____

_____

LEAST POPULAR

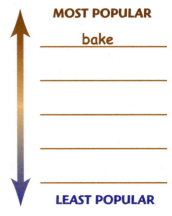

◄ **Reaching Out!**

Preparing Food

Choose a food that you like to eat. List all the ways you can prepare it. Which is your favorite way? Why? Which is the healthiest way? Compare with a classmate.

A ACTIONS IN THE KITCHEN

Match the cooking action with the utensil.

_c_	**1.** chop	**a.**	skillet
____	**2.** stir	**b.**	beater
____	**3.** boil	**c.**	knife
____	**4.** fry	**d.**	wooden spoon
____	**5.** peel	**e.**	cookie sheet
____	**6.** bake	**f.**	pot
____	**7.** mix	**g.**	peeler

B WHERE ARE THEY?

Look at page 59 of the Picture Dictionary. Decide if each sentence is True (T) or False (F).

_T_ **1.** The whisk is in the mixing bowl.

____ **2.** The bottle opener is between the can opener and the garlic press.

____ **3.** The ladle is to the left of the strainer.

____ **4.** The wok is in front of the double boiler.

____ **5.** The cookie cutter is in the measuring cup.

____ **6.** The lid is on the colander.

C JULIE AND DAN'S GIFT REGISTRY

Julie and Dan are getting married. They're at The Kitchen Store today, and they're setting up a "gift registry"—a list of kitchen utensils and cookware their friends and family can buy for them at the store. Here is a list of the items they want for their new home.

2 bottle openers	2 casserole dishes	3 lids	2 pots	2 saucepans
3 cake pans	1 colander	2 measuring cups	1 roasting pan	2 skillets
1 can opener	1 ice cream scoop	1 measuring spoon	1 roasting rack	2 spatulas
1 carving knife	1 kitchen timer	3 paring knives	1 rolling pin	1 steamer

Look at the items they already have in their kitchens, and look at the list above. Which items do they need, and how many? Help them complete the checklist.

The Kitchen Store Checklist

ITEM	NEED?	QUANTITY
saucepan	yes [ ] no [✔]	
skillet	yes [✔] no [ ]	1
pot	yes [ ] no [ ]	
lid	yes [ ] no [ ]	
steamer	yes [ ] no [ ]	
roasting pan	yes [ ] no [ ]	
roasting rack	yes [ ] no [ ]	
casserole dish	yes [ ] no [ ]	
cake pan	yes [ ] no [ ]	
rolling pin	yes [ ] no [ ]	
spatula	yes [ ] no [ ]	
colander	yes [ ] no [ ]	
measuring cup	yes [ ] no [ ]	
measuring spoon	yes [ ] no [ ]	
kitchen timer	yes [ ] no [ ]	
bottle opener	yes [ ] no [ ]	
can opener	yes [ ] no [ ]	
ice cream scoop	yes [ ] no [ ]	
paring knife	yes [ ] no [ ]	
carving knife	yes [ ] no [ ]	

Make a list of the ten utensils and cookware items you use the most and the foods you use them with. Then compare with a classmate. How are your lists the same? How are they different?

Reaching Out!

Your Kitchenware

A INGREDIENTS

Match the fast food with the ingredient.

__c__ 1. nachos
____ 2. french fries
____ 3. hamburger
____ 4. ketchup
____ 5. milkshake
____ 6. chili
____ 7. salad
____ 8. pizza

a. cheese
b. lettuce
c. tortilla chips
d. ground beef
e. beans
f. tomatoes
g. potatoes
h. ice cream

B CATEGORIES

For each word below, write the following:
F = Food, C = Condiment, P = Paper Product/
Utensil.

__F__ 1. frozen yogurt
____ 2. mustard
____ 3. paper cups
____ 4. mayonnaise
____ 5. hot dog
____ 6. plastic utensils
____ 7. straws
____ 8. relish
____ 9. taco
____ 10. napkins
____ 11. lids
____ 12. ketchup

C NUTRITIONAL INFORMATION

This chart gives the nutritional information for one serving of six popular fast-food items—fried chicken, a salad, salad dressing, a fish sandwich, a cheeseburger, and french fries. Look at the chart and complete the lists below.

g = gram

mg = milligram

	Calories	Fat	Salt (Sodium)
	420	24 g.	1120 mg.
	90	4 g.	170 mg.
	170	16 g.	530 mg.
	400	18 g.	640 mg.
	520	26 g.	1155 mg.
	525	25 g.	335 mg.

MOST CALORIES

french fries
____
____
____
____
____

FEWEST CALORIES

MOST FAT

____
____
____
____
____
____

LEAST FAT

MOST SALT

____
____
____
____
____
____

LEAST SALT

Reaching Out!

Healthier Choices

What are some fast foods that you and your family like to eat? For each one, list a healthier option that you could eat. For example, *fried chicken—baked chicken*. Compare with a classmate.

A THE SUNSHINE CAFE

Look at the signs at this coffee shop. Then write the correct price for each item.

THE SUNSHINE CAFE

85¢ $1.75 $1.50 75¢

$3.50 99¢ $2.75 $4.00

All Drinks $1.25

waffles	$3.50
coffee	
donut	
toast	
croissant	
muffin	
milk	
egg salad sandwich	
danish	
ham and cheese sandwich	

B DO THEY SELL IT?

Look at the signs above. Circle the items they have at the Sunshine Cafe.

iced tea	danish	bacon	waffles
bun	lemonade	muffin	pancakes
sausages	eggs	sandwiches	toast

C BREAKFAST OR LUNCH?

Do you eat the following items for breakfast, lunch, or both? Write them in the correct circle.

bacon
bagel
biscuit
corned beef sandwich
coffee
donut
eggs
home fries
iced tea
lemonade
muffin
pancakes
roast beef sandwich
roll

Breakfast

Breakfast & Lunch

Lunch

What are your five favorite breakfast foods? Do you make them at home, or do you order them at a coffee shop or fast-food restaurant? Make a list and then compare your list with a classmate's.

Reaching Out!

Breakfast Foods

A WHICH IS DIFFERENT?

1. **a.** waiter	**b.** chef	**c.** dinner fork	**d.** busperson
2. **a.** booth	**b.** tray	**c.** high chair	**d.** booster seat
3. **a.** water glass	**b.** wine glass	**c.** cup	**d.** napkin
4. **a.** dishroom	**b.** soup spoon	**c.** kitchen	**d.** dining room
5. **a.** butter knife	**b.** salad fork	**c.** teaspoon	**d.** bread basket
6. **a.** table	**b.** soup bowl	**c.** salad plate	**d.** saucer

B WHAT DO THEY DO?

Look at pages 62 and 63 of the Picture Dictionary. Write the restaurant actions below on the correct line.

clears the table	pays the check	seats the customers	sets the table
leaves a tip	pours the water	serves the meal	takes the order

1. hostess   <u>seats the customers</u>

2. customer   _____   _____

3. server   _____   _____

4. busperson   _____   _____   _____

C WHAT'S IN THE RESTAURANT?

Think of a restaurant you know. Put a check next to each of these items the restaurant has.

☐ host	☐ booths	☐ high chairs	☐ bread baskets	☐ dessert cart
☐ hostess	☐ tables	☐ booster seats	☐ salad bar	

D CUSTOMER SATISFACTION

Fill out the form for Emily and Bill.

   Last night Emily and Bill went to a new restaurant called Marissa's Kitchen. There were many things they liked about it. For example, the host and the waitress were very friendly, and the dining room was neat and clean. Also, there were many things to choose from on the menu. However, there were some problems. The salad bar was small, and the vegetables weren't fresh. Also, the food was cold. The only thing they liked were the desserts, which were delicious!

MARISSA'S KITCHEN

CUSTOMER SATISFACTION

Did you like it?	YES	NO
1. Host	—	—
2. Server	—	—
3. Dining Room	—	—
4. Menu	—	—
5. Salad Bar	—	—
6. Food	—	—
7. Dessert Tray	—	—

Reaching Out!

Setting a Table

Work with a partner. Give directions for how to set a table. (Put the . . .) Have your partner draw a diagram based on your directions. Check to see if your partner followed your instructions.

A FRED'S FAMILY RESTAURANT

Complete the menu below. Write the heading for each section.

Appetizers	Desserts	Entrees
Salads	Side dishes	

Fred's Family **Restaurant** ★

Salads

tossed salad	$3.00
Greek salad	$4.00
Caesar salad	$4.25

fruit cup	$3.50
potato skins	$4.95
tomato juice	$2.00

baked chicken	$7.95
meatloaf	$6.25
roast beef	$8.25
broiled fish	$6.50

baked potato	$1.75
rice	$1.95
french fries	$2.50
mixed vegetables	$3.25

ice cream	$2.25
apple pie	$3.95
jello	$2.75
pudding	$2.95

B ON THE MENU

Which of these items are on the menu?

antipasto	
apple pie	✔
baked chicken	
baked potato	
broiled fish	
chicken wings	
chocolate cake	
fruit cup	
Greek salad	
ice cream	
jello	
mashed potatoes	
meatloaf	
mixed vegetables	
nachos	
noodles	
potato skins	
pudding	
rice	
roast beef	
shrimp cocktail	
spinach salad	
tomato juice	
tossed salad	

C THE RESTAURANT BILL

Look at the menu above, and write the names of the foods next to the prices on each of the bills.

Fred's Family Restaurant	
tomato juice	$2.00
	$4.95
	$6.25
	$8.25
	$3.25
	$2.25
	$2.75
Total:	$29.70

Fred's Family Restaurant	
	$3.50
	$3.00
	$6.50
	$1.95
	$2.95
Total:	$17.90

Fred's Family Restaurant	
	$4.00
	$4.25
	$1.75
	$2.50
	$7.95
	$6.50
	$3.95
Total:	$30.90

Reaching Out!

You and a classmate are opening your own restaurant! What foods will you serve? What will the prices be? Create a menu and share it with the class.

A Perfect Menu!

Types of Restaurants

Restaurants are everywhere! When people don't want to eat at home, they can go to many different kinds of restaurants. There are fast-food restaurants, family restaurants, fine dining restaurants, buffet restaurants, sandwich shops, pizza shops, and many others.

Fast-food restaurants are quick and easy. They offer hamburgers, cheeseburgers, hot dogs, tacos, french fries, chili, and other foods. These are called fast foods because they are usually prepared before a customer orders them. Customers stand in line, order the food at a counter, wait a short time, and then receive the food. The person at the counter usually asks, "Is that for here or to go?" Based on the answer, customers either receive the food on a tray or in a bag. If customers order a drink, they sometimes receive an empty cup and fill it themselves at a soda machine. Many people like fast-food restaurants because they're quick and cheap.

At family restaurants, patrons sit at tables and order food from a menu. A waiter or waitress serves the meal. These restaurants usually offer meat, poultry, and seafood dishes that are cooked in different ways. The chef might steam, saute, bake, boil, broil, fry, stir-fry, or grill different dishes. Typical side dishes include rice, potatoes, and vegetables. Fine dining restaurants are like family restaurants, but they are usually fancier and more expensive.

Buffet restaurants are very popular in some areas. At these restaurants, customers serve themselves and pay a set price for all the food they eat. There is usually a large salad bar with fresh uncooked vegetables such as lettuce, spinach, tomatoes, and cucumbers. There is also a hot buffet section with cooked foods and side dishes. Many buffet restaurants also have a section with fruit such as cantaloupe and watermelon and a section with desserts such as cake, pudding, jello, and ice cream. Many people love to eat at buffet restaurants, especially when they're hungry!

1. People go to fast-food restaurants because _____.
   a. they're quick
   b. they're expensive
   c. they're fancy
   d. they have hot buffet sections

2. If a customer orders food "to go," the customer will probably _____.
   a. sit at a table
   b. take food from a buffet
   c. receive the food in a bag
   d. receive the food on a tray

3. One typical side dish at a restaurant is _____.
   a. a hot dog
   b. rice
   c. poultry
   d. seafood

4. The hot buffet section usually has _____.
   a. fruit
   b. dessert
   c. a salad bar
   d. cooked food

5. A salad bar DOESN'T usually have _____.
   a. tomatoes
   b. baked potatoes
   c. lettuce
   d. cucumbers

6. Waiters and waitresses probably receive bigger tips in _____.
   a. fast-food restaurants
   b. buffet restaurants
   c. fine dining restaurants
   d. family restaurants

A DECORATE YOUR APARTMENT!

You're decorating your new apartment. What colors are you going to use?

Living Room	Dining Room	Kitchen	Bedroom
Carpet turquoise	Walls light green	Counters navy blue	Carpet gold
Walls _____	Drapes _____	Walls _____	Walls _____
Drapes _____	Rug _____	Cabinets _____	Curtains _____
Sofa _____	Chairs _____	Curtains _____	Bedspread _____
Armchairs _____	Tablecloth _____	Refrigerator _____	Armchair _____
Pillows _____	Dishes _____	Stove _____	Sheets _____

B COLORS AND EMOTIONS

You're an artist, and you paint pictures that show how you feel. What colors are you going to choose to show the following emotions? Compare your answers with a classmate's.

1. You just had a big fight with a friend. You're very angry. _____

2. You're feeling sad and lonely. _____

3. You're going to start a new job tomorrow, and you're very excited. _____

4. You worked hard all day, and now you're hungry and exhausted. _____

5. You have nothing to do today. You're bored. _____

C COLORS AND FLAGS

What colors do you see on flags? The chart on the left shows the percentage of flags that have these seven colors. Write the correct colors under the bars in the graph.

yellow	43%
blue	50%
red	74%
black	22%
white	71%
green	42%
orange	5%

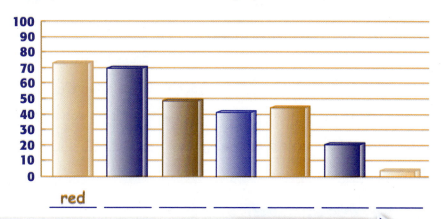

red _____ _____ _____ _____ _____ _____

Take a class survey. What are students' favorite colors? Make a bar graph that shows each color and the number of students who say it's their favorite.

Reaching Out!
Popular Colors

A WHAT ARE THEY WEARING?

Look at page 66 of the Picture Dictionary and choose the correct answer.

1. A woman is wearing a blouse and a ((skirt)   shirt).
2. The man at the bus stop is wearing a (sport shirt   sport jacket).
3. A woman and man are talking. The woman is wearing a green (dress   suit).
4. The police officer is wearing (a uniform   overalls).
5. A young girl is wearing a (jumpsuit   jumper).

B TWO CLOTHING SALES

Look at the ads from Martin's Department Store and The Casual Shop. Then complete the chart.

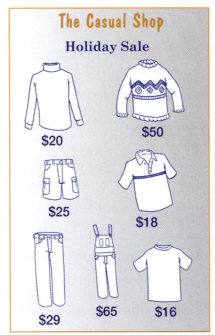

Clothing	Price
dresses	$65
	$45
blazers	
shorts	
	$35
	$16
three-piece suits	
	$50
overalls	
	$40
turtlenecks	
	$30
	$29
jerseys	

1. Robert needs to buy a new suit. He also needs a new shirt and tie. Which store should he

   go to? _____ How much will he spend? _____

2. Barbara wants to buy a sweater and a pair of pants for her son. Which store should she

   go to? _____ How much will she spend? _____

3. Alice wants to buy a new skirt, blouse, and dress for work. Which store should she go to?

   _____ How much will she spend? _____

4. Carl wants to buy a pair of shorts and a jersey for his son and a turtleneck for his

   daughter. Which store should he go to? _____

   How much will he spend? _____

Reaching Out!

Holiday Shopping

You're buying holiday gifts for your friends and family. Look at the two holiday ads. What are you going to buy? Who are you buying each item for? How much are you going to spend? Compare with a classmate.

A WHAT ARE THEY WEARING?

Look at page 67 of the Picture Dictionary and choose the correct answer.

1. The woman with a dog is wearing a (jacket   (coat)).
2. A woman in the park is wearing a jacket and (ear muffs   a muffler).
3. A girl is wearing a sweater jacket and (sunglasses   tights).
4. The vendor is wearing a leather jacket and a (cap   hat).
5. The man with the umbrella is wearing a (poncho   trench coat).
6. A woman is wearing a ski mask and a (down jacket   parka).

B CLOTHING FOR DIFFERENT PLACES

Mr. and Mrs. Garcia live in Canada. They're going to Hawaii for a vacation. It's warm in Hawaii, but it sometimes rains. It's never cold. What should Mr. and Mrs. Garcia take to Hawaii? Look at the list of outerwear they have in their closet. Put an H next to each item they should take to Hawaii, and put an C next to each item they should leave in Canada.

Mr. Garcia	
H baseball cap	___ overcoat
C down vest	___ rain hat
___ ear muffs	___ ski hat
___ gloves	___ ski jacket
___ leather jacket	___ raincoat

Mrs. Garcia	
___ down jacket	___ rain boots
___ hat	___ scarf
___ mittens	___ ski mask
___ parka	___ sweater jacket
___ poncho	___ windbreaker

C OUTERWEAR SALE

Forbes Clothing Store is having a big sale. Everything is half-price. Fill in the sale prices in the ad, and then complete the chart.

FORBES CLOTHING STORE **Save 50% on everything!**

Regular Price $14
Sale Price $ _7_

Regular Price $40
Sale Price $____

Regular Price $12
Sale Price $____

Regular Price $18
Sale Price $____

Regular Price $30
Sale Price $____

Regular Price $8
Sale Price $____

Regular Price $22
Sale Price $____

Regular Price $20
Sale Price $____

Clothing Item	Regular Price	Sale Price
caps	$14	$7

Clothing Item	Regular Price	Sale Price

What outerwear do you own? Look in your drawers and closets, and make a list of all your outerwear items. Compare lists with a classmate.

Reaching Out!

Outerwear Inventory

A WHICH DEPARTMENT?

Which clothing items can you buy in the following departments?

bikini panties	camisole	nightgown	pantyhose	slip
boxers	jockey shorts	nightshirt	robe	undershirt
bra	jockstrap	pajamas		

Sleepwear _____

Men's Underwear _____

Women's Underwear _____

B WHICH IS DIFFERENT?

1. a. athletic supporter   b.) bra   c. jockstrap   d. boxers
2. a. camisole   b. full slip   c. half slip   d. slippers
3. a. knee socks   b. tights   c. knee-highs   d. socks
4. a. pajamas   b. nightgown   c. bikini panties   d. bathrobe
5. a. camisole   b. tights   c. stockings   d. pantyhose

C HOW MUCH WILL THEY SPEND?

Van's Clothing Store is having a big sale. Look at the ad and answer the questions.

VAN'S CLOTHING STORE *On Sale This Week!*

3 for $24   3 for $15   3 for $25   3 for $10

$20 (Buy 2, get one free!)   3 for $21 $14   2 for $10

$30 $25 $35 $2

1. Susan is looking for a bra and two pairs of pantyhose.

   She'll spend _____$30_____.

2. Bob needs three pairs of jockey shorts and a pair of slippers.

   He'll spend _____.

3. Ann is looking for three pairs of briefs and a half slip.

   She'll spend _____.

4. John wants to buy three undershirts and six pairs of boxer shorts.

   He'll spend _____.

5. Ed wants to buy a pair of pajamas, a bathrobe, and three pairs of socks.

   He'll spend _____.

6. Rose needs a new nightgown and three bras.

   She'll spend _____.

◀ **Reaching Out!**

Things to Buy   You need to buy several sleepwear and underwear items. Make a list. Then look at ads in a newspaper, go to a department store, or look at a department store website and find out how much you will have to pay.

A WHAT ARE THEY WEARING?

Look at page 69 of the Picture Dictionary and choose the correct answer.

1. A man is wearing a red (T-shirt   (tank top)).
2. The boy on the bicycle is wearing black (lycra shorts   sweatpants).
3. The woman who is sitting is wearing a pink (cover-up   leotard).
4. A boy is wearing a yellow and red (warm-up suit   bathing suit).
5. A girl is wearing a jogging suit and a (sweatband   sweatshirt).
6. The (high-tops   high heels) are red.
7. The (thongs   sandals) are blue.
8. The (tennis shoes   running shoes) are white, green, and orange.
9. The (cowboy boots   work boots) are dark brown.

B YOUR CLOTHING CHECKLIST

Which of these clothing items do you own? Put one check next to each item you own. Put two checks next to each item you wear often.

boots	jogging suit	running shoes	sweatpants
cowboy boots	leotard	running shorts	swimsuit
heels	loafers	sandals	tank top
hiking boots	lycra shorts	sneakers	tennis shoes
high-tops	moccasins	sweatband	work boots
flip-flops	pumps	sweatshirt	

C WHAT SHOULD THEY WEAR?

It's Saturday morning, and these people are going to do different activities today. Help them decide what they should wear. Compare answers with your classmates.

1. Linda is going to go jogging. She should wear _____.
2. Ahmed is going to ride his bicycle. He should wear _____.
3. Ruth is going to go swimming. She should wear _____.
4. Tom is going to play tennis. He should wear _____.
5. Amanda is going to exercise at a health club. She should wear _____.
6. Roger is going to clean his garage. He should wear _____.

What kinds of footwear and outerwear do you own? Make a list. Then share your list with other classmates. Which items are the most popular?

Reaching Out!

What's Popular?

A WHICH ITEM?

1. Maria is wearing a beautiful (makeup bag (necklace)).
2. I have twenty-five dollars in my (wallet   wrist watch).
3. There are three keys on my key (ring   pin).
4. I keep all my important papers in my (belt   briefcase).
5. If you need some quarters, I have some in my (chain   change purse).
6. My notebook and my textbook are in my (backpack   brooch).
7. My favorite pieces of jewelry are my pearls and my (locket   purse).

B WHAT'S IN THE BAG?

__c__ 1. makeup bag
____ 2. briefcase
____ 3. change purse
____ 4. shoulder bag
____ 5. wallet
____ 6. backpack

a. pennies, nickels, dimes, and quarters
b. dollar bills, credit cards, and photographs
c. lipstick, mascara, eye shadow
d. papers, books, pens, pencils
e. books, lunch, homework, sweater, shoes
f. wallet, change purse, handkerchief, key chain

C MRS. NELSON'S JEWELRY

Mrs. Nelson has insurance for all the expensive jewelry she owns. When she bought the insurance, she took these pictures and wrote down the price of each piece of jewelry.

Yesterday there was a robbery. Mrs. Nelson filed the following police report. Look at the pictures of Mrs. Nelson's jewelry and then complete the police report.

$500
$700
$150
$300
$400
$800
$200
$250
$100
$350
$1000

Name:	Evelyn Nelson	
Address:	44 Main Street, Brandon, NJ	
Date	5/29	
Time of Robbery:	6:30 P.M.	
Items Stolen		**Value**
diamond necklace		$1,000
gold cuff links		
engagement ring		
silver bracelet		
earrings		
silver brooch		
gold chain		
beads		

What **didn't** the robbers take? _____

Reaching Out!

Class Inventory

What kinds of jewelry and accessories do your classmates have with them today? Look around the classroom and make a list. Then do a class inventory—make a list of the items and the total number of each item in the classroom.

A WHICH ONE DOESN'T BELONG?

1. jacket	a. solid green	b. corduroy	(c.) pierced	d. extra-large
2. sweater	a. wool	b. striped	c. cardigan	d. leather
3. socks	a. crewneck	b. cotton	c. ankle	d. knee-high
4. pants	a. denim	b. solid blue	c. turtleneck	d. medium
5. shirt	a. polyester	b. long-sleeved	c. plaid	d. clip-on

B COMPLETE THE STORE SIGNS

Circle the correct words to complete the store signs for these clothing items.

1.  All ((striped)   checked)
(short–sleeved   sleeveless)
(cardigan   cotton) blouses
on sale today!

3.  Special sale today on
our extra–(linen   large)
(print   solid)
(leather   cotton) jerseys!

2.  (Solid black   Solid white)
(wool   straw)
(V–neck   turtleneck)
(sweaters   shirts) on sale!

4. Summer sale on all
(sleeveless   pierced)
(corduroy   floral)
100% (linen   large) dresses!

C YOUR STORE SIGNS

You work at a department store! Today you're making sale signs for the clothing items below. Make a sign for these shirts and a sign for these blouses.

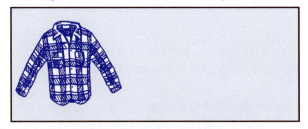

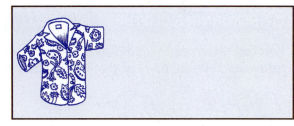

D FIND THE RIGHT PERSON!

Find somebody in the class who is wearing one of the following clothing items. Write the person's first name in the blank.

_____ pierced earrings	_____ a sleeveless blouse	_____ something striped
_____ white crew socks	_____ a turtleneck	_____ a solid blue shirt
_____ blue denim pants	_____ something plaid	_____ something wool
_____ brown leather shoes	_____ a short-sleeved shirt	_____ something polka-dotted

Describe what three people in your class are wearing today, but *don't* say the people's names. (Describe the color, the patterns, and the materials of the clothing items.) Your classmates must guess who you're talking about.

Reaching Out!

Guess Who?

A FIND THE OPPOSITE

1. too fancy   too baggy
2. too tight   too low
3. too heavy   too narrow
4. too wide   too plain
5. too high   too light

B HOW CAN I FIX IT?

1. The dress is too long.   Take it in.
2. The skirt is too short.   Clean it.
3. The collar is stained.   Shorten it.
4. The jacket is too loose.   Let it out.
5. The blazer is too tight.   Lengthen it.

C SAM'S BARGAIN BASEMENT

At Sam's Bargain Basement the clothes are very cheap because they all have defects. Look at the clothes carefully and find the problems. Then complete the sentences.

broken	buttonholes	large	pocket	sleeve	zipper
button	lapel	missing	ripped	stained	

1. The pants have a ___**ripped**___ _____.
2. The jacket has a _____ _____.
3. The shirt has a _____ _____.
4. The _____ on the skirt is _____.
5. The _____ on the blouse's _____ are too _____.

D RETURNING CLOTHES

You can return clothing at Ray's Department Store, but you have to tell the store why you want to return each item. Look at the clothes that people are returning and complete the chart.

RAY'S DEPARTMENT STORE RETURNS	December 15
ITEM	**REASON FOR RETURN**
shoes	The heels are too ___high_____.
shirt	The collar is _____.
jacket	The sleeve is _____.
tie	It's too _____ and too _____.
sweater	The sleeves are too _____.
pants	They're too _____.

Reaching Out!

Sewing Survey

Take a class survey. How many students in the class can shorten pants? lengthen sleeves? fix a seam? take in a shirt? let out pants? repair a broken zipper? sew on a missing button? make buttonholes?

A   LAUNDRY INSTRUCTIONS

Ellen is leaving a note for her son with laundry instructions. Fill in the missing words.

bleach	clothespins	fabric softener	laundry detergent	sort	unload
closet	dark	fold	lint trap	spray starch	wet
clothesline	drawer	iron	put away	static cling remover	wrinkled

Thanks for doing the laundry! Here are some instructions. Don't forget to _____sort_____¹ the laundry first. Wash _____² colors separately. Turn on the washing machine and add ½ cup of _____³. If the white shirts and sheets look a little yellow, add some _____⁴. Add _____⁵ to the baby's clothes to keep them soft. When you _____⁶ the washer, hang the bras and nightgowns on the _____⁷. If there aren't enough _____⁸, look in the cabinet on the porch. Put the rest of the _____⁹ clothes in the dryer. Don't forget to clean out the _____¹⁰ and add _____¹¹. You'll need to _____¹² the _____¹³ clothing. Use a little _____¹⁴ on the shirts and blouses. Hang up the shirts in the _____¹⁵. Then _____¹⁶ and _____¹⁷ the sheets in the _____¹⁸.

B   CLOTHING CARE

Read the following labels and answer the questions.

Jersey	Blouse	Jacket	Pants	Sweater
Machine wash in cold water. No bleach or softeners. Dry at low temperature and remove from dryer right away. Do not iron.	Hand wash in cold water. Do not bleach. Iron at low temperature. Do not hang. Dry flat.	Machine wash warm. Only non-chlorine bleach when needed. Tumble dry low. Remove from dryer immediately. Use warm iron.	Hand wash cool. Mild soap. No bleach. Hang to dry. Cool iron if needed.	Hand or machine wash in cold water. No bleach. If machine drying, dry at low temperature. Cool iron if necessary.

1. Which clothing items can you wash in the washing machine? _____jersey, jacket, sweater_____

2. Which clothing items can you dry in the dryer? _____

3. Which clothing items can you iron? _____

4. Which clothing item should you dry on a clothesline? _____

5. Which clothing item can you use bleach on? _____

Take a class survey. Which laundry items on page 73 of the Picture Dictionary do students use? What are students' favorite brands of laundry detergent? fabric softener? bleach?

Reaching Out!

Laundry Survey

A Successful Business

The Sirivong family came to the United States from Laos ten years ago, and they now own a very successful dry-cleaning business. Mr. and Mrs. Sirivong work together there, and their children help in the store after school. Mr. Sirivong cleans all the clothes that people bring to the store. Mrs. Sirivong fixes clothing problems and does alterations. She fixes broken zippers and torn pockets. She sews on missing buttons. She lets out or takes in pants and jackets, and she shortens or lengthens sleeves, skirts, and other clothing items. Mr. and Mrs. Sirivong work very hard.

Every day many different customers bring their clothing to the dry cleaners. Andrea Weston is the Sirivongs' best customer. She owns a large clothing store in town, and she's always so busy that she doesn't have time to do laundry at home. Ms. Weston brings her sleepwear, underwear, and exercise clothing to a laundry business across the street from the Sirivongs' shop, but she brings all her other clothing to the Sirivongs for dry cleaning.

Their most interesting customers are Mr. and Mrs. Anderson. Mrs. Anderson has very colorful clothing, but Mr. Anderson doesn't. Mrs. Anderson sometimes brings in a red jacket, a blue sweater, purple or turquoise skirts, yellow or orange blouses, and dresses that are pink, green, white, or many other colors. On the other hand, Mr. Anderson usually brings in brown clothing. All his suits, his sport coats, his pants, and his sweaters are brown. His shirts are all white, but everything else is brown—even his tuxedo!

Customers like to bring their clothing to the Sirivongs' dry-cleaning business. The family works very hard, and they like all their customers very much. It's a very successful business.

1. From the story you know that _____.
   a. the Sirivongs are in Laos
   b. the Sirivongs own a clothing store
   c. the Sirivongs have children
   d. the Sirivongs wear colorful clothing

2. An example of a clothing alteration is _____.
   a. fixing a torn pocket
   b. fixing a broken zipper
   c. sewing on a missing button
   d. lengthening a skirt

3. When Ms. Weston goes to the dry cleaners, she sometimes brings her _____.
   a. nightgowns
   b. blouses
   c. running shorts
   d. stockings

4. Ms. Weston is their best customer because _____.
   a. she brings a lot of clothing there
   b. she owns a clothing store
   c. her clothing is colorful
   d. she doesn't own a washer or dryer

5. From the story you know that Mrs. Anderson owns _____.
   a. a blue skirt
   b. a white blouse
   c. a green jacket
   d. a pink dress

6. Mr. Anderson probably doesn't own _____.
   a. white undershirts
   b. brown shoes
   c. blue socks
   d. a brown tie

A WHICH DEPARTMENT?

Where can you find the following items? Write each item next to the correct department.

boxer shorts	food processor	necklace	sofa
earrings	hamburger	necktie	stereo system
end table	iron	refrigerator	stove
evening gown	nachos	skirt	television

Electronics Department	**stereo system**
Jewelry Counter	
Furniture Department	
Women's Clothing Department	
Household Appliances Department	
Snack Bar	
Men's Clothing Department	
Housewares Department	

B WHAT'S IN THE DEPARTMENT STORE?

Think of a department store you know. Put a check next to each of these items the store has.

- [ ] store directory
- [ ] escalator
- [ ] elevator
- [ ] snack bar
- [ ] customer pickup area
- [ ] customer assistance counter
- [ ] gift wrap counter
- [ ] water fountain

C THE STORE DIRECTORY

Julia is shopping at the Marcy Department Store. Look at the store directory below. Which floor should Julia go to if she . . .

1. wants to buy a new blouse? __1__
2. wants to buy a VCR? ____
3. is hungry and wants to eat? ____
4. wants to buy her baby a dress? ____
5. needs to use the bathroom? ____
6. wants to buy perfume? ____
7. wants to drink water? ____
8. wants to buy a table? ____
9. wants to put the table in her car? ____
10. wants to buy her husband a tie? ____
11. wants to buy a new refrigerator? ____

Departments	Floor	Services	Floor
Children's Clothing	3	Customer Pickup Area	1
Electronics	4	Customer Service	5
Home Furnishings	3	Gift Wrap Counter	5
Household Appliances	4	Ladies' Room	5
Housewares	4	Men's Room	5
Jewelry Counter	1	Snack Bar	5
Men's Clothing	2	Water Fountain	5
Perfume Counter	1		
Women's Clothing	1		

Make a list of ten things you want to buy in a department store and the departments where you think you can find them. Then go to a store and see if you are right. Compare lists with a classmate.

Reaching Out!

Departments

A WHICH IS FIRST?

Look at the shopping actions below. Circle the one that comes first.

1. a. return   (b.) buy
2. a. buy   b. get some information about
3. a. try on   b. return

4. a. pay for   b. exchange
5. a. exchange   b. buy
6. a. pay for   b. try on

B WHERE CAN YOU FIND THEM?

Look at page 75 of the Picture Dictionary. What information is on the sign, price tag, labels, and receipt? Write the words on the correct lines.

care instructions	material	regular price	sales tax	total price
discount	price	sale price	size	

1. sale sign   _____**discount**_____
2. price tag   _____   _____
3. labels   _____   _____   _____
4. receipt   _____   _____   _____

C COMPARING RECEIPTS

Nina always shops at Waldo's Clothing Mart, and Jackie always shops at Women's World Clothes. They bought the same dress and the same jeans, but they paid different prices. Look at their receipts and check who paid more.

Waldo's Clothing Mart

dress	$50.00
20% off	-$10.00
sale price	$40.00
+ 5% tax	$2.00
cash	$42.00

women's World Clothes

dress	$60.00
40% off	-$24.00
sale price	$36.00
+ 7% tax	$2.52
cash	$38.52

The Dress:

Whose Was More?	Nina	Jackie
discount		✔
original price		
sales tax		
sale price		
total price		

Waldo's Clothing Mart

jeans	$35.00
30% off	-$10.50
sale price	$24.50
+ 5% tax	$1.23
cash	$25.73

women's World Clothes

jeans	$42.00
10% off	-$4.20
sale price	$37.80
+ 7% tax	$2.65
cash	$40.45

The Jeans:

Whose Was More?	Nina	Jackie
discount	✔	
original price		
sales tax		
sale price		
total price		

Reaching Out!

A Shopping Trip

Tell about the last time you went shopping. Where did you go? Did you buy anything? Was anything on sale? (Try to use at least five of the words in this lesson.) Compare with a classmate.

A VIDEO OR AUDIO?

Check whether each item is video or audio equipment.

	Video	Audio
1. tape deck	____	✔
2. DVD player	____	____
3. headphones	____	____
4. radio	____	____
5. boombox	____	____
6. VCR	____	____
7. speakers	____	____
8. camcorder	____	____
9. shortwave radio	____	____

B MATCHING EQUIPMENT

Circle the item that goes with each of the following pieces of video or audio equipment.

1. DVD: portable stereo system   (DVD player)
2. videotape: VCR   battery charger
3. video game system: video game   tape deck
4. turntable: portable CD player   record
5. microphone: DVD   tape recorder
6. TV: remote control   battery pack
7. stereo system: camcorder   speakers
8. portable cassette player: audiotape   tuner
9. VCR: personal digital audio player   TV
10. CD player: clock radio   compact disc

C CONSUMER RATINGS

Look at the consumer ratings of different televisions. Decide if each sentence is True (T) or False (F). (5 stars = best; 1 star = worst)

CONSUMER RATINGS

Item	Picture	Sound
Plasma TV	★★★	★★★
LCD TV	★★★	★★★★★
Projection TV	★★★★★	★★★★
Portable TV	★	★

T 1. The LCD TV has the best sound.

____ 2. The plasma TV has the best picture.

____ 3. The sound on the LCD TV is better than the sound on the projection TV.

____ 4. The portable TV has the worst sound.

____ 5. The picture on the portable TV is better than the picture on the LCD TV.

____ 6. The picture on the projection TV is better than its sound.

____ 7. The picture on the plasma TV is better than the picture on the LCD TV.

____ 8. The sound on the plasma TV is the same as the sound on the projection TV.

Make a list of the video and audio equipment you have. Then rate each item using 1–5 stars like the ratings above. Compare with a classmate.

Reaching Out!

Rating Products

A MATCHING

Match the equipment that goes together.

__d__ 1. digital camera   **a.** film

____ 2. cell phone   **b.** movie screen

____ 3. camera   **c.** battery

____ 4. answering machine   **d.** memory disk

____ 5. slide projector   **e.** telephone

B YOUR ELECTRONICS

Put a check next to each of the following items you own.

☐ tripod   ☐ adapter

☐ adding machine   ☐ battery charger

☐ PDA   ☐ digital camera

☐ cell phone   ☐ pager

☐ zoom lens   ☐ cordless phone

C A BIG SALE!

Satellite Electronics is having a big sale this week! Here is their newspaper ad. First, decide if an item is camera equipment or telephone equipment. Then make a list of the camera equipment from most expensive to least expensive. Finally, make a list of the telephone equipment from most expensive to least expensive.

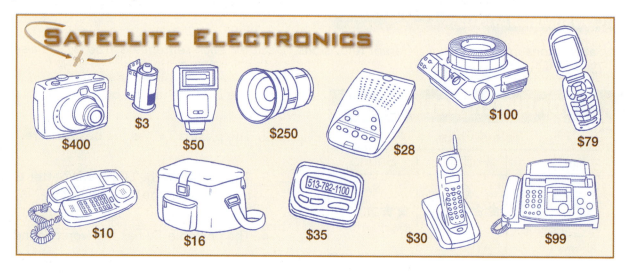

SATELLITE ELECTRONICS

$400 $3 $50 $250 $28 $100 $79

$10 $16 $35 $30 $99

CAMERA EQUIPMENT

MOST EXPENSIVE

digital camera

_____

_____

_____

_____

_____

LEAST EXPENSIVE

TELEPHONE EQUIPMENT

MOST EXPENSIVE

_____

_____

_____

_____

_____

LEAST EXPENSIVE

Reaching Out!

Sharing Photographs

Bring to class some favorite photographs you have taken. When did you take the photographs? What kind of camera did you use? Where did you buy it? Show your photographs to a classmate and tell about them.

A WHICH COMPUTER ITEMS?

1. Insert the CD-ROM in the (disk   (CD-ROM drive)).

2. You need to attach the printer to the computer with a (scanner   cable).

3. Some people like to use a mouse when they do word processing on their computer. Others prefer to use a (track ball   modem).

4. You should get a (computer game   spreadsheet program) if you want to keep information about how much money you spend every month.

5. If you want to play this computer game, you'll need to buy a (flat panel screen   joystick).

6. We want to buy this (educational software program   spreadsheet program) for our daughter. She's six years old, and she's learning to read.

7. If you want to connect to the Internet, you'll need to buy a (surge protector   modem).

8. I'm looking for a good (word-processing program   CD-ROM). I type a lot of letters and documents.

B SHOPPING AT TECH-CITY COMPUTERS

These people shopped at Tech-City Computers. What items did they buy? Check the items in the chart.

Angela went to Tech-City Computers last weekend. She bought the following items: a central processing unit, a monitor, a modem, and a word-processing program.

Mario went to Tech-City Computers last night. He bought the following items: a notebook computer, a printer, and a scanner.

Sarah went to Tech-City Computers this morning. She bought an LCD screen and a mouse. She wanted to buy a printer and a scanner, but they didn't have any left!

Item	Angela	Mario	Sarah
	✔		

Do you own a computer, or do you sometimes use one? Make a list of all of the parts on the computer you use. If you don't use a computer, draw a picture of your *dream* computer and describe it. Compare with a classmate.

Reaching Out!

Computers and You

A TYPES OF TOYS

Put the toys below in the correct group. (You can put the same toy in more than one group.)

bicycle	hula hoop	pail and shovel	science kit	toy truck
coloring book	jump rope	paint set	skateboard	train set
construction paper	markers	play house	stuffed animal	tricycle
construction set	matchbox car	racing car set	swing set	wagon
crayons	model kit			

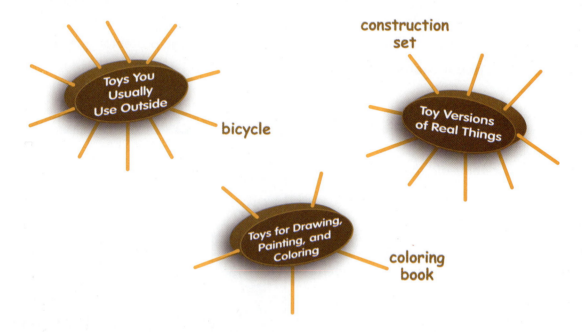

Toys You Usually Use Outside — bicycle

Toy Versions of Real Things — construction set

Toys for Drawing, Painting, and Coloring — coloring book

B RECOMMENDED AGES

Look at the graph below to see the recommended age for each toy. Then make a list of the toys in the order of the recommended ages, from oldest to youngest.

OLDEST

walkie-talkie set

_____

_____

_____

_____

YOUNGEST

Reaching Out!

Which Toys?

Which toys on Picture Dictionary page 79 do you recommend for the following types of children: a child who likes to build things? a very active child? an artistic child? a child who likes to be outdoors? Make a list. Then compare lists with a classmate.

The Mall of America

The Mall of America is the largest shopping mall in the United States. It is located in Bloomington, Minnesota. People from all over the world visit the complex, which contains more than 500 stores and 70 restaurants!

Major department stores are located in each corner of the mall. In each department store, a store directory shows customers where to find women's clothing, men's clothing, household furnishings, and all the other departments. These stores also have customer service counters (where people can return or exchange items) and gift wrap counters (where people can bring store items they buy to give as presents, and someone from the store will wrap them).

Specialty shops are located on every floor of the mall. Jewelry stores are full of rings, necklaces, and earrings. Electronics stores offer a wide variety of items, from the largest new TVs to the smallest cell phones and cameras. Music and video stores have CDs, videotapes, and DVDs. There are also book stores, toy stores, computer stores, shoe stores, kitchenware stores, and stores that specialize in clothing for men, women, teenagers, or little children. In addition to the stores, there are kiosks throughout the mall. At each of these little stands, a person usually sells just one type of item. There's a kiosk with watches, a kiosk with purses, one with children's puzzles, another with baseball caps, and many others. People like to stop at the kiosks as they walk through the mall. They have interesting things that sometimes aren't for sale in the regular stores.

The Mall of America is a convenient and friendly place to visit. There are big parking lots and parking garages around the complex. Glass elevators carry customers from the 1st floor to the 4th floor. Men's rooms and ladies' rooms are on every floor. In addition to all the restaurants, there are snack bars everywhere and specialty food stands where people can buy fresh-baked cookies, large pretzels, ice cream, and other good things to eat. The mall even has its own post office! People say it's like a small city. That's why people from all over the world come to Minnesota to see the largest mall in the United States.

1. Customers can find departments in a department store when they _____.
   a. go to the customer service counter
   b. go to the gift wrap counter
   c. ask a person at a kiosk
   d. look at the store directory

2. In the second paragraph, the word *presents* means _____.
   a. stores
   b. gifts
   c. customers
   d. friends and family members

3. A jewelry store is an example of a _____.
   a. department store
   b. mall
   c. specialty shop
   d. customer service counter

4. According to the story, a person probably CAN'T buy men's clothing _____.
   a. at a kiosk
   b. in a department store
   c. in a men's clothing department
   d. at a specialty store for men

5. People at the mall don't eat _____.
   a. at snack bars
   b. at food stands
   c. at restaurants
   d. at kitchenware stores

6. A good reason for people to say the Mall of America is like a city is that _____.
   a. it has glass elevators
   b. it has men's and ladies' rooms
   c. it has a post office
   d. it has a parking lot

A WHICH ITEMS?

1. I'd like to cash this (account   (check)), please.
2. You need to fill out this (deposit   withdrawal) slip if you want to put money in your account.
3. If you want to take money out of your account, you need to fill out a (deposit   withdrawal) slip.
4. You need to speak with a (security guard   bank officer) if you want to apply for a loan.
5. When I buy things in stores, I usually pay with a (bankbook   credit card).
6. You need to sign your name on each (traveler's check   currency).

B GETTING HELP AT A BANK

Look at the list of things you can do at a bank. Write T for things a teller helps you with, T/ATM for things a teller or ATM can help you with, and B for things a bank officer helps you with.

__T__ 1. cash a check   ____ 4. get traveler's checks   ____ 6. make a withdrawal

____ 2. apply for a loan   ____ 5. open an account   ____ 7. exchange currency

____ 3. make a deposit

C CHOOSING A BANK

Cathy is looking for a new bank. She's deciding between Best Bank and Star Bank. Look at the pictographs that describe each bank's services. Check which bank has more of each service.

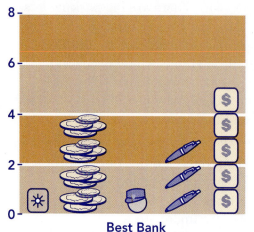

Best Bank

tellers
ATMs
security guards
vaults
bank officers

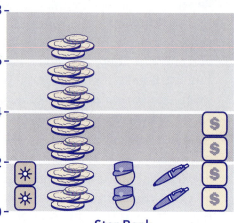

Star Bank

Which Has More?	Best Bank	Star Bank
vaults		✔
security guards		
bank officers		
ATMs		
tellers		

Reaching Out!

Your Bank

What bank do you use? How many of the people and services above does your bank have? Compare your information with a classmate who uses a different bank. Which bank is better? Why?

A TAKING CARE OF FINANCES

1. I'm going to balance my (money order   (checkbook)) today.
2. After you insert your ATM card, you need to enter your (PIN   bank) number.
3. Did we receive our (monthly statement   rent) from the bank?
4. Our largest household bill is our (check register   mortgage payment).
5. I use an ATM machine to (transfer funds   bank online).
6. The grocery store around the corner accepts only (cash   check numbers).

B FORMS OF PAYMENT

Blake's Department Store lets you pay many different ways. Look at their sign and check the different payment types that they take.

We take the following forms of payment:

- [ ] traveler's checks
- [ ] credit cards
- [ ] online banking
- [ ] checks
- [ ] cash
- [ ] money orders

C HOUSEHOLD BILLS

These pie charts show how much Allison and Charlie spend on their household bills. In each line of the table below, fill in the numbers 1–5 to show how much each person spends. (1 = most money spent; 5 = least money spent)

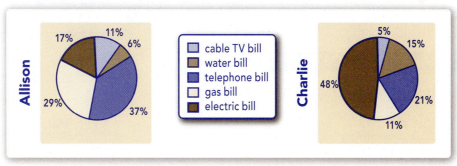

Allison: 17%, 11%, 6%, 37%, 29%

Legend:
- cable TV bill
- water bill
- telephone bill
- gas bill
- electric bill

Charlie: 5%, 15%, 21%, 11%, 48%

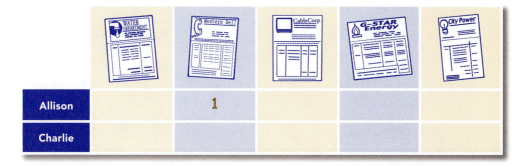

	WATER DEPARTMENT	Western Bell	CableCorp	G-STAR Energy	City Power
Allison		1			
Charlie					

Which household bills do you spend the most money on? the least money? Make a list of your household bills and how much you spend on each of them every month. Then make a pie chart to show this information.

Reaching Out!

Your Bills

A POSTAL RATES

Fill in the missing post office items and prices.

42¢ $8.40 $4.20   27¢ $42   65¢

book of stamps	$8.40
sheet of stamps	
postcard	
	65¢
stamp	
	$42

B ADDRESSING A LETTER

Label the parts of the address on the envelope below.

| mailing address | postmark | return address | stamp | zip code |

Sara Turner
26 Washington St.
Jamestown, NY 14701

Abby Fine
4238 Center St.
Oakland, CA 94605

C SENDING MAIL AT THE POST OFFICE

Cross out three items in each group that don't belong.

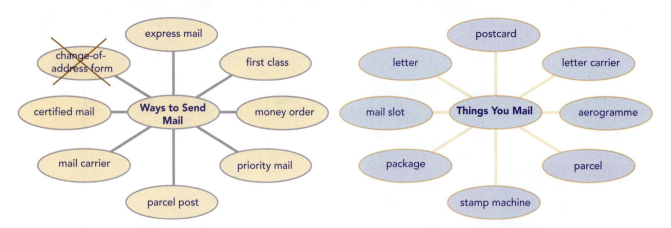

Ways to Send Mail
express mail
~~change-of-address form~~
first class
certified mail
money order
mail carrier
priority mail
parcel post

Things You Mail
postcard
letter
letter carrier
mail slot
aerogramme
package
parcel
stamp machine

Reaching Out!

Your Mail

What time does your mail usually arrive? Where does the mail carrier leave it? On a typical day, how many bills do you receive? How many letters? How many packages? How many advertisements? Compare with a classmate.

A BORROWING FROM THE WESTFORD LIBRARY

You can borrow many things from the Westford Library, but you have to pay a fine if you don't return them on time. Look at the chart and decide if each sentence is True (T) or False (F).

Item	Loan Period	Daily Late Fee
book	3 weeks	15¢
magazine	3 weeks	10¢
videotape DVD	1 week	50¢
audiotape book on tape CD software	2 weeks	20¢
dictionary atlas encyclopedia	must remain in library	

T 1. If you keep a book more than 3 weeks, you pay 15¢ a day.

____ 2. If you return a CD late, you pay 10¢ a day.

____ 3. If you return a DVD 2 days late, you pay $1.00.

____ 4. You can keep reference books for 3 weeks.

____ 5. You don't pay anything if you keep software for 2 weeks.

____ 6. You can keep books on tape longer than books.

____ 7. You can't borrow any periodicals from the library.

____ 8. If you return an audiotape a day late, you pay 50¢.

B WHAT FLOOR?

Read about a day at the Westford Public Library and fill in the correct floor on the floor directory.

It's a typical day at the Westford Public Library. On the first floor, people are reading newspapers, journals, and magazines. A family is taking out books. They're talking to the library clerk. A few people are trying to find books. They're checking the titles and authors. On the second floor, parents are reading books to their children, teenagers are listening to audiotapes, and a young man is looking for a computer program. It's very quiet on the third floor. Some students are writing papers. They're looking through encyclopedias and atlases and making copies of the important pages. A man nearby is reading a document on microfilm. Across the hall some people are reading books in Spanish, French, and Arabic.

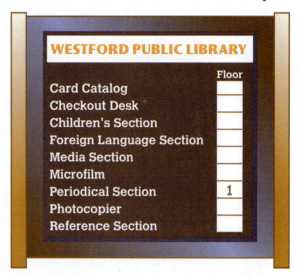

WESTFORD PUBLIC LIBRARY

	Floor
Card Catalog	
Checkout Desk	
Children's Section	
Foreign Language Section	
Media Section	
Microfilm	
Periodical Section	1
Photocopier	
Reference Section	

C WHAT'S ON THE CARD?

J8
123.6

Mary Susan Welles
Buddy Finds A Friend
A little girl gets a dog
for her birthday.

32 pages

1. The card on the left is from ____.

    a. a library card   b. a card catalog   c. an online catalog

2. The title of the book is _____.

3. The author of the book is _____.

4. You can find the book in the _____ section.

Go to your local library and find out the following information: What materials can you borrow? How long can you keep them? How much are the fines? Compare information with a classmate.

Reaching Out!

Your Library

A WHICH IS DIFFERENT?

1. a. police station   b. paramedic   c. fire station   d. hospital
2. a. ambulance   b. police car   c. dump   d. fire engine
3. a. church   b. mosque   c. synagogue   d. senior center
4. a. emergency operator   b. activities director   c. EMT   d. nursery
5. a. game room   b. gym   c. emergency room   d. playroom
6. a. sanitation worker   b. city manager   c. firefighter   d. recycling center
7. a. hospital   b. child-care center   c. mayor   d. town hall

B WHAT DOES WATERVILLE NEED?

The people of Waterville are having a meeting about next year's budget. They're telling the mayor what they think their city needs. Read what they're saying and complete the statements.

ambulances	emergency room	gym	paramedics	police officers
eldercare workers	fire engines	nursery	police cars	sanitation workers

1. "Our city isn't safe anymore. We need to hire more __police officers__, and we need to give them newer _____. "

2. "Hire more _____ to keep our streets clean."

3. "The people in our town don't get enough exercise. We should build a new _____."

4. "The child-care center needs a new _____."

5. "We should buy more _____ and hire more _____ to get patients quickly and safely to the hospital."

6. "Our firefighters are doing a fine job, but they don't have enough _____."

7. "Mr. Mayor, we need to build a new _____ for our hospital."

8. "What about our senior citizens? I think we should hire more _____ to help them."

C IT'S UP TO YOU

Which budget items do YOU think are the most important? Number these budget items from 1 (the most important) to 10 (the least important). Compare answers with a classmate.

☐ ambulances	☐ emergency room	☐ gym	☐ paramedics	☐ police officers
☐ eldercare workers	☐ fire engines	☐ nursery	☐ police cars	☐ sanitation workers

Reaching Out!

Your Community

Work with a small group of students to find answers to the following questions: Where is the nearest police station, fire station, and hospital in your community? What other community institutions are in your city or town? Make a list of the places you know, and look in the telephone directory to add to your list. Report your information to the class.

A WHAT'S THE HEADLINE?

Read the following newspaper headlines and circle the correct word.

1. (BURGLARY   (ROBBERY)) AT MIDTOWN BANK—TELLER HANDS OVER $1,000 IN CASH
2. (GAS LEAK   EXPLOSION) BLOWS ROOF OFF HOUSE
3. (VANDALISM   DRUG DEALING) AT LOCAL HIGH SCHOOL—REPAIRS WILL COST $2,000
4. (CAR ACCIDENT   TRAIN DERAILMENT) TEN MILES FROM STATION SENDS 50 PASSENGERS TO HOSPITAL
5. (KIDNAPPING   CHEMICAL SPILL) ON HIGHWAY 6—TRUCK WAS CARRYING TOXIC WASTE
6. (WATER MAIN BREAK   DOWNED POWER LINE) PUTS LIGHTS OUT ALL OVER TOWN
7. FOUR-ALARM (FIRE   MUGGING) DESTROYS THREE BUILDINGS

B CRIME IN FIVE CITIES

The chart below shows the crime rates last year in five large cities. The crime rate is the number of crimes for every 100,000 residents of the city.

City	Murder	Robbery	Assault	Burglary
Yorkville	8.2	351.5	471.3	393.4
Greenbrier	15.6	456.1	879.0	682.7
Paxton	22.9	633.3	877.2	892.1
Riverton	19.7	685.3	703.1	1,697.1
Bradbury	11.9	328.1	295.4	902.1

Write the names of the cities from highest to lowest crime rate for each of the crimes below.

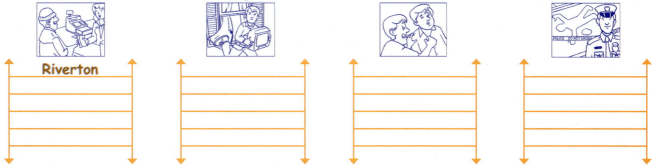

Riverton

C WHAT'S YOUR OPINION?

How long should people go to jail for each crime? Compare answers with your classmates.

Crime	Jail Time
drug dealing	
vandalism	
drunk driving	
car jacking	
kidnapping	

Crime	Jail Time
mugging	
assault	
burglary	
bank robbery	
murder	

What crimes and emergencies did you worry about where you lived before? What crimes and emergencies do you worry about now? Compare with a classmate.

Reaching Out!

Then and Now

A Popular Postal Clerk

Jack Fitzgerald is a postal clerk at the Central Avenue Post Office. He works at the window counter Monday through Friday from 8 A.M. to 4 P.M., and he's always busy.

Many people come to Jack's counter to buy stamps. Some people buy just a few stamps or a book of stamps. Others buy sheets of stamps or whole rolls of stamps when they have a lot of mail to send. (Sheets usually have 20 or more stamps. Rolls usually contain 100 stamps.) When people bring packages to the counter, Jack weighs them on a scale and asks if they want to send their packages priority mail, express mail, or parcel post. Some people choose priority mail because they want their packages to arrive in two or three days. Other people choose express mail so their packages will arrive the next day. Many people choose parcel post. It's slower than express or priority mail, but it's cheaper. When people have important letters to send, Jack tells them to send the letters certified mail since that's the safest way to send them. He also helps people when they need change-of-address forms, selective service registration forms, or passport application forms.

Jack's job may sound dull, but he makes it interesting and enjoyable for his customers and for himself. In fact, people come to the Central Avenue Post Office from many miles away just to see Jack! He always has a smile on his face and a funny story to tell. He's helpful, he's friendly, and he cares about his customers. He always asks them about their families, and they ask him about his.

Sometimes, the post office gets very crowded. However, most people choose to see Jack rather than go to a stamp machine or outside mailbox. The Central Avenue Post Office has the largest number of customers in the city. That's because Jack Fitzgerald works there.

1. This is a story about a popular _____.
   a. letter carrier
   b. mail carrier
   c. postal worker
   d. mailbox

2. A person probably spends the most money on _____.
   a. a roll of stamps
   b. a book of stamps
   c. a sheet of stamps
   d. a few stamps

3. In the second paragraph, in the sentence, "Jack weighs them on a scale . . . ," *them* refers to _____.
   a. stamps
   b. customers
   c. counters
   d. packages

4. According to the story, the fastest way to send a package is by _____.
   a. certified mail
   b. express mail
   c. priority mail
   d. parcel post

5. A good way to send an important letter is by _____.
   a. change-of-address form
   b. passport application form
   c. parcel post
   d. certified mail

6. In the third paragraph, the word *customers* refers to _____.
   a. Jack's family
   b. the packages
   c. the people who come to the post office
   d. the other clerks at the post office

THE BODY

DICTIONARY PAGES 86–87

A WHICH IS DIFFERENT?

1. a. ear   b. elbow   c. mouth   d. nose
2. a. gums   b. tooth   c. hips   d. tongue
3. a. chin   b. chest   c. cheeks   d. forehead
4. a. pelvis   b. skull   c. ribcage   d. brain
5. a. hair   b. esophagus   c. eyelashes   d. eyebrows
6. a. thumb   b. throat   c. knuckle   d. fingernail
7. a. heart   b. liver   c. pancreas   d. finger
8. a. jaw   b. iris   c. cornea   d. pupil
9. a. knee   b. calf   c. wrist   d. shin

B WHAT IS IT?

a. brain   c. eyelid   e. heart   g. palm   i. shoulder   k. thigh
b. chest   d. forehead   f. knuckle   h. pupil   j. tooth   l. wrist

__i__ 1. It's between your neck and arm.

____ 2. It's between your lungs.

____ 3. It's between your hand and your arm.

____ 4. It's between your eyebrows and hair.

____ 5. It's between your hip and knee.

____ 6. It's in the middle of your finger.

____ 7. It's inside your skull.

____ 8. It's between your wrist and fingers.

____ 9. It's inside the jaw.

____ 10. It's in front of the eye.

____ 11. It's in the center of the iris.

____ 12. It's between your neck and abdomen.

C FIND THE EXERCISE

A   B   C   D   E

__C__ 1. Lie on your back. Place your hand behind your thigh and pull it toward your chest.

____ 2. Lie on your stomach. Place your arms at your sides with your hands next to your hips. Raise your head and shoulders.

____ 3. Rest your buttocks on your heels and stretch your arms out in front of you.

____ 4. Lie on your stomach. Bend your knee. Raise your thigh and foot toward the ceiling. Keep your hips on the floor.

____ 5. Lie on your stomach with your arms above your head. Raise one arm with your thumb pointing up.

What exercises do you know for the eyes, neck, shoulders, chest, arms, wrists, back, hips, abdomen, thighs, calves, buttocks, lungs, heart, or other body parts? Describe the exercises and show how to do them.

Reaching Out!

Exercises You Know

A TRUE OR FALSE?

Look at page 88 of the Picture Dictionary.
Answer True (T) or False (F).

__F__ 1. The woman on the stairs has a fever.

____ 2. The man in the chair has the chills.

____ 3. The boxer has a runny nose.

____ 4. The man with glasses has a wart.

____ 5. The man in the bathroom has laryngitis.

____ 6. The boy is crying because he cut his finger.

____ 7. The woman with long curly hair has
cramps.

____ 8. The boy in the sweater has chest pains.

B FIND THE AILMENTS

Look at page 89 of the Picture Dictionary.
Match the ailment with the part of the body.

__d__ 1. twisted	a. feet
____ 2. burned	b. shoulder
____ 3. swollen	c. wrist
____ 4. scratched	d. ankle
____ 5. dislocated	e. fingers
____ 6. scraped	f. hand
____ 7. bruised	g. knees
____ 8. itchy	h. eye
____ 9. sprained	i. arm

C TIME TO CALL THE DOCTOR

Read these guidelines from a clinic and circle the correct answers.

Symptom:	When to Call the Doctor:
1. (dislocated itchy) eyes	If it happens often and medicine doesn't help.
2. cuts and (scrapes burps)	If (bleeding bloating) doesn't stop.
3. colds	If the (cough sneeze) lasts more than a week. If you have shortness of (rash breath).
4. headaches	If you have a high (fever bruise). If you have a (stiff scratched) neck.
5. (sore throat twisted ankle)	If it lasts more than three days. If you have difficulty breathing or speaking.
6. sunburn	If there are (warts blisters) on large areas of the skin. If you develop an (infection insect bite).
7. diarrhea or (vomiting hiccups)	If fluids like juice and water don't stay down. If you feel (laryngitis dizzy).
8. (cavities sprains)	If swelling lasts more than three days. If you have difficulty moving the part of the body that hurts.

Reaching Out!

What Do You Do?

What do you do when you have the ailments, symptoms, and injuries on pages 88 and 89 of the Picture Dictionary? When do you call the doctor? When do you go to the emergency room? When do you stay home from school or from work? Compare answers with your classmates.

Are you in good health? Fill out the medical questionnaire below.

Medical Questionnaire

1.	Do you have frequent headaches?	yes ☐	no ☐
2.	Do you have frequent stomachaches?	yes ☐	no ☐
3.	Do you have frequent backaches?	yes ☐	no ☐
4.	Do you have frequent colds?	yes ☐	no ☐
5.	Do you have frequent cramps?	yes ☐	no ☐
6.	Do you sometimes have shortness of breath?	yes ☐	no ☐
7.	Do you sometimes have chest pains?	yes ☐	no ☐
8.	Do you sometimes feel faint or dizzy?	yes ☐	no ☐
9.	Do you often feel exhausted?	yes ☐	no ☐
10.	Do you have any rashes?	yes ☐	no ☐
11.	Did you ever break a bone?	yes ☐	no ☐
12.	Did you ever have a bad sprain?	yes ☐	no ☐
13.	Did you ever have a severe burn or cut?	yes ☐	no ☐

The Acme Company wants to keep a record of how many employees miss work each month and why. Read about the following workers and add their information to the graph.

Mrs. Jones called to say she cut herself while she was making breakfast. She's at the emergency room. Mr. Martinez didn't come to work because he has a bad cough. Ms. Lewis sprained her ankle while she was jogging. She's at home in bed. Miss Phillips called to say she's congested and has laryngitis. Mr. Franklin couldn't come to work because he has a stomachache. Mrs. Green is at the clinic because she has a bad bruise on her knee. Mrs. Smith has terrible cramps and has been throwing up all morning. Mr. Chen is at the doctor's because he burned his hand. Mrs. Lorenzo woke up this morning with a high temperature and called in sick.

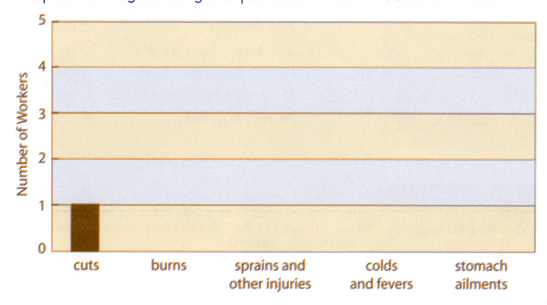

A THE WHITMAN SCHOOL

The Whitman School checks their first-aid kit every month to see what they have and what they need to buy. Look at their first-aid supplies and check everything they have.

- ☑ adhesive tape
- ☐ antihistamine cream
- ☐ antiseptic wipes
- ☐ antibiotic ointment
- ☐ Band-Aids
- ☐ elastic bandage
- ☐ first-aid manual
- ☐ gauze
- ☐ hydrogen peroxide
- ☐ pain reliever
- ☐ splint
- ☐ tweezers

B WHAT CAN THEY USE?

Some students at the Whitman School need first aid. Write down the first-aid supplies they need for each problem.

1. Peter cut his finger. _____
2. Jane has a splinter (a small piece of wood) in her finger. _____
3. Rosita has a burn. _____
4. Charlie has a sprained wrist. _____
5. Edith has a very bad rash. _____

C WHAT DO THEY NEED?

The Whitman School 🏫
First-Aid Supplies to Buy

_____
_____
_____

D WHAT'S THE REMEDY?

__d__ 1. He's choking.
____ 2. She doesn't have a pulse.
____ 3. He's bleeding very badly.
____ 4. She has a broken thumb.
____ 5. He isn't breathing.

a. tourniquet
b. rescue breathing
c. splint
d. Heimlich maneuver
e. CPR

Reaching Out!

Your First-Aid Supplies

What first-aid supplies do you have? Look in your home and check everything you have. Then make a list of the first-aid supplies you need to buy. Go to a pharmacy and find out how much these items cost. Compare with a classmate.

A HOW DID IT HAPPEN?

_d_ 1. He was moving heavy furniture.

____ 2. He fell asleep at the beach.

____ 3. The baby found a bottle of bleach.

____ 4. He ate some strawberries.

____ 5. He went skiing without a ski mask.

____ 6. He touched a wire.

____ 7. He fainted and fell down the stairs.

____ 8. He was suffering from depression.

a. He has heatstroke.

b. He's having an allergic reaction.

c. He got an electric shock.

d. He had a heart attack.

e. He's unconscious.

f. He overdosed on drugs.

g. He has frostbite.

h. He swallowed poison.

B YOUR MEDICAL HISTORY

Fill out the patient health form.

MEDICAL HISTORY

Name: _____ Date of Birth: _____/_____/_____

Please check (✓) if you had any of the following illnesses.

☐ chicken pox	☐ mumps	☐ heart disease	☐ tuberculosis	☐ cancer
☐ measles	☐ diabetes	☐ asthma	☐ high blood pressure	☐ depression

FAMILY HISTORY:

Please check (✓) if anyone in your family had any of the following illnesses and indicate the relationship (mother, father, grandmother, etc.).

Family history of …	Relationship			Relationship
☐ diabetes		☐ asthma		
☐ heart disease		☐ cancer		
☐ high blood pressure		☐ depression		

RECORD OF IMMUNIZATIONS:

Please check (✓) if you had any of the following vaccinations or tests and fill in the year of the most recent ones.

	Year		Year
☐ measles		☐ tuberculosis test	
☐ mumps		☐ influenza	
☐ chicken pox			

C ARE THEY CONTAGIOUS?

A contagious disease _is a disease that one person can get from another person._ Look at the diseases on page 91 of the Picture Dictionary. Which are contagious? Which are not contagious?

Contagious _____

Not Contagious _____

Which medical emergencies and illnesses in this lesson is it possible to prevent? In your opinion, what can you do to prevent them? Compare ideas with a classmate.

Reaching Out!

Medical Prevention

A THEY GO TOGETHER

1. Measure your height and weight.
2. Take your temperature.
3. Draw some blood.
4. Listen to your heart.
5. Examine your eyes.
6. Take a chest X-ray.
7. Check your blood pressure.

stethoscope
X-ray machine
blood pressure gauge
scale
syringe
eye chart
thermometer

B HOW ABOUT YOU?

1. My height is _____.
2. My weight is _____.
3. My temperature is _____.
4. My blood pressure is _____.
5. My vision is _____.
6. My cholesterol* is _____.

* *Cholesterol* is a material in our blood. Too much of the bad kind of cholesterol can cause heart disease.

C WHAT ARE THEY DOING?

Match what the doctor and other medical workers are saying and what they're doing.

__e__ 1. "Stand on this scale."

____ 2. "Cover your left eye."

____ 3. "Stick out your tongue and say Ah."

____ 4. "Roll up your sleeve."

____ 5. "Don't move."

____ 6. "Make a fist."

____ 7. "Have a seat."

a. taking a chest X-ray

b. checking your blood pressure

c. asking some questions about your health

d. examining your throat

e. measuring your height and weight

f. examining your eyes

g. drawing some blood

D WHO DOES IT?

When you have a medical exam in the United States, who usually does the following things: the doctor, the nurse, or a technician? Check D for Doctor, N for Nurse, or T for Technician.

	D	N	T
Who listens to your heart?			
Who takes your temperature?			
Who checks your blood pressure?			
Who takes a chest X-ray?			
Who asks you some questions about your health?			
Who draws blood?			
Who measures your height and weight?			
Who examines your eyes, ears, nose, and throat?			

E THE DOCTOR'S BAG

What can the doctor carry in his or her medical bag? Cross out what doesn't belong.

thermometer
scale
needles
~~examination table~~
blood pressure gauge
stethoscope
X-ray machine

Reaching Out!

The Doctor's Questions

What are some questions about your health that the doctor asks? Work with a small group of classmates and make a list of questions.

A WHICH IS DIFFERENT?

1. a. physician   b. receptionist   c. patient   d. nurse
2. a. anesthetic   b. sling   c. cast   d. brace
3. a. insurance card b. stitches   c. prescription d. medical history form
4. a. Novocaine   b. injection   c. alcohol   d. shot
5. a. drill   b. clean   c. close   d. dress
6. a. dental hygienist b. cavity   c. dentist   d. tape

B DOCTOR, DENTIST, OR BOTH?

Who does the following—the doctor, the dentist, or both? Write DO for Doctor, DE for Dentist, or B for Both.

__B__ 1. Who has a waiting room?
____ 2. Who drills cavities?
____ 3. Who can give prescriptions?
____ 4. Who gives a patient crutches?
____ 5. Who wears gloves?
____ 6. Who gives Novocaine?
____ 7. Who has a receptionist?
____ 8. Who puts your arm in a cast or sling?
____ 9. Who dresses wounds?
____ 10. Who has a hygienist?
____ 11. Who fills your teeth?
____ 12. Who takes insurance?

C WHEN DOES IT HAPPEN?

Put these events in the correct order. Number them from 1–10.

__ The doctor closed the wound with three stitches.
__ The doctor gave the patient a prescription.
_1_ The patient went into the waiting room.
__ The doctor dressed the wound.
__ The doctor got some cotton balls and alcohol and cleaned the wound.
__ The nurse took her to an examination room.
__ She showed her insurance card to the receptionist.
__ The doctor examined her wound.
__ She filled out a medical history form.
__ The doctor got some gauze and some tape.

D DID YOU EVER . . . ?

Interview a classmate. Put a check next to the things that happened to you and to your partner. Tell each other about your experiences.

You	Classmate	You	Classmate	You	Classmate
□ have stitches? □	□ use crutches?	□	□ wear a brace?	□
□ wear a cast? □	□ have a filling without Novocaine?	□	□ wear a sling?	□

Reaching Out!

Class Survey

Use the information from Exercise D to take a class survey. Then make a graph that shows how many students in the class had stitches, wore a cast, used crutches, had a filling without Novocaine, wore a brace, and wore a sling.

A BAD ADVICE

Cross out the bad advice for the following problems

1. a cold: a. take vitamins   b. ~~see a specialist~~   c. use a humidifier
2. frequent backaches: a. gargle   b. get acupuncture   c. use a heating pad
3. a cavity: a. see a dentist   b. rest in bed   c. get a filling
4. allergies: a. have tests   b. use a walker   c. use an air purifier
5. trouble walking: a. use a cane   b. get physical therapy   c. drink fluids
6. overweight: a. get braces   b. go on a diet   c. exercise

B GOOD ADVICE

Look at page 94 of the Picture Dictionary. In your opinion, what's the best advice for the following problems?

1. a sore throat _____   6. overweight _____
2. a cold _____   7. a dislocated shoulder _____
3. frequent backaches _____ 8. a sore throat _____
4. allergies _____   9. high blood pressure _____
5. trouble walking _____   10. depression _____

C TRYING TO MAKE THINGS BETTER

Put a check next to each of the following remedies you tried. What was the ailment or problem?

Remedy	Reason
☐ 1. I went on a diet.	
☐ 2. I saw a specialist.	
☐ 3. I got acupuncture.	
☐ 4. I used a heating pad.	
☐ 5. I used a humidifier.	
☐ 6. I used an air purifier.	
☐ 7. I had physical therapy.	
☐ 8. I had surgery.	
☐ 9. I had counseling.	
☐ 10. I wore braces.	
☐ 11. I used a cane or a walker.	
☐ 12. I used a wheelchair.	

◄ **Reaching Out!**

Easy or Difficult?

Look at the medical advice on page 94 of the Picture Dictionary. In your opinion, which advice is easy to follow? Which advice is difficult to follow? Discuss with a classmate.

A AILMENTS AND MEDICINE

Match the ailment with the medicine to treat it.

_e_ 1. I have a cough.
____ 2. I have a headache.
____ 3. I have a runny nose.
____ 4. I have a sore throat.
____ 5. I have itchy eyes.
____ 6. I have a rash.
____ 7. I have a stomachache.
____ 8. I have dry skin.
____ 9. I have a cold.

a. You should use throat lozenges.
b. You should use antacid tablets.
c. You should take aspirin.
d. You should take cold medicine.
e. You should use cough drops.
f. You should use lotion.
g. You should use nasal spray.
h. You should use ointment.
i. You should use eye drops.

B WHAT'S THE DOSAGE?

tab. = tablet	1x / day = once a day
cap. = capsule	2x / day = twice a day
tsp. = teaspoon	3x / day = 3 times a day

A   B   C   D   E   F

Look at the medicine labels and choose the correct medicine.

_B_ 1. Take one tablet twice a day.
____ 2. Take three teaspoons twice a day.
____ 3. Take one pill three times a day.
____ 4. Take one capsule once a day.
____ 5. Take three tablets once a day.
____ 6. Take this four times a day.

C FOLLOW THE INSTRUCTIONS

Match the instruction with the correct medicine.

_c_ 1. Spray into your nose.
____ 2. Take two with a glass of water.
____ 3. Rub this on your skin.
____ 4. Take two teaspoons.
____ 5. Keep this in your mouth.

a. aspirin
b. cough syrup
c. nasal spray
d. throat lozenge
e. ointment

> **Reaching Out!**
>
> *Medicine and You*

What medicines do you use when you get sick? Make a list of the ones on page 95 of the Picture Dictionary that you use. What other medicines do you use to get better? Compare with a classmate.

A SPECIALISTS AND WHAT THEY TREAT

Match the specialists with who or what they treat.

_f_	**1.** pediatrician	**a.**	ears
____	**2.** chiropractor	**b.**	heart
____	**3.** ophthalmologist	**c.**	women
____	**4.** cardiologist	**d.**	back
____	**5.** orthodontist	**e.**	stomach
____	**6.** audiologist	**f.**	children
____	**7.** gerontologist	**g.**	teeth
____	**8.** gastroenterologist	**h.**	elderly people
____	**9.** gynecologist	**i.**	eyes

B SPECIALISTS AND YOU

Check the specialists you have seen.

- ☐ orthodontist
- ☐ allergist
- ☐ gynecologist
- ☐ acupuncturist
- ☐ physical therapist
- ☐ orthopedist
- ☐ gerontologist
- ☐ chiropractor

C INSURANCE COVERAGE OF SPECIALISTS

Sometimes you can go to a specialist directly, and sometimes you need a referral from your regular doctor. Look at the information about this health plan's benefits. Then complete the chart. For each specialist, do you need a referral? Answer Yes or No. How much of the specialist's bill will the health plan pay? Write the percent.

GOOD NEIGHBORS HEALTH PLAN

SUMMARY OF BENEFITS

Most Specialists
ENT specialist
cardiologist
orthopedist
gastroenterologist

A referral from your family doctor is needed. With a referral, we will pay 100%.

Mental Health
therapist
psychiatrist

No referral needed. We will pay 80%.

Gynecologist

One visit per year, no referral needed. We will pay 100%.

Chiropractor

No referral needed. We will pay 60%.

Acupuncturist

No referral needed. Not covered. We pay 0%.

Medical Specialist	Referral?	% paid
	Yes	100%

Reaching Out!

Your Health Insurance

Do you have health insurance? If so, does your insurance pay for you to go to a medical specialist? How much does it pay? Do you need a referral from your family doctor? Compare answers with a classmate.

A IN A PATIENT'S ROOM

Look at this patient's hospital room and check the things you see.

- ✓ bed control
- ☐ bed pan
- ☐ bed table
- ☐ call button
- ☐ dietitian
- ☐ doctor
- ☐ hospital bed
- ☐ hospital gown
- ☐ I.V.
- ☐ medical chart
- ☐ patient
- ☐ vital signs monitor

B PERSON, PLACE, OR THING?

Is each of these hospital words a person, a place, or a thing? Write PER for Person, PL for Place, and T for Thing.

☐ orderly	☐ gurney	☐ call button	☐ ER	☐ midwife
☐ lab	☐ radiologist	☐ surgeon	☐ bed pan	☐ I.V.

C WHERE IN THE HOSPITAL?

This is the floor directory for Springfield Memorial Hospital. Write the floor number where you can find the following people.

Springfield Memorial Hospital

	Floor
Birthing Room	3
Emergency Room	1
Laboratory	2
Nurse's Station	6
Operating Room	4
Radiology Department	5

Person	Floor
anesthesiologist	
X-ray technician	
nurse	
lab technician	
surgical nurse	
EMT	
obstetrician	

Reaching Out!

World Hospitals

With a small group of classmates, talk about hospitals in different countries you know. Compare patients' rooms, emergency rooms, other departments, and hospital workers. Then discuss as a class. Make a class chart to compare hospitals around the world.

A WHICH PRODUCT?

1. I wear (a shower cap   shampoo) when I take a shower so my hair doesn't get wet.
2. I gargle with (mouthwash   cologne) every morning.
3. I always use (bubble bath   aftershave) when I take a bath.
4. I usually style my hair with a (curling iron   styptic pencil).
5. I often use an (electric shaver   emery board) when I do my nails.
6. If you want to have soft hands, you should use (nail polish   hand lotion).
7. That (barrette   mascara) looks very good in your hair.
8. Alice likes to wear makeup. Every day she puts on foundation, rouge, and (eyeliner   soap).
9. When my shoes look dull, I put on some (shoe polish   shoelaces).
10. My dentist says it's important to use (a toothbrush   dental floss) after I brush my teeth.

B WHICH IS DIFFERENT?

1. a. bubble bath	b. shampoo	c. razor blade	d. soap
2. a. teeth whitener	b. toothbrush	c. dental floss	d. bobby pin
3. a. emery board	b. face powder	c. nail polish	d. nail brush
4. a. styptic pencil	b. aftershave	c. shaving cream	d. mascara
5. a. shoe polish	b. nail clipper	c. razor	d. scissors
6. a. blush	b. eyeliner	c. hair gel	d. eyebrow pencil

C PERSONAL HYGIENE SURVEY

The students in Mr. Montero's class took a survey of their personal hygiene habits. Look at the chart and complete the bar graph.

Personal Hygiene Activity	Number of Students
take a shower or bath in the morning	6
take a shower or bath in the evening	4
brush their teeth every day	10
use dental floss every day	6
use a hair dryer	5
put on cologne or perfume	2

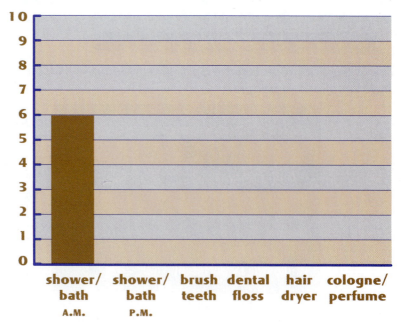

Reaching Out!

Class Survey

Take a survey of the personal hygiene habits of students in your class. Decide what you want to ask about. As a class, make a chart and a graph to show all the information.

A WHAT DO YOU USE?

Put these words into the correct groups.

baby lotion	bib	diaper pins	ointment
baby powder	bottle	formula	training pants
baby shampoo	cotton swabs	nipple	wipes

Feed the Baby	Change the Baby	Bathe the Baby
bib		

B BABYSITTING

Amanda is a new babysitter. What instructions did the baby's mother give Amanda?

__c__ 1. When the baby is dirty, . . .
____ 2. When the baby is hungry, . . .
____ 3. When the baby's diaper is dirty, . . .
____ 4. After you change the baby, . . .
____ 5. If the baby is crying, . . .
____ 6. When the baby is bored, . . .

a. dress the baby.
b. change the baby's diaper.
c. bathe the baby.
d. play with the baby.
e. feed the baby.
f. hold the baby.

C NEWBORN BABY INVENTORY

*Julie is going to have a baby. Look at the list of baby items the Coolidge Hospital recommends.
Check the items Julie already has, and then make a shopping list of things she needs to buy.*

COOLIDGE HOSPITAL
Items to buy for your new baby

☐ baby lotion   ☐ diapers
☐ baby powder   ☐ diaper pins
☐ baby shampoo ☐ ointment
☐ bottle   ☐ pacifier
☐ cotton swabs ☐ wipes

Shopping List
baby shampoo

*In your opinion, what are the eight most useful baby items in this
lesson? Compare lists with a classmate.*

Reaching Out!
Useful Baby Items

A Community Health Center

The Crosstown Clinic is a large community health center in the downtown section of Southington. This medical facility offers many services to local residents. People visit the clinic when they have ailments such as an earache or symptoms such as a high fever or a bad cough. They can also go to the clinic once a year for an annual physical. During this medical exam, a nurse measures a person's height and weight and checks the person's blood pressure, and a doctor examines the person and asks questions about his or her health.

When people have medical emergencies such as a broken bone or other serious injury, they don't go to the community health center. They go to the emergency room at the hospital across the street from the clinic. However, sometimes people show up at the emergency room with ailments and symptoms that aren't very serious. When that happens, the emergency room receptionist sends them across the street to the clinic.

The clinic's services are available to everyone in the community. It has a sliding scale fee system. Patients pay for services based on their annual income—the amount of money they make in a year. Very poor patients don't have to pay anything. Most patients pay at least some of the cost of the services they receive. This fee system works well because it helps all people stay healthy.

The Crosstown Clinic has excellent facilities. It has ten examination rooms, a large reception area, and a radiology department that does patients' X-rays. It also has its own laboratory, so they don't have to send patients' blood tests to a different facility. Once or twice a week, different specialists come to the clinic. A cardiologist is there every Monday and Thursday, an orthopedist comes every Tuesday and Friday, and an allergist is there every Wednesday. A pediatrician and a gynecologist work there every day. Since patients need to visit at different times, the clinic is open weekdays from 8 A.M. to 9 P.M. and from 9 A.M. to noon on Saturdays. The people of Southington are very proud of their community health center, and they should be. It's one of the best public health clinics in the country.

1. In the first paragraph, the word *physical* means _____.
   a. an ailment or symptom
   b. an examination
   c. a health clinic
   d. a doctor or nurse

2. A broken bone is an example of _____.
   a. a symptom
   b. an emergency room
   c. a serious injury
   d. an X-ray

3. In the first paragraph, the word *annual* means _____.
   a. medical
   b. downtown
   c. every month
   d. once a year

4. A sliding scale fee system means that _____.
   a. the clinic has a scale in each exam room
   b. wealthy patients don't pay fees
   c. nobody pays for services
   d. patients pay what they can

5. Patients with heart problems can see a specialist at the clinic _____.
   a. on Thursdays
   b. on Fridays
   c. on Tuesdays
   d. on Wednesdays

6. In the fourth paragraph, the word *facilities* refers to the clinic's _____.
   a. patients
   b. rooms and departments
   c. doctors and nurses
   d. specialists

A WHAT'S THE ORDER?

Put the schools in order from 1–6.

- [ ] high school
- [1] preschool
- [ ] graduate school
- [ ] college
- [ ] middle school
- [ ] elementary school

B LAST SCHOOL ATTENDED

What was the last school you and members of your family attended? Write the type of school and its name.

your mother _____

your father _____

your siblings _____

_____

your grandparents _____

_____

you _____

C AVERAGE NUMBER OF YEARS IN SCHOOL

This graph shows the average number of years students spend in different types of schools. Use the graph to complete the chart.

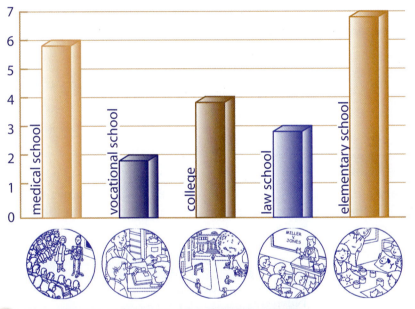

Most Years in School

elementary school

_____

_____

_____

_____

Least Years in School

D SCHOOLS IN YOUR CITY

Look in the telephone book or on the Internet to find different types of schools in your community. Write the names of one or two schools for each category.

1. nursery school _____
2. elementary school _____
3. middle school / junior high school _____
4. high school _____
5. adult school _____
6. community college _____

Make a list of the types of schools in your country and the average number of years it takes to complete them. Then list five ways that schools are the same as those in the U.S. and five ways that they are different. Compare with a classmate.

Reaching Out!

Different Schools

A WHERE DO THEY WORK?

Write the people's names next to the places where they work in a school.

coach	librarian	nurse	principal	science teacher
counselor	lunchroom monitor	P.E. teacher	secretary	teacher

1. principal's office   *principal*
2. field
3. guidance office
4. science lab
5. cafeteria

6. main office
7. gym
8. classroom
9. library
10. nurse's office

B WHO WORKS IN YOUR SCHOOL?

Look at the list of people who work in a school. Which ones work at the school where you study English? Circle the ones that work there, and ~~cross out~~ the ones that don't.

principal	custodian	cafeteria worker	counselor	coach
assistant principal	librarian	security officer	teacher	

C BUILDING AN ADDITION

The Henderson School is small and very old, but soon it will be larger. This diagram shows what will be in the old building and what will be in the new section. Use the diagram to complete the chart. Will each room be in the old or new section of the building?

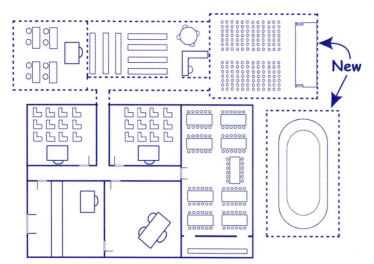

New

Room	Old	New
auditorium		✔
cafeteria		
classrooms		
library		
main office		
track		
science lab		
principal's office		

Reaching Out!

Your School

Draw and label a diagram of the school you go to now. Then draw and label a diagram of a school you went to before. How are they the same, and how are they different? Compare diagrams with a classmate.

A WHICH SUBJECT?

1. My favorite science class is ((chemistry) government).
2. We're studying prepositions in (physics   Spanish) now.
3. We're studying parts of the body in (health   history) class.
4. I'm learning to cook in my (shop   home economics) class.
5. We paint and draw in (art   industrial arts) class.
6. We're learning about South America in our (biology   geography) class.
7. There are many disk drives in our (computer science   driver's education) class.

B CLASS SCHEDULES

Here is the schedule of classes for students at Jefferson High School. Use the schedule to complete the statements below.

Period	10th grade Class	11th grade Class	12th grade Class
1	history	geography	computer science
2	English	chemistry	physics
3	health	math	English
4	math	business education	government
5	biology	English	business education
6	geography	history	math

1. Sandra is in 11th grade, and it's 2nd period. She's in _____chemistry_____ class.
2. Joseph is in 12th grade, and it's 4th period. He's in _____ class.
3. It's 1st period, and Benjamin is in history class. He's in _____ grade.
4. Maria is in 12th grade, and it's 2nd period. She's in _____ class.
5. It's 3rd period, and Franco is in math class.   He's in _____ grade.
6. Theresa is in 11th grade, and it's 1st period. She's in _____ class.
7. It's 4th period, and Robert is in government class. He's in _____ grade.
8. Alice is in 10th grade, and it's 5th period. She's in _____ class.
9. The students in the _____ grade go to business education before they go to math class.
10. The students in the _____ grade go to English after they go to history class.
11. The students in the _____ grade go to a science class after they go to geography class.

Make a list of ten school subjects and number them from 1 (the easiest) to 10 (the most difficult). Then compare lists with a classmate.

Reaching Out!

Easy and Difficult Subjects

A WHICH ACTIVITY?

1. I write for the (school newspaper   A.V. crew).
2. My daughter sings in the school (band   chorus).
3. My son plays the piano in the school (orchestra   pep squad).
4. Look in the (choir   yearbook). You'll see pictures of all the students in our class.
5. When the (international   computer) club meets, we usually bring in food from different countries.
6. There's an important (chess club   student government) meeting this afternoon to talk about some problems in our school.
7. The (debate   community service) club is going to paint some old buildings near our school.

B THE WEBSTER HIGH SCHOOL YEARBOOK

The Webster High School yearbook has pictures of all the students in the 12th grade. With each picture is a list of the student's extracurricular activities and the number of years the student did the activity. Look at the yearbook listings for Amy and Jenny and complete the chart. Fill in the number of years they did an activity, and mark with an X an activity they didn't do.

Amy Jackson
choir 3, pep squad 2,
international club 4,
yearbook 1, drama 2

Jenny Stratton
international club 1,
computer club 3, band 4,
student government 2,
drama 3, debate club 3

Activity	Amy	Jenny
student government	X	2
band		
international club		
drama		
pep squad		
debate club		
choir		
computer club		
yearbook		

C EXTRACURRICULAR ACTIVITIES AND YOU

Complete the chart below about your extracurricular activities now or in the past. For each activity, put a check in the Yes or No column. Then in the last column, write Yes or No to show if schools in your country offer the activity. After you complete the chart, compare with your classmates.

Extracurricular Activity	Yes	No	Schools in My Country Offer This
debate club			
community service			
band			
yearbook			
football			
international club			
computer club			
school newspaper			

Reaching Out!

Activities to Try

Make a list of three extracurricular activities you would like to try and tell why. Then compare lists with a group of classmates.

A) ARITHMETIC MATCHING

Draw lines to match the equal amounts in each column.

50 plus 50	FIVE	100 divided by 10
40 divided by 2	100	10 times 10
1 times 1	20	4 plus 1
10 minus 5	ten	2 minus 1
5 plus 5	one	36 divided by 2
9 times 2	18	30 minus 10

B) MAKING 100

There are many ways to make the number 100. Circle each math sentence that equals 100.

30 minus 70	10 times 10	108 minus 8	40 plus 60	1000 times 10
⟨200 divided by 2⟩	50 plus 2	500 divided by 5	100 minus 0	99 plus 1

C) ON SALE!

Write the equivalent fraction next to the sale sign.

1/4	2/3	1/2	1/10	3/4	1/3

1/2 **1.** 50% off all men's clothes

_____ **3.** **Sale** 25 percent off

_____ **5.** 10% off all skirts

_____ **2.** 66% discount

_____ **4.** 33% off everything!

_____ **6.** 75 PERCENT DISCOUNT

D) HIGH SCHOOL MATH

This graph shows the percent of West High School students currently taking each math subject. Look at the graph and number the pictures from 1 (highest percent) to 5 (lowest percent).

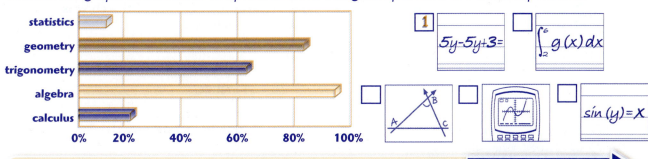

Write four arithmetic sentences to show four different ways to make the number 1000—using addition, subtraction, multiplication, and division. Compare with a classmate, and check each other's work.

Reaching Out!

Making 1000

A WHICH ONE DOESN'T BELONG?

1. measurements: a. height   b. length   c. side   d. width
2. lines: a. straight   b. center   c. parallel   d. curved
3. geometric shapes: a. circle   b. square   c. triangle   d. yard
4. solid figures: a. pyramid   b. cube   c. ellipse   d. cone
5. types of angles: a. radius   b. acute   c. obtuse   d. right
6. circle: a. diameter   b. base   c. radius   d. center

B WHICH SHAPES?

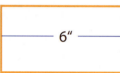

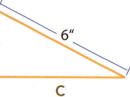
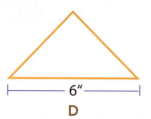
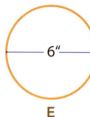

A — 3"   B — 6"   C — 6"   D — 6", 6"   E — 6"

__A,B__ 1. It has 4 right angles.
____ 2. It has 3 sides.
____ 3. It's a rectangle.
____ 4. It's a triangle.
____ 5. It's an isosceles triangle.

____ 6. It has 4 sides.
____ 7. It's a square.
____ 8. Its width is 3".
____ 9. Its hypotenuse is 6".
____ 10. It's a circle.

____ 11. Its diameter is 6".
____ 12. It has parallel sides.
____ 13. It has an obtuse angle.
____ 14. Its radius is 3".
____ 15. It has one right angle.

C JENNY'S LIVING ROOM

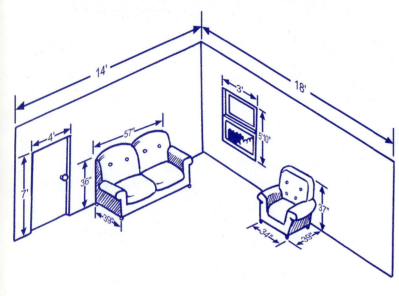

1. The width of the room is __14 feet__.
2. The length of the room is _____.
3. The height of the door is _____.
4. The width of the door is _____.
5. The width of the window is _____.
6. The length of the sofa is _____.
7. The depth of the sofa is _____.
8. The height of the sofa is _____.
9. The _____ of the chair is 39 inches.
10. The height of the chair is _____.
11. The _____ of the chair is 34 inches.
12. The _____ of the window is 5 feet 10 inches.

Reaching Out!

Your Living Room

Measure your living room and the furniture in it. Draw a diagram like the one in Exercise C. Show all the measurements. Share your diagram with a classmate and tell about it.

A CAN YOU FIND IT?

How to Bake an Apple Pie [1]

Apple pie is a very popular dessert. [3]   Do you know

2 { how to bake it? [4]   It's the easiest thing in the world! [5]

Follow these simple instructions. [6]

_____2_____ paragraph

_____ title

_____ interrogative sentence

_____ imperative sentence

_____ exclamatory sentence

_____ declarative sentence

B WHAT'S WRONG?

The English teacher corrected the students' sentences. What did she say about each sentence?

__d__ 1. What did you do on your vacation (?)

_____ 2. I bought apples (,) oranges, and pears.

_____ 3. I get up (at) 6:00 every morning.

_____ 4. My brother is (a) doctor.

_____ 5. I think (it) is going to snow.

_____ 6. We (are) very happy today.

_____ 7. I want to speak English (well) ~~good~~.

_____ 8. It's my (brother's) ~~brothers~~ birthday tomorrow.

_____ 9. Mary isn't happy (:) she misses her family.

_____ 10. I really love my English class (!)

_____ 11. The people on my street are interesting (✗).

_____ 12. (")I don't understand,(") said Susan(.)

a. Don't forget the exclamation point.

b. You need an article before the noun.

c. You need a pronoun in this sentence.

d. End a question with a question mark.

e. Use a semi-colon.

f. You need an adverb here.

g. Don't forget to use a comma.

h. You need quotation marks and a period.

i. Don't forget to use an apostrophe.

j. This sentence needs a preposition.

k. This sentence doesn't have a verb.

l. Adjectives are never plural.

C I WROTE TODAY

I worked on a (preposition <u>composition</u>)[1] about my family today. First I (brainstormed edited)[2] some ideas, and then I (organized made)[3] them. I wrote a first (comma draft)[4], and then I (revised found)[5] it. I got (quotation marks feedback)[6] from my teacher. She showed me the (mistakes marks)[7] I made in some of my (titles sentences)[8]. I made (corrections semi-colons)[9], and then I wrote a (final first)[10] copy.

Reaching Out!

Writing a Composition

Write a composition about your English class. Brainstorm ideas. Organize your ideas. Choose a title. Write a first draft. Edit your work. Pay special attention to punctuation marks. Get feedback from your classmates and rewrite. Which step was the easiest for you? the most difficult? the most useful?

A MATCHING

Match each statement with the correct form of literature or writing.

__c__ **1.** I really enjoyed that book. It was very exciting. And everything was true!

_____ **2.** I just finished a very interesting book about the life of Christopher Columbus.

_____ **3.** Our neighbors want us to come to a party at their house next weekend.

_____ **4.** I got a short note from my boss. She wants all the employees to come in early tomorrow.

_____ **5.** Someday I'm going to write a book about everything that happened in my life.

_____ **6.** We received it from our friends who are on vacation in Puerto Rico. There's a photograph of a beautiful beach on the front.

a. invitation

b. autobiography

c. non-fiction

d. postcard

e. biography

f. memo

B YOUR READING HABITS

Fill out the questionnaire and then compare with a classmate.

How often do you read . . . ?
(o = often, s = sometimes, r = rarely, n = never)

	o	s	r	n
1. novels	☐	☐	☐	☐
2. short stories	☐	☐	☐	☐
3. poetry	☐	☐	☐	☐
4. biographies	☐	☐	☐	☐
5. autobiographies	☐	☐	☐	☐
6. newspaper articles	☐	☐	☐	☐
7. editorials	☐	☐	☐	☐
8. magazine articles	☐	☐	☐	☐

C YOUR WRITING HABITS

Fill out the questionnaire and then compare with a classmate.

How often do you write . . . ?
(o = often, s = sometimes, r = rarely, n = never)

	o	s	r	n
1. letters	☐	☐	☐	☐
2. memos	☐	☐	☐	☐
3. thank-you notes	☐	☐	☐	☐
4. e-mail	☐	☐	☐	☐
5. instant messages	☐	☐	☐	☐
6. poems	☐	☐	☐	☐
7. essays	☐	☐	☐	☐
8. reports	☐	☐	☐	☐

D MORE READING HABITS

Answer the questions with words from page 108 of the Picture Dictionary.

What do you read . . .

1. at school? _____

2. at work? _____

3. at home? _____

4. on vacation? _____

E MORE WRITING HABITS

Answer the questions with words from page 108 of the Picture Dictionary.

What do you write . . .

1. at school? _____

2. at work? _____

3. at home? _____

4. on vacation? _____

Reaching Out!

What We Want to Learn!

Take a class survey. What kind of fiction and non-fiction do students like to read? What do they want to learn to write? (letters? poems? essays? etc.) Discuss as a class the results of the survey. Have students tell the reasons for their choices.

GEOGRAPHY

A LAND OR WATER?

bay	desert	lake	ocean	plains	river
canyon	island	meadow	peninsula	pond	stream

LAND		WATER	
canyon		bay	

B WHAT ARE THEY?

__d__ 1. Atlantic, Pacific

____ 2. Himilayas, Andes, Alps

____ 3. Nile, Mississippi, Amazon

____ 4. Everest, Kilimanjaro

____ 5. Sahara, Kalahari

____ 6. Japan, Hawaii, Cuba

____ 7. Superior, Victoria, Baikal

____ 8. Niagara, Angel

a. lakes

b. rivers

c. waterfalls

d. oceans

e. mountain peaks

f. mountain ranges

g. deserts

h. islands

C ADD YOUR OWN

1. lake: _____

2. river: _____

3. waterfall: _____

4. ocean: _____

5. mountain peak: _____

6. mountain range: _____

7. desert: _____

8. island: _____

D WHAT'S ON THE MAP?

Put a check next to everything you see on the map.

☐ desert	☐ canyon	☐ lake	☐ river	☐ seashore	☐ rainforest	☐ waterfall
✔ ocean	☐ jungle	☐ bay	☐ island	☐ peninsula	☐ plateau	☐ mountain peak

Draw a map of the region where you live. Include lakes, rivers, and mountains on your map. Write and tell about the geography of the region. Compare with a classmate.

Reaching Out!

Where You Live

111

A NEW SCIENCE EQUIPMENT

Ms. Martinez, the science teacher at Waterville High School, is ordering new equipment for the science lab. How much is she going to spend for each item? Fill in the prices on her list.

Equipment to Order	
24 funnels	$40
12 flasks	$
12 beakers	$
24 graduated cylinders	$
48 test tubes	$
12 Petri dishes	$

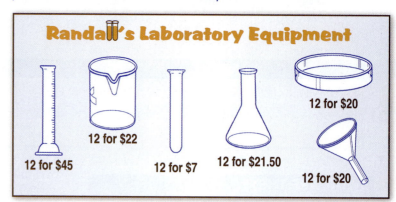

Randall's Laboratory Equipment

12 for $45
12 for $22
12 for $7
12 for $21.50
12 for $20
12 for $20

B WHAT ARE THEY USING?

These students are working in the science lab. What are they using?

1. Peter is heating some chemicals. He's using a (⟨Bunsen burner⟩   magnet).
2. Gina is examining some slides. She's using a (beaker   microscope).
3. Tai is experimenting with sunlight. He's using (forceps   a prism).
4. Orlando is picking up a hot test tube. He's using (crucible tongs   a scale).
5. Marina is putting chemicals into a test tube. She's using a (slide   dropper).
6. Arnold is pouring liquid into a flask. He's using a (funnel   magnet).
7. Rhonda is growing bacteria. She's using a (graduated cylinder   Petri dish).
8. Tony is weighing some chemicals. He's using a (balance   computer).

C A SCIENCE EXPERIMENT

__c__ 1. State the problem.

____ 2. Form a hypothesis.

____ 3. Plan a procedure.

____ 4. Do a procedure.

____ 5. Make observations.

____ 6. Draw conclusions.

a. "I was right. Fresh orange juice has more vitamin C than frozen orange juice."

b. "I'll have to get test tubes and chemicals and learn how to test for vitamin C."

c. "Do fresh orange juice and frozen orange juice have the same amount of vitamin C?"

d. "The fresh juice in this test tube looks lighter than the frozen juice in that test tube."

e. "I think that fresh orange juice has more vitamin C than frozen orange juice."

f. "I'm adding ten drops of fresh orange juice to this test tube."

Reaching Out!

A Class Science Fair

Work with a classmate and think of an idea for a science experiment. State a problem, and form a hypothesis. Think of the procedure you will use and the materials you will need. Present your idea to the class. Vote as a class to choose the best idea for an experiment.

A TRUE OR FALSE?

Answer True (T) or False (F).

__T__ 1. Mercury is the closest planet to the sun.

____ 2. An asteroid is someone who goes into space.

____ 3. A constellation is a group of stars.

____ 4. The Big Dipper is the name of a comet.

____ 5. An astronomer can look at the universe through a telescope.

____ 6. A space station is a large satellite that people can live in.

____ 7. In a lunar eclipse the sun passes between Earth and the moon.

____ 8. In a solar eclipse the moon passes between the sun and Earth.

B FROM SMALL TO LARGE

Number these from small to large.

☐	planet
☐	universe
1	meteor
☐	solar system
☐	Sun
☐	galaxy
☐	asteroid

C WHICH PLANET?

Look at the chart and complete each sentence with the name of the correct planet.

Planet	Average Distance from Sun	Time to Circle Sun	Diameter	Number of Moons
Mercury	36,000,000 m.	.241 y.	3,030 m.	0
Venus	67,000,000 m.	.615 y.	7,523 m.	0
Earth	93,000,000 m.	1.00 y.	7,926 m.	1
Mars	142,000,000 m.	1.881 y.	4,222 m.	2
Jupiter	483,000,000 m.	11.857 y.	88,846 m.	63
Saturn	888,000,000 m.	29.4 y.	74,898 m.	31
Uranus	1,784,000,000 m.	84.02 y.	31,763 m.	27
Neptune	2,794,000,000 m.	164.79 y.	30,775 m.	13
Pluto	3,647,000,000 m.	247.92 y.	1,485 m.	1

1. _____**Venus**_____ is about 67 million miles from the Sun.

2. _____ is the fourth planet from the Sun.

3. It takes _____ almost 165 years to circle the Sun.

4. _____ circles the Sun in about a quarter of a year.

5. _____ and _____ don't have any moons.

6. The smallest planet is _____.

7. _____ and _____ are larger than Uranus.

D WHAT KIND OF MOON?

Look at the chart and fill in the correct dates.

3/26/09	3/29/09	4/2/09	4/9/09	4/17/09

crescent moon: ____3/29/09____

full moon: _____

new moon: _____

first quarter moon: _____

last quarter moon: _____

Reaching Out!

Take a class survey. How many students have seen a solar eclipse? a lunar eclipse? a comet? a meteor shower? a U.F.O.? How many students have visited an observatory? How many constellations can everybody name and identify?

Class Survey

A Very Special Teacher

Abdi Ibrahim is a very special teacher. He teaches science at Wilson High School. He teaches four science classes every day: two biology classes for 10th graders, a chemistry class for 11th graders, and a physics class for 12th graders. He works very hard, and all of his students say that he is one of the best teachers at Wilson High.

Mr. Ibrahim has a very interesting background. He is from Somalia. His family moved to the United States when he was 13 years old. When he went to his first day of middle school in his new country, he didn't speak one word of English. He learned quickly, though, and he worked very hard during his years in high school. Science was his favorite subject, and he was in the school band, he played football, and he was a leader in the student government. During his years in college, he decided to become a science teacher. He remembered the teachers who helped him during his years in school, and he decided to help students in the same way. He looked for a job in a school with students from many countries, and he was very happy to find a position at Wilson High, where the students come from more than forty different nations.

In addition to teaching science, Mr. Ibrahim is a football coach at Wilson High, and he also works with students on the yearbook and the school newspaper. After school, if he isn't in the science lab or on the football field, students know they can usually find him in his classroom. Students who don't speak English very well especially like to go to his classroom after school. Mr. Ibrahim gives them extra help with their science homework, and he goes with them to the guidance office if they have problems with their schedules. All the new students know that he understands how they feel in school because he was once a new student himself. In his students' eyes, Mr. Ibrahim is indeed a very special teacher.

1. When Abdi Ibrahim arrived in the United States, he first went to _____.
   a. nursery school
   b. elementary school
   c. middle school
   d. high school

2. Students at this school usually take their science classes in the following order: _____.
   a. physics, chemistry, biology
   b. chemistry, biology, physics
   c. biology, physics, chemistry
   d. biology, chemistry, physics

3. According to the story, when Mr. Ibrahim was a high school student, he _____.
   a. played in the band
   b. played basketball
   c. worked on the school newspaper
   d. worked on the yearbook

4. He decided to become a science teacher when he was in _____.
   a. high school
   b. college
   c. middle school
   d. the guidance office

5. According to the story, Abdi Ibrahim ISN'T _____.
   a. a football coach
   b. a biology teacher
   c. a guidance counselor
   d. a chemistry teacher

6. New students from other countries like Mr. Ibrahim because _____.
   a. he understands all their different languages
   b. he understands what it's like to be a new student
   c. he doesn't give his students homework
   d. he doesn't speak English

A WHICH IS DIFFERENT?

1. **a.** food-service worker   **b.** baker   **c.** fisher   **d.** chef
2. **a.** janitor   **b.** housekeeper   **c.** custodian   **d.** carpenter
3. **a.** construction worker   **b.** garment worker   **c.** factory worker   **d.** assembler
4. **a.** carpenter   **b.** construction worker   **c.** mason   **d.** delivery person
5. **a.** home attendant   **b.** accountant   **c.** babysitter   **d.** health-care aide

B WHAT CAN THEY DO?

Look at pages 111 and 112 of the Picture Dictionary. Find as many jobs as you can for each of these people.

1. Nick likes to work with food. _____ food-service worker, cook, baker, butcher _____
2. Gregory is very strong and healthy. _____
3. Diane is good with people. _____
4. Alan is very good with numbers. _____
5. Jessica loves children. _____
6. Olivia is good with her hands. _____
7. Mohamed loves science and technology. _____
8. Sonia is very neat and organized. _____

C HOW MUCH DO THEY MAKE?

Look at the list of occupations on the left. (Don't look at the chart on the right.) Which occupation do you think pays the most? Which pays the least? Number the occupations from 1 (highest salary) to 12 (lowest salary) in the boxes on the left.

	accountant	
	actor	
	architect	
	artist	
	barber	
	carpenter	
	cashier	
	construction worker	
	cook	
	farmer	
	firefighter	
	janitor	

Now look at the chart on the right. It shows the average yearly salary in the U.S. for each occupation. Use the chart to number the occupations again from 1 (highest salary) to 12 (lowest salary) in the boxes on the right. How many occupations did you guess correctly?

accountant	$61,139
actor	$45,614
architect	$59,160
artist	$38,294
barber	$21,291
carpenter	$37,181
cashier	$17,077
construction worker	$29,206
cook	$33,129
farmer	$24,292
firefighter	$37,222
janitor	$20,138

Interview a classmate about the occupations on pages 111–112 of the Picture Dictionary. In your classmate's opinion, what are the five most interesting occupations? the five least interesting occupations? Why?

Reaching Out!

Interesting Occupations

A WHICH IS DIFFERENT?

1. a. salesperson   b. instructor   c. storekeeper   d. stock clerk
2. a. mail carrier   b. letter carrier   c. telemarketer   d. postal worker
3. a. waiter   b. server   c. servicewoman   d. waitress
4. a. translator   b. courier   c. mail carrier   d. messenger
5. a. security guard   b. police officer   c. serviceman   d. lawyer

B THE WRONG JOB

These people are looking for work. Which of the three occupations is wrong for them? Cross it out.

1. Harry wants to work for a newspaper.   reporter   ~~painter~~   photographer
2. Fernando is a good boss.   supervisor   medical assistant   manager
3. Margarita has good telephone skills.   receptionist   telemarketer   machine operator
4. Kim speaks five languages fluently.   tailor   interpreter   language instructor
5. Diane wants a job in the health field.   pharmacist   physician assistant   sanitation worker
6. Ellen has to sit at work.   travel agent   stock clerk   secretary
7. Andy speaks and writes well.   welder   journalist   lawyer
8. Amal likes cars and trucks.   truck driver   repairperson   mechanic

C GETTING A LICENSE

The following chart shows how much it costs to get a license from the state of Georgia to work in these occupations. Use this information to number the occupations in the list from 1 (the least money) to 8 (the most money).

Occupation	Fees	Occupation	Fees
lawyer	$150	security guard	$70
manicurist	$50	teacher	$20
pharmacist	$175	truck driver	$65
physician assistant	$200	veterinarian	$100

 _____    _____   1   _____

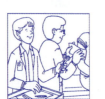 _____    _____   _____   _____

Reaching Out!

Finding Jobs

Work with a classmate. Look at the job listings in your local newspaper. Which occupations in this lesson can you find? How many job listings for each occupation are there? Which occupations have the most job listings?

A WHAT DO THEY DO?

1. Artists   sew.
2. Tailors   clean.
3. Farmers   draw.
4. Architects   grow vegetables.
5. Housekeepers   sell things.
6. Stock clerks   design buildings.
7. Salespeople   take inventory.

8. Pilots   type.
9. Managers   deliver things.
10. Secretaries   supervise people.
11. Interpreters   fly airplanes.
12. Carpenters   cook.
13. Couriers   build things.
14. Chefs   translate.

B EXPLORING OCCUPATIONS

Interview three classmates. Ask them about their skills. Then recommend one or more jobs. Write about your interviews below.

Name	Skills	Recommended Jobs

C WHAT ARE THEIR SKILLS?

The students in Ms. Crane's English class did a class survey to find out everybody's skills. The graph below shows the results of the survey. Complete the sentences about the students in the class.

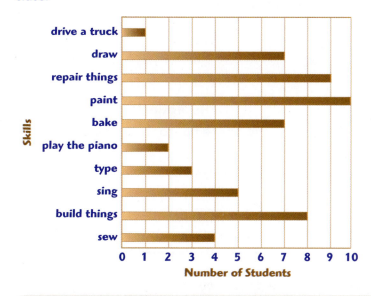

10 students can _____**paint**_____.

9 students can _____.

8 students can _____.

7 students can _____.

  and _____.

5 students can _____.

4 students can _____.

3 students can _____.

2 students can _____.

Only 1 student can _____.

Take a class skills survey. Ask about ten different skills. Then make a graph like the one above.

Reaching Out!

Skills in Your Class

A JOB SEARCH ADVICE

Mario is looking for his first job in the United States. His friend Eric is telling him about all the things he needs to do.

__d__ 1. Request information.

_____ 2. Request an interview.

_____ 3. Prepare a resume.

_____ 4. Dress appropriately.

_____ 5. Fill out an application.

_____ 6. Talk about your skills and qualifications.

_____ 7. Talk about your experience.

_____ 8. Ask about the salary and benefits.

_____ 9. Write a thank-you note.

a. When you finish the letter, sign it "Yours truly."

b. Tell the interviewer what you can do.

c. You should wait until the end of the interview before you ask these questions.

d. Call the company and ask, "Is the job still available?"

e. Tell the interviewer about the job you have now and the jobs you had before.

f. Answer all the questions on the form, and write neatly.

g. Wear a suit and tie.

h. Say, "I'd like to come in for an interview."

i. Write about your education and work experience. Type carefully.

B WANT ADS

Complete the want ads with the correct abbreviations. Then decide if the sentences below are True (T) or False (F).

| avail. | F | FT | Excel. | eves. | exper. | hr. | prev. | req. |

Dishwashers Wanted

PT and __FT__ positions. $5 /_____
No _____ exper. req. Must work weekends and _____

Call Ronald's Restaurant. 555-693-2251.

Receptionist

Position _____ in busy office. M–_____
3 years _____ and computer skills _____
_____ benefits.

Call Ms. Ricardi at 555-689-3311

Dishwashers

__T__ 1. They can work part time or full time.

_____ 2. They have to work evenings.

_____ 3. They must have previous experience.

_____ 4. They don't have to work on Saturdays and Sundays.

Receptionist

_____ 5. He or she has to work on Saturdays and Sundays.

_____ 6. This person must be able to use a computer.

_____ 7. Experience isn't necessary.

_____ 8. He or she probably gets sick days, vacations, and health insurance.

Reaching Out!

Want Ad Abbreviations

Find some want ads in the newspaper and bring them to class. Work with a classmate or in a small group. Underline all the abbreviations in your ads. Then make a list of the abbreviations and the full words. Compare lists as a class. Who has the longest list of abbreviations?

A WHERE ARE THEY?

Look at page 119 of the Picture Dictionary. Where are these things? Write E for Employee Lounge, C for Conference Room, W for Work Area, M for Mailroom, and R for Reception Area.

[R] coat closet	[ ] conference table	[ ] message board	[ ] postal scale
[ ] coat rack	[ ] copier	[ ] paper cutter	[ ] presentation board
[ ] coffee machine	[ ] file cabinet	[ ] paper shredder	[ ] vending machine
[ ] computer workstation	[ ] mailbox	[ ] postage meter	[ ] water cooler

B WHAT ARE THEY DOING?

Look at page 119 of the Picture Dictionary and choose the correct answers.

1. The office assistant is ((sorting)   filing) mail.
2. A woman in the work area is using a (paper cutter   paper shredder).
3. A woman in the employee lounge is looking at a (message board   presentation board).
4. Someone is standing in front of the (coffee machine   vending machine).
5. A man in a cubicle is using (an adding machine   a computer).

C THE FIRST DAY AT WORK

Howard is starting a new job as a secretary at the Casco Company. His boss is telling him about the workplace and his job. Fill in the missing words.

assistant	closet	cooler	lounge	message	photocopier	supply	type
cabinet	conference	cubicles	make	office	rack	swivel chair	vending

Welcome to the Casco Corporation. Hang up your coat on the coat ____**rack**____ 1 or in the coat _____ 2, and come into my _____ 3. This is Tessa, our administrative _____ 4. She can answer all your questions. You're going to work in one of the _____ 5. It's a little small, but we'll get you a comfortable _____ 6. If you need any more paper, pens, or pencils, you can get them from the _____ 7 room. Use the _____ 8 in the work area to _____ 9 copies of the letters you _____ 10. Then file the copies in the file _____ 11. As you know, we have meetings every Tuesday in the large _____ 12 room. We expect you to work hard, but on your break you can relax in the employee _____ 13. Buy yourself a drink or some candy from the _____ 14 machine, or have some water from the water _____ 15. Don't forget to read the announcements on the _____ 16 board.

Which of the people, places, and things on page 119 of the Picture Dictionary can you find in your school? Make a list of all the things you find and where you find them. Compare lists with a classmate.

Reaching Out!

What's in Your School?

A THESE SUPPLIES ARE IMPORTANT

1. I write the dates and times of meetings in my ((appointment book)   mailer).
2. I use (thumbtacks   paper clips) to hold my papers together.
3. Please put those letters in a (file folder   rotary card file).
4. The name of our company is at the top of our (letter tray   stationery).
5. When I make a mistake while I'm typing, I fix it with (correction fluid   glue).
6. Use a (clipboard   pushpin) to put that notice on the bulletin board.
7. If you're planning to take notes at the meeting, don't forget to take a (memo pad   desk pad) with you.

B WHAT SHOULD HE BUY?

Carl's office is a mess! He needs your help. Tell him what office supplies to buy. Use as many items as you can from page 120 of the Picture Dictionary.

1. Carl often forgets things because he doesn't write them down.	memo pad, legal pad, Post-It note pad, index cards
2. His desk and office are very messy, and he can't find the papers he needs.	
3. He often forgets his plans for the day, and he misses important meetings.	
4. He often forgets important addresses and phone numbers.	
5. When he writes long memos, he loses some of the pages.	
6. He receives a lot of mail, but he doesn't answer it.	

C TAKE INVENTORY!

What's in the supply cabinet? Take inventory, and check the office supplies you see.

✔ cellophane tape	☐ mailers	
☐ clipboards	☐ mailing labels	
☐ correction fluid	☐ packing tape	
☐ desk calendars	☐ paper clips	
☐ envelopes	☐ pushpins	
☐ file folders	☐ rotary card files	
☐ index cards	☐ rubber stamps	
☐ legal pads	☐ stationery	
☐ glue sticks	☐ staplers	
☐ ink cartridges	☐ staples	

Reaching Out!

Your Office Supplies

What office supplies do you use at home and at school? Make a list. Check your desk and closet to see what supplies you have. Make a list of any supplies you need to buy. Compare with a classmate.

THE FACTORY

DICTIONARY PAGE **121**

A HOW MANY?

Look at the factory on page 121 of the Picture Dictionary and count how many you see.

- ☐ people on the loading dock
- ☐ people in the employee lounge
- ☐ time cards
- ☐ union notices
- ☐ boxes on the forklift
- ☐ boxes on the dolly

B WHERE IN THE FACTORY?

Look at the factory on page 121 of the Picture Dictionary and circle the correct answer.

1. The packer is working in the . . .   locker room.   warehouse.
2. The suggestion box is to the right of the . . .   union notices.   time cards.
3. The line supervisor is at the . . .   freight elevator.   assembly line.
4. The shipping clerk is at the . . .   loading dock.   payroll office.
5. The factory workers are sitting at the . . .   shipping department.   work stations.
6. The loading dock is below the . . .   personnel office.   warehouse.

C PERSON, PLACE, OR THING?

Write these factory words in the correct categories below.

conveyor belt	line supervisor	payroll office	shipping department
factory worker	loading dock	personnel office	suggestion box
freight elevator	locker room	quality control supervisor	time clock
hand truck	packer	shipping clerk	warehouse

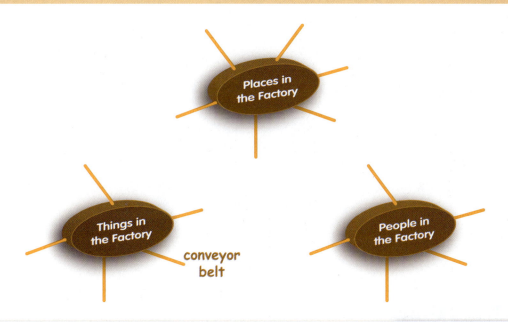

Places in the Factory

Things in the Factory
conveyor belt

People in the Factory

Reaching Out!

Are there any factories in your area? Look in the telephone book or on the Internet to find out. How many factories are there? What do they produce? Compare information with your classmates.

Factories in My Area

A AT THE CONSTRUCTION SITE

1. Two construction workers are standing on the (~~scaffolding~~   shovel).
2. Did you draw these (beams   blueprints)?
3. Who is operating the (concrete   concrete mixer) today?
4. Put those bricks in the (wheelbarrow   drywall).
5. I know how to operate a (girder   backhoe).
6. I'm wearing a (toolbelt   pipe) around my waist.
7. When you use a (pneumatic drill   trowel), it makes a lot of noise.
8. Carol is over there. She's standing on a (sledgehammer   ladder).
9. If you want to know the length of that wall, use this (tape measure   pickax).

B COMPARING CONSTRUCTION SITES

Look at the two construction sites below. Compare the tools and machines you see in each site.
Write the items in the correct groups below.

Construction Site 1

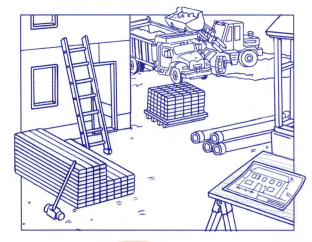

Construction Site 2

Site 1

_____
_____
_____
_____

Sites 1 & 2

_____
_____
_____
_____

Site 2

_____
_____
_____
_____

Reaching Out!

A Construction Site

Find a construction site in your city or town. What are they building?
What equipment, tools, and materials do you see? Make a list, and
draw a diagram of the site like the ones above. Then give the diagram
to a classmate. Can your classmate name all the things on your list?

A WHAT DOES IT PROTECT?

Write the body part that each safety item protects. You can use some body parts more than once.

ears	head	hands	eyes	mouth	body	back	feet

1. goggles _____ *eyes* _____
2. latex gloves _____
3. safety earmuffs _____
4. back support _____
5. respirator _____
6. helmet _____

7. mask _____
8. safety glasses _____
9. toe guard _____
10. safety vest _____
11. safety boots _____

B WARNING SIGNS

Match the warning sign with what it means.

A   B   C   D   E   F   G   H

☐	flammable	☐	corrosive	☐	hazardous	☐	biohazard
☐	dangerous	☐	radioactive	☐	poisonous	☐	electrical hazard

(D flammable)

C WHICH WORKPLACE IS SAFER?

The following graph compares the safety items at two different companies. Use the graph and put checks in the chart below to show which company has more of each safety item.

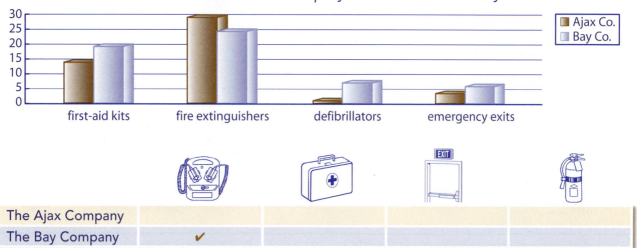

	defibrillators	first-aid kits	emergency exits	fire extinguishers
The Ajax Company				
The Bay Company	✔			

Reaching Out!

Safety Inventory

Work with a small group of classmates. Do a "safety inventory" of your school. What safety items does your school have? How many? What items does your school need? Share your information with people in the school office.

Looking for a Job

Amy Lewis became 16 years old last week, and now she is looking for her first job. Amy is a high school student, and she plans to go to college. She wants to become an architect or a lawyer some day. Her family doesn't have much money, so Amy wants to work after school in the evening and on weekends. She plans to save all of her salary to pay for college.

Each day when Amy walks home from school, she looks at help wanted signs in the windows of local businesses. Sometimes she sees job notices on the bulletin board at the supermarket, but these are usually for jobs such as gardeners, home health aides, or full-time babysitters—jobs that she can't take because she goes to school on weekdays. Amy also checks the classified ads in the newspaper. There are many job openings for cashiers, hairdressers, cooks, and other types of work, but almost all of the ads say that previous experience is required.

However, last Sunday, Amy saw an ad in the paper for a stock clerk in a supermarket and another ad for a salesperson in a clothing store. Both ads said "no experience required," so Amy decided to apply for both jobs. The ad for a stock clerk said to apply in person, so Amy went there after school on Monday, filled out an application form, and spoke with the manager of the supermarket. Unfortunately, they only had a full-time job available.

The ad for the position in the clothing store included a telephone number. Amy called and requested an interview. She dressed appropriately, and she arrived 15 minutes early. After she filled out the application form, the owner of the store asked her questions about her classes and activities at school. Amy also talked about the types of clothing young people like these days. The store owner was very impressed, and Amy got the job! She will work Thursday and Friday evenings and all day each Saturday. The part-time hours are perfect because she will still have plenty of time for her homework. Amy's first day of work is tomorrow. She's very excited, and she's very proud.

1. According to the story, Amy is going to start working tomorrow as _____.
   a. an architect
   b. a lawyer
   c. a salesperson
   d. a stock clerk

2. Most of the jobs in the want ads _____.
   a. were part-time
   b. were full-time
   c. were on bulletin boards
   d. required previous experience

3. In the third paragraph, *apply in person* means _____.
   a. call to request an interview
   b. go to the place and ask about the job
   c. there is one job available
   d. you must know a person at the job

4. In the fourth paragraph, the word *position* means _____.
   a. manager
   b. job
   c. application
   d. interview

5. Amy probably arrived early for her interview because _____.
   a. she didn't want to be late
   b. she applied for two jobs
   c. she dressed appropriately
   d. the application form was long

6. The new job is perfect for Amy because _____.
   a. the clothing store is near her school
   b. she wants to be a store owner some day
   c. the job isn't full-time
   d. the salary is very good

A WHICH GROUP?

Put these words into the correct groups.

arrival and departure board	bus stop	passenger	taxi driver	timetable
bus	cab	platform	taxi stand	token
bus driver	conductor	subway	ticket	train
bus route	fare card			

Forms of Transportation

bus

People

Places to Wait

Things That Cost Money

Things That Give Information

B GOING PLACES

1. Many people are waiting for the bus at the ((bus stop)   bus fare).
2. You need to buy a (turnstile   fare card) to get on the subway.
3. You need to show your ticket to the (cab driver   conductor).
4. Eleven people were standing on the (platform   track) and waiting for the train.
5. The passenger gave the (ticket counter   transfer) to the bus driver.
6. If you want to find out where the Number Fifteen bus goes, look at the (bus route   meter).

C GETTING TO THE MID-CITY MALL

The new Mid-City Mall is opening this week. This newspaper ad gives directions for how to get there. Look at the ad and decide if the statements are True (T) or False (F).

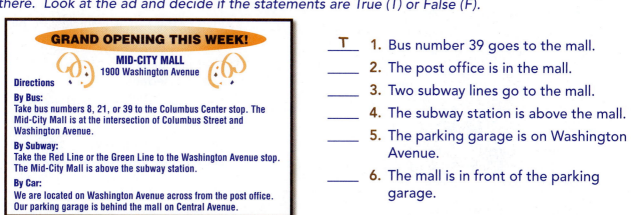

GRAND OPENING THIS WEEK!

MID-CITY MALL
1900 Washington Avenue

Directions

By Bus:
Take bus numbers 8, 21, or 39 to the Columbus Center stop. The Mid-City Mall is at the intersection of Columbus Street and Washington Avenue.

By Subway:
Take the Red Line or the Green Line to the Washington Avenue stop. The Mid-City Mall is above the subway station.

By Car:
We are located on Washington Avenue across from the post office. Our parking garage is behind the mall on Central Avenue.

___T___ 1. Bus number 39 goes to the mall.

_____ 2. The post office is in the mall.

_____ 3. Two subway lines go to the mall.

_____ 4. The subway station is above the mall.

_____ 5. The parking garage is on Washington Avenue.

_____ 6. The mall is in front of the parking garage.

What forms of public transportation do you use? How many times per week do you use them? Make a list, and then compare with a classmate.

Reaching Out!

Transportation

A PUT THEM IN ORDER

Put the vehicles in order.

← **From Smallest to Largest. 1 = Smallest, 6 = Largest** →

| van | | semi | | **1** motorcycle | | truck | | minivan | | hatchback |

← **From Slowest to Fastest. 1 = Slowest, 4 = Fastest** →

| sports car | | moped | | bicycle | | sedan |

← **From Least Expensive to Most Expensive. 1 = Least Expensive, 5 = Most Expensive** →

| hatchback | | motor scooter | | R.V. | | minivan | | S.U.V. |

B WHICH VEHICLE?

Circle the best answer.

1. George needs to buy a ((minivan)   sports car) because he has a large family.
2. I can put a lot of groceries in the back of my (station wagon   moped).
3. I like to put the top down in my (hatchback   convertible).
4. Our car won't start. We need a (pickup truck   tow truck).
5. We have a bed, a small stove and sink, and a small bathroom in our (R.V.   S.U.V.).
6. Do you prefer a (sedan   motor scooter) with two doors or four doors?

C TOP 10 BEST-SELLING VEHICLES

This chart shows the top 10 vehicles in the United States in a recent year. Use the chart to decide if the statements are True (T) or False (F).

Company	Model	Type	Number
1. Ford	F-Series	pickup truck	845,586
2. Chevrolet	Silverado	pickup truck	684,302
3. Dodge	Ram	pickup truck	449,371
4. Toyota	Camry	sedan	413,296
5. Honda	Accord	sedan	397,750
6. Ford	Explorer	S.U.V.	373,118
7. Ford	Taurus	sedan	300,496
8. Honda	Civic	sedan	299,672
9. Chevrolet	Impala	sedan	267,882
10. Chevrolet	TrailBlazer	S.U.V.	261,334

Source: *Automotive News*

__T__ 1. The most popular vehicle is made by Ford.

____ 2. Five of the top 10 vehicles are pickup trucks.

____ 3. Honda makes two of the most popular sedans.

____ 4. Chevrolet sells more S.U.V.s than sedans.

____ 5. Among the top 10 vehicles, more sedans are sold than pickup trucks.

Reaching Out!

Vehicle Evaluation

Make a list of five vehicles you are familiar with (yours, friends', family members'). In your opinion, which of these is the most comfortable? the most beautiful? the safest? Compare with a classmate.

DICTIONARY PAGES 126–127

A WHERE IN THE CAR?

Where is each of these items in a car? Write **O** if it's outside the car, **H** if it's under the hood, and **I** if it's inside the driver's section.

[H] spark plugs	☐ dashboard	☐ air filter	☐ bumper	☐ heater
☐ visor	☐ headlight	☐ license plate	☐ battery	☐ alternator
☐ fender	☐ steering wheel	☐ hubcap	☐ engine	☐ tire
☐ radiator	☐ side mirror	☐ headrest	☐ dipstick	☐ ignition

B TYPES OF CAR PARTS

Some parts of a car are necessary to operate a car, some are for safety, and some are a luxury and are not necessary. Write each part in the correct category below.

radio	battery	transmission	navigation system	sunroof	gas pedal
fan belt	air conditioning	CD player	seat belt	brake light	engine
air bag	brake pedal	rearview mirror	shoulder harness	door lock	roof rack

Necessary to Operate a Car	Safety Items	Luxury Items
fan belt		

C THE STATE INSPECTION

Many states require an inspection for all vehicles. Look at the inspection form for this car to see what passed and what needs to be fixed. Then circle all the parts of the car that need to be fixed.

Jack's Repair Shop State Inspection	okay
brakes	✓
taillights	
backup lights	✓
windshield wipers	
turn signals	✓
parking lights	
tires	✓
headlights	
side mirrors	
seat belts	✓

What is your "dream car"? Make a list of all the items it would have. Then compare with a classmate. Which of your choices are the same? Which are different?

Reaching Out!

Your Dream Car

A ON THE STREETS

1. Hector is walking, and he wants to cross the street. He should use ____.
   a. an overpass   (b.) a crosswalk   c. a median

2. Ruby is driving on the interstate, and she needs to stop. She should stop on the ____.
   a. shoulder   b. right lane   c. center lane

3. Susan is behind a slow driver, and she wants to pass. She should make sure there's a ____.
   a. double yellow line   b. broken line   c. solid line

4. Ken is driving on a road that goes through a mountain. He's in ____.
   a. an underpass   b. a bridge   c. a tunnel

5. Fatima is driving, and she has to pay to use the road. She's at ____.
   a. a divider   b. an intersection   c. a tollbooth

6. Andrew had to stop at an intersection because there was a ____.
   a. traffic light   b. corner   c. block

B INTERSTATE HIGHWAYS AND CITY STREETS

Compare the things you find on interstate highways and city streets. Write each item in the correct category below.

block	crosswalk	exit ramp	median	speed limit sign
bridge	double yellow line	exit sign	route sign	tollbooth
corner	entrance ramp	intersection	shoulder	traffic light

Interstates Only
____
____
____
____

Interstates & Streets
____
____
____

Streets Only
____
____
____
____
____

C ROAD INVENTORY

How many of each of the following do you see between your home and your school? Count them, and then write the number next to each item.

[ ] speed limit signs   [ ] bridges   [ ] overpasses
[ ] crosswalks   [ ] traffic lights   [ ] route signs

Reaching Out!

Class Chart

Compare your "road inventory" answers from Exercise C with a classmate. Who sees more of each? Does your classmate see things that you don't see?

A OPPOSITE PREPOSITIONS

Match the preposition with its opposite.

__c__ 1. around   a. out of

____ 2. on   b. over

____ 3. under   c. through

____ 4. into   d. up

____ 5. down   e. off

B YOUR COMMUTE

Check what you do on your way to English class.

- ☐ I walk across a street.
- ☐ I go under an overpass.
- ☐ I drive onto an entrance ramp.
- ☐ I get into a bus.
- ☐ I go over a bridge.
- ☐ I go up a hill.

C TRAVELING

1. Jim drives his car ((through)   on) a tunnel every day.
2. Kelly gets (onto   under) the subway at the 14th Street station.
3. Helen walks (up   over) a bridge to get to her son's school.
4. Terence drives (out of   down) a hill every day.
5. Margaret walks (around   over) many buildings on her way to work.
6. Jonathan goes (into   onto) his office building Monday through Friday.
7. Emilio drives (across   past) a school every day on his way to English class.

D HOW JULIA GETS TO WORK

This map shows how Julia gets to work. Decide if each statement is True (T) or False (F).

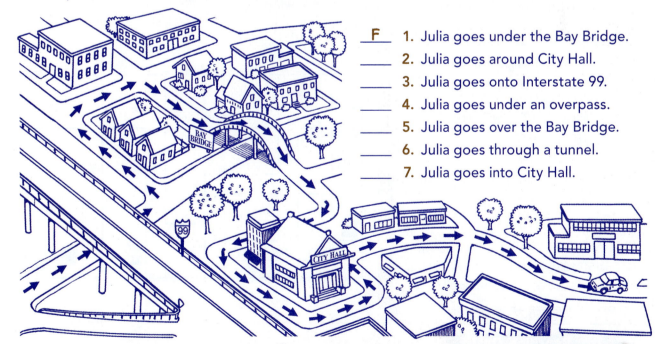

__F__ 1. Julia goes under the Bay Bridge.

____ 2. Julia goes around City Hall.

____ 3. Julia goes onto Interstate 99.

____ 4. Julia goes under an overpass.

____ 5. Julia goes over the Bay Bridge.

____ 6. Julia goes through a tunnel.

____ 7. Julia goes into City Hall.

Make a list of all the actions you do every day that you can describe with the "prepositions of motion" in this lesson. Write a full sentence for each action. Compare lists with your classmates. Who is the "most active" person?

Reaching Out!

Your Actions

A GETTING A DRIVER'S LICENSE

In order to get a driver's license, it's necessary to take a written test and a driving test. For this part of the written test, write the letter next to each traffic sign.

A Merging Traffic
B No Right Turn
C No U-Turn
D Pedestrian Crossing
E Railroad Crossing
F School Crossing
G Slippery When Wet
H Handicapped Parking Only

D

B INVENTORY OF SIGNS

How many of each sign do you see between your home and your school?

| One Way | Do Not Enter | Stop | Yield | Detour | Right Turn Only |

C DRIVING DIRECTIONS

Carla needed directions from her home at 32 Jefferson Avenue to the Northville Public Library. She went online and got these directions from www.mapit.com. On the route map, start at Carla's house, follow the directions, and draw a line where she will drive.

Start: 32 Jefferson Ave., Northville, AZ
End: 49 Main St., Northville, AZ

1: Go EAST on JEFFERSON AVE. to ELM ST.

2: Turn LEFT onto ELM ST.

3: Turn LEFT onto SUMMER AVE.

4: Turn RIGHT onto OAK ST.

5: Turn RIGHT onto WESTON AVE.

6: Go STRAIGHT until MAIN ST.

7: Go RIGHT onto MAIN ST.

8: Go STRAIGHT. End at 49 Main St., Northville, AZ.

Total Time: 12 Minutes   **Total Distance:** 3.5 Miles

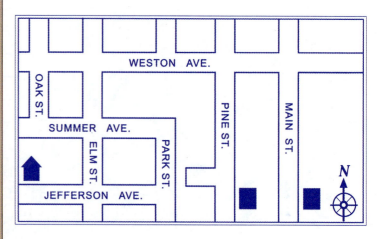

Reaching Out!

Drawing a Route Map

Work with a classmate. Give directions from your home to the school, and your classmate will draw a route map. Check the route map to see if it is correct. Then switch: Your classmate gives directions, and you draw the route map.

A AT THE AIRPORT

Match the sentence and the correct group of words.

__g__ 1. These people work at the airport.

____ 2. You find these at a security checkpoint.

____ 3. You carry your clothing in these.

____ 4. You need these to get on the airplane.

____ 5. These are places in the airport.

____ 6. These are for your suitcases.

____ 7. You only need these when you go to a foreign country.

a. metal detector, X-ray machine, security officer

b. boarding area, baggage claim area, gate

c. ticket, identification, boarding pass

d. garment bag, suitcase, carry-on bag

e. baggage claim check, luggage cart

f. visa, customs declaration form, passport

g. ticket agent, immigration officer, security officer, customs officer

B AIRPORT SIGNS AND MONITORS

There are many flights each day from Chicago to Miami. Look at the signs and monitors in each airport and fill out the chart for each of the people below.

In Chicago

Ticket Counters

Airline	Floor
Air Pleasant (AP)	2
All Sky Airways (ASA)	3
In-Transit Airways (ITA)	2
Safety Airlines (SA)	3
Trans-Air (TA)	3
World Airways (WA)	2

In Miami

Baggage Claim Area

Airline	Carousel
Air Pleasant (AP)	A
All Sky Airways (ASA)	D
In-Transit Airways (ITA)	B
Safety Airlines (SA)	B
Trans-Air (TA)	A
World Airways (WA)	C

DEPARTURES

FLIGHT	CITY	TIME	GATE
ASA 28	Memphis	2:30	67
WA 151	Miami	1:25	18
ASA 82	Miami	2:15	72
TA 726	Miami	2:45	32
TA 267	New York	2:00	35
SA 589	New York	2:20	23B

ARRIVALS

FLIGHT	CITY	TIME	GATE
AP 724	Boston	6:05	17
WA 151	Chicago	5:35	78
ASA 82	Chicago	6:10	36
TA 726	Chicago	6:45	14
WA 11	Columbus	6:00	79
ITA 268	Detroit	6:25	21

Flight	Ticket Counter Floor	Departure Gate	Departure Time	Arrival Gate	Arrival Time	Baggage Carousel
Theresa is on All Sky Airways flight 82.	3					
Chen is on World Airways flight 151.						
Carlos is on Trans-Air flight 726.						

Describe an airport you know in the U.S. and an airport in another country. How are they the same? How are they different? Compare with a classmate.

Reaching Out!

Comparing Airports

A WHERE DO YOU HEAR THESE?

Check the place where you usually hear each of the following sentences.

Airplane Travel Sentences	At the Gate	At Security	On the Airplane
1. "Put your computer in a tray."		✔	
2. "All passengers can now board the plane."			
3. "Take off your shoes."			
4. "Fasten your seat belt."			
5. "Walk through the metal detector."			
6. "Empty your pockets."			
7. "Please find your seat."			
8. "You need to check in here."			
9. "Please stow your carry-on bag."			
10. "Put your bag on the conveyor belt."			

B ON THE AIRPLANE

Circle the best answer to complete the sentence.

1. The pilot and the co-pilot work in the (lavatory (cockpit)) of an airplane.
2. If you have long legs, you will probably want to sit in the (aisle seat   middle seat).
3. If you need the flight attendant's help, you should push the (call button   life vest).
4. The plane takes off and lands on the (terminal   runway).
5. If you start to feel sick, you can use the (oxygen mask   air sickness bag).
6. People store their carry-on bags in the (overhead compartment   cockpit).

C WHICH DON'T BELONG?

Cross out two items in each group that don't belong.

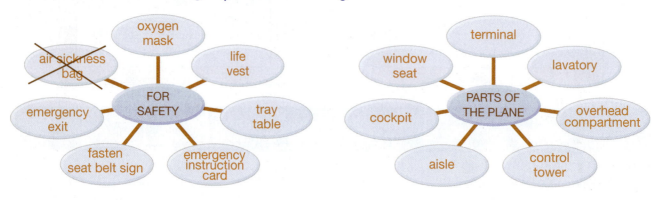

FOR SAFETY: oxygen mask, air sickness bag ~~(crossed out)~~, life vest, emergency exit, tray table, fasten seat belt sign, emergency instruction card

PARTS OF THE PLANE: terminal, window seat, lavatory, cockpit, overhead compartment, aisle, control tower

> ◀ **Reaching Out!**
>
> *Airplane Travel Opinions*
>
> What do you like about airplane travel? What don't you like? Make a list of five things you like and five things you don't like. Compare lists with a classmate.

A TRUE OR FALSE?

Look at page 133 of the Picture Dictionary. Decide if each statement is True (T) or False (F).

__T__ 1. The doorman is opening the door for a hotel guest.

_____ 2. A man is speaking to the desk clerk at the front desk.

_____ 3. The bell captain is putting luggage on a luggage cart.

_____ 4. A woman is speaking with the concierge.

_____ 5. There's an ice machine in the lobby.

_____ 6. The exercise room is near the swimming pool.

_____ 7. There are more people in the meeting room than in the gift shop.

_____ 8. A housekeeper is opening a guest room with a room key.

B THEY DON'T WORK WITH THEM

Cross out the people or things they don't usually work with.

1. concierge: telephones   ~~housekeeping carts~~   guests
2. parking attendant: cars   keys   ice machines
3. housekeeper: computers   sheets   housekeeping carts
4. bellhop: suitcases   luggage carts   room service
5. desk clerk: pools   guests   room keys
6. bell captain: luggage carts   restaurants   bellhops

C HOTEL SERVICES

These advertisements show the services at two hotels in town. Look at the pictures and decide what services these hotels have. Then write each service in the correct place below. Is the service available only in the Drake Hotel, only in the Bedford Inn, or in both?

The Drake Hotel	The Drake Hotel & The Bedford Inn	The Bedford Inn
exercise room	_____	_____
_____	_____	_____

> **Reaching Out!**
>
> Look in the Yellow Pages of the telephone book to find advertisements for two hotels in your city. What services do they offer? If the information isn't in the telephone book, call the hotels and ask. Then share the information and compare hotels with your classmates.
>
> *Hotels in Your City*

Which Is Faster—the Plane or the Bus?

Donald and George are brothers. Donald lives in Chicago, Illinois, and George lives in Indianapolis, Indiana. When Donald visits his brother in Indianapolis, he likes to fly. He usually arrives at the airport two hours before his flight. He waits in a long line at the check-in counter. That's where he receives his boarding pass and checks his large suitcase. Then he goes through the security checkpoint, where he takes off his shoes, empties his pockets, puts his carry-on bag and shoes on the conveyor belt, and walks through the metal detector. Then he walks through the airport to the departure gate. When he arrives at the gate, he sits down in the waiting area, and when they call his flight number, he boards the plane. The flight to Indianapolis takes about one hour. When the plane arrives, it takes five or ten minutes for it to get from the runway to the gate and another ten minutes or more for all the passengers to get off the plane. Then Donald goes to the baggage claim area and waits for his suitcase. Donald finally meets his brother outside the airport in Indianapolis more than four hours after he first arrived at the airport in Chicago.

When George travels from Indianapolis to Chicago to visit his brother, he prefers to go by bus. He gets to the bus terminal about ten minutes before his bus leaves. He doesn't have to wait in any long lines, and there aren't any security checkpoints. He goes to the bus terminal, buys his ticket at the ticket window, waits for the boarding announcement, hands his luggage to the bus driver, and gets on the bus. He sits and looks out the window and enjoys the 3 1/2-hour ride to Chicago. When the bus arrives, the driver opens the baggage compartment, and George gets his luggage right away. He meets his brother about 3 hours and 40 minutes after he first arrived at the bus station in Indianapolis.

Donald's plane trip takes longer than George's bus trip. These days, bus travel can be faster than air travel!

1. Donald checks his suitcase _____.
   a. at the security checkpoint
   b. at the gate
   c. at the baggage claim area
   d. at the check-in counter

2. Donald doesn't wear his shoes when he _____.
   a. waits at the departure gate
   b. walks on the conveyor belt
   c. goes through the metal detector
   d. boards the plane

3. Donald boards the plane _____.
   a. when they call him on the phone
   b. at the security checkpoint
   c. at the gate
   d. when he arrives in Indianapolis

4. According to the story, George doesn't have to _____.
   a. buy a ticket
   b. take off his shoes
   c. go to a terminal
   d. travel to visit his brother

5. From the story, you know that _____.
   a. Donald travels with a suitcase and a carry-on bag
   b. George is afraid to fly
   c. George and Donald don't have a sister
   d. George likes the bus because it's cheaper

6. Another good title for this story is _____.
   a. "George's Bus Trip"
   b. "The Flight to Indianapolis"
   c. "Suitcases and Luggage"
   d. "Two Brothers and How They Travel"

DICTIONARY PAGES 134–135

A CRAFT, HOBBY, OR GAME?

Are these activities a craft, a hobby, or a game? Write C for craft, H for hobby, and G for game.

C knit	☐ Monopoly	☐ photography	☐ backgammon
☐ astronomy	☐ sew	☐ make pottery	☐ do origami
☐ chess	☐ collect stamps	☐ do needlepoint	☐ cards

B WHAT DO YOU USE?

1. When I sew I use   a sketch pad.
2. When I paint I use   yarn.
3. When I draw I use   a thimble.
4. When I do pottery I use   binoculars.
5. When I knit I use   glue.
6. When I build models I use   a canvas.
7. When I go bird-watching I use clay.

C WHICH IS DIFFERENT?

1. a. watercolor	(b.) clay	c. oil paint	d. acrylic paint
2. a. magnifying glass	b. telescope	c. web browser	d. binoculars
3. a. coin catalog	b. backgammon	c. stamp album	d. field guide
4. a. do needlepoint	b. sew	c. do embroidery	d. do origami
5. a. pattern	b. easel	c. canvas	d. paintbrush

D COURSES AT EASTVILLE

The Eastville Center for Adult Education has some interesting courses this year. Look at the course descriptions in the school catalog, and fill in the name of each course.

Astronomy	Bird-watching	Needlepoint	Origami	Photography	Pottery	Woodworking

EASTVILLE CENTER FOR ADULT EDUCATION

Bird-watching	Sat. 6:00-8:00 A.M.	We will take trips to Fern Park. Bring a field guide and binoculars.
	Sun. 4:00-5:00 P.M.	If you like to sew, you will love this class.
	Mon. 6:00- 8:00 P.M.	Learn to take beautiful pictures. Bring a camera and film to class.
	Tues. 7:00-9:00 P.M.	Work with clay. Make your own cups, bowls, and plates.
	Wed. 5:00-7:00 P.M.	Learn the Japanese art of making birds and animals from paper.
	Wed. 10:00-12:00 P.M.	View the stars through the observatory's powerful telescope.
	Thurs. 8:00-10:00 P.M.	You will build tables and chairs. We'll supply the tools.

Interview a classmate. What crafts can your classmate do? What hobbies and games does he or she like? Take notes. Then tell the class about your classmate.

Reaching Out!

Classmate Interview

A THE WRONG PLACE!

Cross out the place that doesn't belong.

1. Places where you can look at art: art gallery   ~~planetarium~~   museum
2. Places to see animals or fish: zoo   aquarium   flea market
3. Places to go on a rainy day: play   concert   yard sale
4. Places where you can go shopping: movies   swap meet   craft fair
5. Places where you can enjoy nature: botanical gardens   play   mountains
6. Places that are educational: planetarium   historic site   carnival

B WHERE CAN YOU GO?

Put a check next to the places and events people in your community can go to this weekend. Use the phone book and newspaper listings if you need information.

☐ amusement park	☐ beach	☐ craft fair	☐ movies	☐ play
☐ aquarium	☐ carnival	☐ flea market	☐ museum	☐ yard sale
☐ art gallery	☐ concert	☐ historic site	☐ park	☐ zoo

C TRUE OR FALSE?

Look at the park on page 137 of the Picture Dictionary and decide if the statements are True (T) or False (F).

__T__ 1. There are nine children on the playground.

_____ 2. A woman is sitting on the swings and feeding the birds.

_____ 3. There are two trash cans in the picnic area.

_____ 4. The ballfield is next to the tennis court.

_____ 5. There's one bicycle in the bike rack.

_____ 6. Two people are running on the bicycle path.

_____ 7. Two children are on the seesaw, and one child is on the slide.

D CROSS OUT TWO!

1. You get food from them.	snack bar stand	vendor	~~boogie board~~	cooler	refreshment	~~swimmer~~
2. These are people at the beach.	vendor	cooler	swimmer	sunbather	life preserver	surfer
3. They protect you from the sun.	beach umbrella	sun hat	lifeguard	sunglasses	surfboard	sunblock
4. You take them to the beach.	wave	blanket	suntan lotion	lifeguard stand	towel	beach chair

Reaching Out!

Your Recommendations

Friends are visiting your community this weekend. Which museums, historic sites, parks, beaches, amusement parks, and other places should they visit? Why? Compare recommendations with a classmate.

A THEY GO TOGETHER

_g_	1. weightlifting	a.	racket, shuttlecock
____	2. hockey	b.	paddle, table, net, ball
____	3. horseback riding	c.	life vest, sailboard, sail
____	4. gymnastics	d.	rod, reel, net, bait
____	5. archery	e.	saddle, reins, stirrups
____	6. hiking	f.	life jacket, oars, boat
____	7. camping	g.	barbell, weights
____	8. scuba diving	h.	harness, rope, boots
____	9. fishing	i.	bow and arrow, target
____	10. windsurfing	j.	thermos, basket, blanket
____	11. ping pong	k.	horse, parallel bars, balance beam, trampoline
____	12. skiing	l.	bat, batting helmet, catcher's mitt, catcher's mask
____	13. rowing	m.	tent, tent stakes, sleeping bag, lantern
____	14. baseball	n.	wet suit, tank, mask
____	15. rock climbing	o.	skates, puck, stick, glove
____	16. badminton	p.	backpack, compass, canteen, boots, trail map
____	17. picnic	q.	boots, bindings, poles

B HOW ARE THEY THE SAME?

1. badminton / volleyball
   a. You use a ball.
   b. There's a net.

2. kayaking / rowing / windsurfing
   a. You wear a life vest.
   b. You wear safety goggles.

3. softball / baseball
   a. You pass the ball.
   b. You pitch the ball.

4. volleyball / tennis / ping pong
   a. You serve the ball.
   b. You dribble the ball.

5. lacrosse / hockey / pool
   a. You use a racket.
   b. You use a stick.

6. soccer / football
   a. You wear shoulder pads.
   b. You kick the ball.

7. basketball / volleyball
   a. You play on a court.
   b. You play on a field.

8. golf / baseball / softball
   a. You catch the ball.
   b. You hit the ball.

9. canoeing / table tennis
   a. You wear a life jacket.
   b. You use a paddle.

10. billiards / ping pong
    a. You play on a table.
    b. There's a net.

11. cycling / figure skating
    a. It's a winter sport.
    b. You can do this alone.

12. windsurfing / sailing
    a. You use a sail.
    b. You're in a boat.

(continued)

137

C WHICH IS DIFFERENT?

1. a. court | (b.) player | c. field | d. rink
2. a. jogging | b. walking | c. bowling | d. running
3. a. canoe | b. surfboard | c. kayak | d. sailboat
4. a. skis | b. bobsled | c. raft | d. skates
5. a. Frisbee | b. basketball | c. barbell | d. softball
6. a. ice skates | b. ski boots | c. roller blades | d. boxing trunks
7. a. bow | b. birdie | c. puck | d. golf ball
8. a. bounce | b. throw | c. dribble | d. jump
9. a. basketball court | b. picnic basket | c. backboard | d. hoop
10. a. exercise bike | b. rowing machine | c. towrope | d. treadmill

D SAFETY FIRST!

Sports and recreation can be dangerous, but you can keep safe with the right equipment. When should you use the following? List as many sports and recreational activities as you can.

1. helmet _____cycling_____
2. gloves _____
3. life jacket _____
4. knee and elbow pads _____
5. safety goggles _____

E MY FAVORITE SPORTS AND RECREATION ACTIVITIES

Complete the following chart. Then compare favorite activities with a classmate.

	Favorite	Reason
Outdoor Recreation Activity		
Individual Sport		
Team Sport		
Winter Sport		
Summer Sport		
Form of Exercise		

F CLASS SURVEY

Take a class survey. Find answers to the following questions.

1. What are the most popular kinds of outdoor recreation? _____
2. What are the most popular individual sports? _____
3. What are the most popular team sports? _____
4. What are the most popular winter sports? _____
5. What are the most popular water sports? _____

Reaching Out!

Sporting Goods Store

You and a classmate are going to open a sporting goods store! Use information from the survey in Exercise F. What will you sell in the winter? What will you sell in the summer? What will you sell all year? Make a list of items. Then compare lists with other classmates.

A FIND THE TICKETS

Look at the tickets. Write the correct ticket price next to each picture.

$30

SCHUBERT THEATER
CHICAGO OPERA COMPANY
8:00 P.M. Thursday, April 24, 2012
$60.00   C5

BRIDGETON COMEDY CLUB
9:00 P.M. Friday, June 4, 2012
$30.00

CARROLL CONCERT HALL
ATLANTA ORCHESTRA
7:00 P.M. Saturday, July 5, 2012
$40.00   H14

MAJESTIC THEATER
Best Play of the Year
THE EAGLE'S SONG
2:00 P.M. Sunday, May 19, 2012
$50.00   J2

B ENTERTAINMENT REVIEWS

Complete these entertainment reviews from the newspaper. Fill in the missing words.

actor	ballet	concert	musicians	opera singer
band	comedian	Concert Hall	orchestra	theater
ballerina	Comedy Club	conductor	opera	screen

Eddie Murray kept the audience laughing at his jokes at the Riverside **Comedy Club** 1 last Saturday night. This young new _____ 2 has a bright future.

You must hear Pavalutti sing in this new production of the _____ 3, Aida. No other _____ 4 can sing the way he does.

Sunday's Bach and Vivaldi _____ 5 at the Royal _____ 6 was magnificent! All the _____ 7 in the _____ 8 played beautifully thanks to their talented _____ 9, Eric Landsdorf.

In "The Unforgotten," Cliff Eastman shows us once again how talented he is. When he's on the _____ 10, you forget that he's a movie _____ 11 and that you're in a _____ 12.

If you enjoy _____ 13, you must see Anna Petrova dance in *Swan Lake.* In our opinion, she's the greatest _____ 14 in the world today.

The Roosters are an exciting new _____ 15. Their music is very lively and fun to dance to.

Interview a classmate. What kinds of entertainment does your classmate like? Who are your classmate's favorite actors, actresses, musicians, singers, and comedians? Take notes. Then share with the class.

Reaching Out!

Pair Interview

A TONIGHT'S TV PROGRAMS

Circle the correct answers in the TV listings.

7:00 ② **THE SINGING CLASSROOM**
Lots of music and games on this new
(children's program   soap opera).

④ **NEWS**

⑤ **THE MILLION DOLLAR QUESTION**
Contestants can win $100,000,000 on this
(shopping program   game show).

⑦ **MOVIE:** "Le Vieux"
This (foreign film   action movie) from West
Africa tells the story of a lonely old man.

7:30 ④ **THE MARY WINDSOR SHOW**
Mary's guests are Jennifer Gomez and Brad Potts.
You won't want to miss this (talk show   tragedy).

8:00 ② **WHAT'S IN OUR FOOD?**
A (science fiction movie   documentary) about
the food we eat.

⑤ **MOVIE:** *Montana Cowboy*
A cowboy protects his home and the woman he
loves in this (western   war movie).

9:00 ② **THE BIRDS OF SOUTH AMERICA**
A beautiful (reality show   nature program).

④ **MOVIE:** *Frankenstein's Monster*
A scary (horror movie   sitcom) that you won't
forget.

⑦ **BASEBALL:** Yankees play the Red Sox
An exciting (sports program   play).

◄ Reaching Out!

TV Listings

Find a TV schedule in the newspaper. Make a list of five programs
you want to watch. What kind of programs are they? Compare lists
with a classmate.

B HOW DO YOU RATE THEM?

Number the following kinds of music from 1 (you like the most) to 12 (you like the least). Then
number the kinds of movies in the same way. Compare answers with a classmate.

☐ bluegrass   ☐ country music   ☐ folk music   ☐ hip hop   ☐ popular music   ☐ reggae
☐ blues   ☐ classical music ☐ gospel music ☐ jazz   ☐ rap music   ☐ rock music

☐ action movies   ☐ documentaries   ☐ horror movies   ☐ science fiction movies
☐ cartoons   ☐ dramas   ☐ musicals   ☐ war movies
☐ comedies   ☐ foreign films   ☐ mysteries   ☐ westerns

C WHAT DO YOU RECOMMEND?

Recommend a movie, a television program, and a music CD. Fill out the chart.

Name of movie:		Kind of movie:	
Name of TV show:		Kind of TV show:	
Name of CD:		Kind of music:	

◄ Reaching Out!

Music We Like

Bring your favorite music CDs to class and play them. What are the
most popular kinds of music in the class?

A INSTRUMENTS OF THE ORCHESTRA

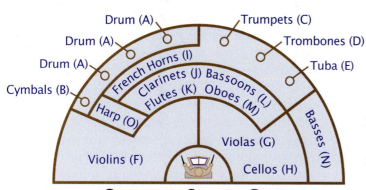

Drum (A), Drum (A), Drum (A), Cymbals (B), Harp (O), French Horns (I), Clarinets (J), Flutes (K), Bassoons (L), Oboes (M), Violins (F), Violas (G), Cellos (H), Basses (N), Trumpets (C), Trombones (D), Tuba (E)

ORCHESTRA SEATING CHART

| brass | woodwinds |
| strings | percussion |

1. The ____brass____ instruments are in the back of the orchestra on the right.

2. The _____ instruments are in the back of the orchestra on the left.

3. The _____ are in the front of the orchestra.

4. The _____ are behind the strings.

B FIND THE INSTRUMENTS

Find each of these instruments in the seating chart above. Write the instrument's letter below the picture.

1. _G_   2. ____   3. ____   4. ____   5. ____

6. ____   7. ____   8. ____   9. ____   10. ____

11. ____   12. ____   13. ____   14. ____   15. ____

C WHICH INSTRUMENTS?

Which instruments on page 150 of the Picture Dictionary often play the following kinds of music?

1. jazz _____   3. country music _____

2. rock music _____   4. your favorite music _____

Find five music CDs or cassettes. What instruments are there on each of them? Make a list. Compare lists with your classmates. Which are the most common instruments? Bring your CDs and cassettes to class and play them.

Reaching Out!

Instruments We Like

Owens City—A Wonderful Place to Live!

The residents of Owens City enjoy living there very much, and one of the reasons is that there are excellent recreational activities in the city and in the surrounding area during every season. Owens City has more than a dozen beautiful parks. In the spring, summer, and fall, people go to the parks to have picnics, play on the ballfields, play tennis, or just walk on the paths or sit on the benches. Each park has a playground with slides, swings, and other equipment that young children enjoy. One of the larger parks in the center of town also has skateboard ramps and a carousel. Most of the parks are connected to each other by bicycle paths and jogging paths. It's possible to bike or jog from one park to another very easily.

In the summer, people pack their cars with beach umbrellas and coolers and drive to the beautiful Owens City beach. It's the only beach in the city, but it's very large and has lots of room for all the swimmers and sunbathers who like to hit the beach, especially on summer weekends. Young children like to collect the beautiful shells, make sand castles, and fly their kites. Teenagers love to play volleyball, ride the waves on their surfboards and boogie boards, or just hang out at the refreshment stand. Parents like the beach because they know their children are safe there, since the city has many lifeguards on duty during the day.

There are beautiful mountains just a short drive from Owens City, so camping, hiking, rock climbing, and mountain biking are very popular activities in the summer and fall. In the winter, those mountains become a wonderful place for downhill skiing and snowboarding. For people who don't want to drive to the mountains, the city itself offers ice skating at a beautiful new skating rink and cross-country skiing on some of the bike paths and jogging paths. The rink is part of a new recreation complex that includes an indoor swimming pool and a workout room with treadmills, rowing machines, and other exercise equipment.

With its beautiful parks, beach, and surrounding mountains as well as its indoor recreation facilities, you can understand why Owens City is one of the most popular places to live in the area. It's a wonderful community.

1. From the story, you know that all of the parks in Owens City have _____.
   a. a carousel
   b. a skateboard ramp
   c. a playground
   d. a bicycle path

2. In the second paragraph, the expression *hit the beach* means _____.
   a. hit a beach ball around the beach
   b. ride the waves
   c. sit on the sand
   d. go to the beach

3. From the story, you know that the beach probably has many _____.
   a. refreshment stands
   b. lifeguard stands
   c. bicycle paths
   d. vendors

4. A popular activity during the autumn is _____.
   a. hiking
   b. sunbathing
   c. skiing
   d. collecting shells

5. The paths around Owens City probably aren't a good place to go _____.
   a. jogging
   b. biking
   c. cross-country skiing
   d. downhill skiing

6. From the story, you know that Owens City residents can _____.
   a. use exercise equipment in every park
   b. go cross-country skiing in the mountains surrounding the city
   c. bike from one park to another
   d. play tennis at the new recreation complex

A THEY GO TOGETHER: Places

c	1. coop	a.	fruit tree
___	2. pen	b.	bee
___	3. stable	c.	chicken
___	4. hive	d.	cows and sheep
___	5. cocoon	e.	pig
___	6. orchard	f.	crops
___	7. pasture	g.	horse
___	8. field	h.	caterpillar

B THEY GO TOGETHER: Animals

d	1. elephant	a.	horn
___	2. moose	b.	quills
___	3. lion	c.	bill
___	4. camel	d.	trunk
___	5. porcupine	e.	tentacles
___	6. octopus	f.	antlers
___	7. rhinoceros	g.	hump
___	8. duck	h.	mane

C WHICH GROUP?

bass	caterpillar	elephant	kangaroo	robin	swordfish
bear	cod	flounder	lion	sea horse	tiger
bee	cricket	fly	mosquito	shark	trout
blue jay	crow	giraffe	moth	sparrow	tuna
butterfly	dog	grasshopper	owl	spider	wasp
camel	eagle	hawk	parrot	stingray	wolf
cardinal	eel	horse	pigeon		

Animals	Birds	Insects	Fish
bear	blue jay	bee	bass

D CROSS OUT TWO!

1. buildings on a farm	barn	~~scarecrow~~	stable	hen house	pig pen	~~farmer~~ farmhouse
2. crops	corn	soybeans	tractor	wheat	cotton	rice barnyard
3. flowers	tulip	orchid	pansy	twig	daisy	carnation koala
4. farm animals	panda	cow	pig	goat	hyena	sheep lamb
5. pets	hamster	canary	slug	puppy	kitten	gerbil prairie dog
6. insects	firefly	squid	tick	cricket	stingray	beetle centipede
7. types of monkeys	baboon	gibbon	chimpanzee	gorilla	chipmunk	bison orangutan

(continued)

E HOW ARE THEY THE SAME?

1. horse / donkey / camel   (a.) You can ride them.   b. They have humps.
2. boa constrictor / cobra   a. They're both reptiles.   b. They're both sea animals.
3. zebra / panda / skunk   a. They're black and white.   b. They have stripes.
4. walrus / elephant   a. They both have trunks.   b. They both have tusks.
5. giraffe / leopard / jaguar   a. They have paws.   b. They have spots.
6. turtle / crab / snail   a. They have gills.   b. They have shells.
7. deer / moose   a. They both have horns.   b. They both have antlers.
8. redwood / poison ivy   a. They both have leaves.   b. They both have bark.
9. geranium / bush / oak   a. They all have roots.   b. They all have petals.

F WHICH ONE?

1. There are goats, turkeys, and (lions   (lambs)) in our barnyard.
2. My son's favorite pet is his (goldfish   jellyfish).
3. Look! There's a (bison   beetle) on your shirt!
4. There are cows and (sheep   sharks) in the field.
5. We're always careful when we go camping. There are (scarecrows   bears) in the woods.
6. We saw swordfish and (whales   leopards) in the water near our boat.
7. We grow (caterpillars   cotton) on our farm.
8. We saw blue jays and (dolphins   robins) when we went bird-watching last weekend.
9. On our visit to the aquarium, we saw sharks and (porcupines   porpoises).

G THE SAN BERNADINO ZOO

Look at the map of the San Bernadino Zoo. Where can you find the following animals? Write the number.

3 baboons	cows	gorillas	lions	parrots
boa constrictors	eagles	iguanas	orangutans	pigs
chickens	flamingos	jaguars	ostriches	sheep
chimpanzees	gibbons	lambs	owls	storks
cobras	goats	leopards	panthers	tigers

Reaching Out!
In Your Opinion

In your opinion, which animals in these lessons are the best pets? Which animals are the most dangerous? Which are the most intelligent? Which are the most beautiful? Discuss with a classmate.

A GOOD OR BAD?

Are these good or bad for the environment? Write G for Good and B for Bad.

- [B] acid rain
- [ ] air pollution
- [ ] carpool
- [ ] conserve energy
- [ ] global warming
- [ ] hazardous waste
- [ ] radiation
- [ ] recycle
- [ ] save water
- [ ] water pollution

B ENERGY AND ENVIRONMENT CHOICES

1. We use ((solar energy)   radiation) to heat our home.
2. You should fix that leaking faucet if you want to save (water   gas).
3. My neighbor and I (carpool   recycle) to work.
4. (Air   Oil) is an important source of energy.
5. I (use   conserve) energy because I'm concerned about the environment.
6. Our community gets some of its energy from (acid rain   hydroelectric power).
7. There are too many cars on our highways. In my opinion, that causes (wind   air pollution).
8. Do you agree that (global warming   geothermal energy) is a serious problem?
9. Some factories in our community are producing (coal   hazardous waste).

C ENERGY FOR ELECTRICITY

These pie graphs show how two states use different amounts of coal, natural gas, nuclear energy, oil, and other energy sources (solar, wind power, etc.) to generate electricity. Fill out the chart below. For each state, number the energy sources from 1 (the highest percentage) through 5 (the lowest percentage).

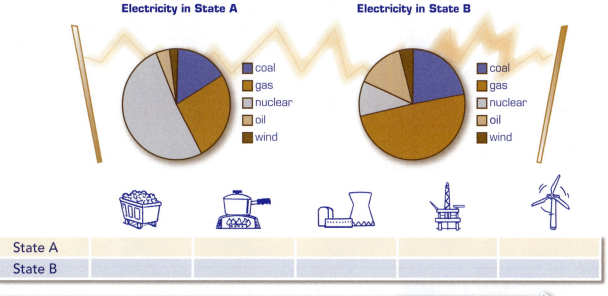

Electricity in State A

- coal
- gas
- nuclear
- oil
- wind

Electricity in State B

- coal
- gas
- nuclear
- oil
- wind

State A					
State B					

Reaching Out!

Recycling

Ask five people you know: What do you do to recycle? What else can people do to reuse or recycle materials? Compare your information with a classmate.

A WHAT'S THE HEADLINE?

1. STRONG WINDS FROM ((HURRICANE)   FLOOD) DAMAGE MANY TREES

2. (EARTHQUAKE   FOREST FIRE) DESTROYS SEVEN DOWNTOWN BUILDINGS

3. WEEKEND (TSUNAMI   BLIZZARD) COVERS CITY WITH 30 INCHES OF SNOW

4. BLACK CLOUDS FROM (MUDSLIDE   TORNADO) FILL THE SKY

5. 10 SKIERS INJURED IN WEEKEND (AVALANCHE   DROUGHT)

6. WATER FROM (VOLCANIC ERUPTION   FLOOD) COVERS CITY STREETS

7. HEAVY RAIN CAUSES MANY (WILDFIRES   MUDSLIDES)

8. (TYPHOON   HURRICANE) HITS JAPAN

9. (TSUNAMI   AVALANCHE) DESTROYS HOMES IN 5 BEACH COMMUNITIES

10. NO RAIN MAY CAUSE SUMMER (FLOOD   DROUGHT)

B NATURAL DISASTERS IN THE UNITED STATES

Look at the map of typical natural disasters in regions of the United States and check the boxes to show where each natural disaster occurs.

Natural Disaster	West	Midwest	South	Northeast
Tornadoes	☐	☑	☑	☐
Hurricanes	☐	☐	☐	☐
Forest Fires	☐	☐	☐	☐
Blizzards	☐	☐	☐	☐
Volcanic Eruptions	☐	☐	☐	☐
Floods	☐	☐	☐	☐
Earthquakes	☐	☐	☐	☐

Reaching Out!

Where Do They Take Place?

Where do different natural disasters commonly take place? In what parts of the world? In what countries? Discuss with a small group of classmates. Then share your information with the class.

There Really Is a MacDonald's Farm!

Old MacDonald had a farm, E-I-E-I-O.
And on this farm he had a cow, E-I-E-I-O.
With a moo-moo here and a moo-moo there.
Here a moo, there a moo,
Everywhere a moo-moo.
Old MacDonald had a farm, E-I-E-I-O.

This is a nursery rhyme that most children in the United States learn before they are four or five years old. The nursery rhyme is about a man named MacDonald who owns a farm filled with many different kinds of animals. The nursery rhyme tells children what kinds of animals live on a farm. It also tells the sounds the animals make.

It turns out that there really is a MacDonald's Farm! An elderly farmer named MacDonald has a very large farm in the state of Oregon. "Old MacDonald's" farm, as people call it, is filled with hundreds of farm animals such as chickens, roosters, turkeys, goats, sheep, and lambs. There are often baby piglets in the pig pen, baby chicks in the chicken coop, and young calves in the pasture with the older cows. There's a pond full of trout, frogs, and turtles behind the farmhouse. The MacDonalds' many pets all live inside the house with Farmer MacDonald and his family. They have dogs, cats, hamsters, and gerbils.

The farm is at the seashore. It sits on a cliff that overlooks the Pacific Ocean. For electricity, the farm uses solar energy, wind energy, and hydroelectric power. The hydroelectric power comes from a dam on a nearby river. Using these energy sources helps the environment and saves money.

Families like to take their children to Old MacDonald's farm. A visit there truly makes the nursery rhyme "come alive"!

1. The nursery rhyme in this story is about ____.
   a. children in the United States
   b. sources of energy
   c. a farmer and his animals
   d. pets

2. From the story, you don't know if this farm has ____.
   a. cows
   b. horses
   c. goats
   d. chickens

3. The fish on this farm live ____.
   a. in the pond
   b. in the farmhouse
   c. in the pasture
   d. in a nearby river

4. The family's pets include ____.
   a. frogs and turtles
   b. dogs and cows
   c. cats and pigs
   d. gerbils and dogs

5. The farm doesn't use energy from ____.
   a. the sun
   b. oil or gas
   c. the wind
   d. water

6. The MacDonald family doesn't own ____.
   a. a pasture
   b. a chicken coop
   c. a dam
   d. a farmhouse

A WHICH FORM?

1. A household bill with your name and address on it is (⟨proof of residence⟩   a visa).
2. Every citizen of the United States can get a U.S. (passport   permanent resident card).
3. Everybody who works here wears (an employee I.D. badge   a work permit).
4. I need to see your (permanent resident card   driver's license) before I can cash your check.
5. All students must show their (student I.D. card   birth certificate) each time they enter the school building.

B YOUR FORMS OF I.D.

Check the forms of I.D. you have. Check the ones you always carry with you. Then write the numbers on each form of I.D.

	I have one	I always carry it with me	Number
1. driver's license	☐	☐	_____
2. permanent resident card	☐	☐	_____
3. employee I.D. badge	☐	☐	_____
4. birth certificate	☐	☐	_____
5. work permit	☐	☐	_____
6. social security card	☐	☐	_____
7. student I.D. card	☐	☐	_____

C THE I-9 FORM

When you apply for a job in the United States, you must complete the I-9 Employment Eligibility Form and show one or two forms of identification. Look at the chart below. You must show one item from List A. Or you must show two items—one from List B and one from List C. Here are the forms of I.D. that seven people are showing. Decide if each person is showing the correct form or forms to get a job. Answer Yes or No.

I-9 Employment Eligibility Form				
List A	**OR**	**List B**	**AND**	**List C**
Passport **or** Permanent Resident Card		Driver's License **or** Student I.D. Card		Social Security Card **or** Birth Certificate

1. __Yes__   2. _____

3. _____   4. _____   5. _____   6. _____   7. _____

◄ **Reaching Out!**

Proving Your Identity

Which forms of identification did you have to show during the past week? Where did you have to show them? Who asked to see them? Why? Compare with a classmate.

A WHO, WHAT, WHERE?

Look at page 161 of the Picture Dictionary and complete the chart.

Who?	Which branch?	Which building?	What do they do?
senators and representatives		Capitol Building	
	judicial		
			enforce the laws

B TRUE OR FALSE?

__T__ 1. The president is in the executive branch.

_____ 2. The chief justice works in the Supreme Court building.

_____ 3. Congressmen and congresswomen explain the laws.

_____ 4. The Supreme Court is in the judicial branch of the government.

_____ 5. The cabinet makes the laws.

_____ 6. Senators work in the Capitol Building.

_____ 7. The vice-president is in the executive branch.

_____ 8. The executive branch enforces the laws.

_____ 9. The senate is larger than the house of representatives.

_____ 10. The Supreme Court justices don't make the laws.

C YOUR GOVERNMENT OFFICIALS

Who are your government officials right now? Write their names below.

President of the United States _____

Vice-president of the United States _____

Chief justice of the Supreme Court _____

Senators from your state _____

_____

Representative from your congressional district _____

Governor of your state _____

Mayor or city manager of your city or town _____

Reaching Out!

Work with a small group of students. Compare the government of the United States with the governments of other countries you know. How are they the same? How are they different? Present your information to the class.

Comparing Governments

149

A WHICH IS CORRECT?

1. The Constitution is the supreme (court (law)) of the land.
2. The Constitution begins with the (Preamble   1st Amendment).
3. After the 16th Amendment passed, people (had to   didn't have to) pay income taxes.
4. The Bill of Rights is the first (ten   seven) amendments to the Constitution.
5. The 1st Amendment (ended   guarantees) freedom of assembly.
6. The Preamble is part of the (Bill of Rights   Constitution).
7. The (1st   13th) Amendment ended slavery.
8. Eighteen-year-old citizens (could   couldn't) vote before the 26th Amendment.
9. The (1st   15th) Amendment guarantees freedom of religion.
10. The 19th Amendment gave (African-Americans   women) the right to vote.

B WHICH AMENDMENT?

Write the correct number to complete each sentence.

1. The __13th__ Amendment ended slavery.
2. The _____ Amendment guarantees people freedom of speech, press, religion, and assembly.
3. The _____ Amendment gave citizens eighteen years and older the right to vote.
4. The _____ Amendment established income taxes.
5. The _____ Amendment gave African-Americans the right to vote.
6. The _____ Amendment gave women the right to vote.

C THE 1ST AMENDMENT

These people are all practicing their rights under the 1st Amendment. Match the situation with the 1st Amendment right.

_____ 1. Sarah is a journalist. She just wrote a newspaper article that tells about problems in her community.

_____ 2. Fernando spoke at a town government meeting yesterday. He said he was very angry about the crime in his neighborhood.

_____ 3. Hundreds of people are meeting in Riverway Park today. They're holding signs that say "Save the earth!" and "Stop pollution!"

_____ 4. In our neighborhood we have a church, a mosque, a temple, and a synagogue.

a. freedom of religion

b. freedom of the press

c. freedom of assembly

d. freedom of speech

Reaching Out!
Voting Around the World

Work with a small group of students. Compare voting rights in different countries you know. Who can vote? Who can't vote? Make a chart. Present your information to the class.

A MATCH THE DATE AND THE EVENT

_b_ 1. 1929   a. George Washington becomes the first president.

____ 2. 1620   b. The stock market crashes, and the Great Depression begins.

____ 3. 1789   c. Astronaut Neil Armstrong lands on the moon.

____ 4. 1776   d. Pilgrims come to the Plymouth Colony.

____ 5. 1863   e. The March on Washington takes place.

____ 6. 1969   f. President Lincoln signs the Emancipation Proclamation.

____ 7. 1607   g. The colonies declare their independence.

____ 8. 1963   h. Colonists come to Jamestown, Virginia.

B WHICH CAME FIRST?

Circle the event that came first. Use the timeline on page 163 of the Picture Dictionary for reference.

1. a. The colonies declare their independence.
   b. Thomas Edison invents the light bulb.

2. a. George Washington becomes the first president.
   b. The civil rights movement begins.

3. a. Representatives write the United States Constitution.
   b. Colonists come to Jamestown, Virginia.

4. a. The March on Washington takes place.
   b. The Vietnam War ends.

5. a. Alexander Graham Bell invents the telephone.
   b. The Civil War begins.

6. a. Pilgrims come to the Plymouth Colony.
   b. The Bill of Rights is added to the Constitution.

7. a. The stock market crashes, and the Great Depression begins.
   b. The Persian Gulf War occurs.

8. a. Women get the right to vote.
   b. World War I ends.

C TIMELINE

Write the event in the correct place on the timeline.

| The Civil War | The Revolutionary War | World War I |
| The Korean War | The Vietnam War | World War II |

The Revolutionary War

1750   1800   1850   1900   1950   2000

Make a list of five important events in the history of your country and the years when they happened. Then work with a small group of classmates or with the entire class. Make a timeline that shows all the important events.

Reaching Out!

Make a Timeline

151

A WHEN ARE THEY?

<u>c</u>   1. Valentine's Day is on

____ 2. Halloween is on

____ 3. Thanksgiving is in

____ 4. Independence Day is on

____ 5. Veterans Day is on

____ 6. Memorial Day is in

____ 7. Christmas is on

____ 8. New Year's Day is on

____ 9. Martin Luther King, Jr. Day is in

a. November.

b. December 25th.

c. February 14th.

d. May.

e. January 1st.

f. July 4th.

g. October 31st.

h. January.

i. November 11th.

B HOLIDAY TRADITIONS

1. Today is (Independence   New Year's) Day. It's time to put a new calendar on the wall.

2. Every year on (Halloween   Thanksgiving), we give candy to children in costumes who knock on our door and say, "Trick or Treat!"

3. All the students in our class give cards to each other on (Valentine's   Veterans) Day.

4. Animals and fruit are symbols of (New Year's Day   Kwanzaa).

5. Our family has a big turkey dinner every (Valentine's Day   Thanksgiving).

6. Every year on (Independence   Memorial) Day, there are fireworks in the sky above our city.

7. Abdi's family doesn't eat until the sun goes down during their holiday of (Thanksgiving   Ramadan).

8. My grandfather died during World War II. Every year we remember him on (Valentine's   Memorial) Day.

9. Americans honor a great man on (Martin Luther King, Jr.   New Year's) Day.

10. We put presents under the tree on (Halloween   Christmas).

11. Soldiers often march in parades on (Veterans   Valentine's) Day.

12. We light candles every night of (Hanukkah   Independence Day).

C HOLIDAYS AND THE CALENDAR

Choose the correct answer.

1. Thanksgiving is always on the (third   fourth) Thursday in November.

2. Memorial Day is always on the (last   first) Monday in May.

3. Martin Luther King, Jr. Day is always on the third Monday in (January   June).

Now look at a calendar for this year and answer the questions.

4. On what date is Thanksgiving this year? _____

5. On what date is Memorial Day this year? _____

6. On what date is Martin Luther King, Jr. Day this year? _____

◀ **Reaching Out!**

Holidays

Have a conversation with a classmate. Talk about different holidays that one of you celebrates but not the other. Or, if you celebrate the same holidays, talk about differences between how you celebrate them. Then share with the class what you learned about your classmate's holiday.

A WHICH HAPPENS FIRST?

Circle the event that usually happens first.

1. **a.** Someone is convicted.   **b.** Someone is booked at the police station.
2. **a.** Someone appears in court.   **b.** Someone is acquitted.
3. **a.** Someone stands trial.   **b.** Someone is released from prison.
4. **a.** Someone hires a lawyer.   **b.** Someone is arrested.
5. **a.** Someone is sentenced.   **b.** Someone is booked at the police station.
6. **a.** Someone appears in court.   **b.** Someone goes to jail.

B GOING THROUGH THE LEGAL SYSTEM

1. police officer   suspect

   The _____**suspect**_____ was arrested by a
   _____**police officer**_____.

2. handcuffs   Miranda rights

   The police officer put _____ on the suspect,
   and he read him his _____.

3. fingerprints   mug shot

   At the police station, they took a _____ of
   the suspect, and they also took his _____.

4. lawyer   suspect

   The police told the _____ he could call a
   _____.

5. bail   defendant   judge

   The _____ appeared in court, and the
   _____ said, "Your _____ is $20,000."

6. prosecuting attorney
   witness

   At the trial, the _____ called a _____
   who said, "I saw the defendant rob a grocery store."

7. defense attorney   evidence
   innocent

   The _____ said, "This man is _____!"
   But he didn't have any _____ to prove it.

8. jury   guilty   verdict

   The _____ reached a _____. "We find the
   defendant _____."

9. fine   jail

   The judge told the defendant, "You must pay a _____
   of $10,000. And you have to go to _____.

10. convict   released

    The _____ was in jail for five years. Then he
    was _____.

Find newspaper articles about people in the legal system—people who
were arrested, stood trial, went to jail, etc. Bring them to class, and work
with a classmate. Make a television news report about the people and
events, and present your news report to the class.

Reaching Out!

In the News

DICTIONARY PAGE 166

A CITIZENSHIP ACTIONS

__c__	**1.** pay	**a.** community life
____	**2.** obey	**b.** citizenship
____	**3.** serve	**c.** taxes
____	**4.** be part of	**d.** a naturalization ceremony
____	**5.** register with	**e.** laws
____	**6.** apply for	**f.** on a jury
____	**7.** attend	**g.** the Selective Service System
____	**8.** recite	**h.** U.S. government and history
____	**9.** learn about	**i.** a citizenship test
____	**10.** take	**j.** the Oath of Allegiance

B WHAT DO THEY HAVE TO DO?

1. Citizens must obey (taxes (laws)).
2. Citizens must serve on (community life a jury).
3. You need to know about current (citizens events).
4. All males 18 to 26 must (vote register) with the Selective Service System.
5. If you want to become a citizen, you need to have a (news naturalization) interview.
6. The new citizens were proud when they recited the Oath of (Service Allegiance).

C MR. SNYDER'S CITIZENSHIP CLASS

Mr. Snyder has 12 students in his citizenship class. The chart below is on the bulletin board in his classroom. It shows where each student is on the path to citizenship. Look at the chart and decide if the statements are True (T) or False (F).

	Eduardo	Tatiana	Lee	Ana	Rosa	Ahmed	Chen	Ryoko	Joanne	Ayla	Christos	Laura
apply for citizenship	✔	✔	✔	✔	✔	✔	✔	✔	✔	✔	✔	✔
take a citizenship test		✔	✔	✔		✔		✔	✔	✔		✔
have a naturalization interview		✔		✔				✔	✔			✔
attend a naturalization ceremony		✔						✔				✔

__F__ **1.** All the students are now citizens.

____ **2.** Eight students took a citizenship test.

____ **3.** Seven students need to have a naturalization interview.

____ **4.** Nine students have attended their naturalization ceremonies.

____ **5.** Three students have completed the path to citizenship.

◀ **Reaching Out!**

Rights & Responsibilities

Have a discussion with a group of classmates. Compare citizens' rights and responsibilities in different countries you know. How are these rights and responsibilities the same? How are they different? Later, report to the class about what your group discussed.

The Constitution and the Bill of Rights

The United States Constitution is called the supreme law of the land. It established the nation's system of government more than 200 years ago. The introduction to the Constitution is called the Preamble. It begins with three very famous words: We the People. These three words describe the power of the people in the government of the country. The people give power to the government. The government serves the people.

The Constitution established the three branches of government—legislative, executive, and judicial. The legislative branch makes the laws. It has two parts: the senate and the house of representatives. There are two senators from each state. There are 435 representatives. States with more people have more representatives, while states with fewer people have fewer representatives. The executive branch enforces the laws. The President is the chief of the executive branch and is also Commander-in-Chief of the armed forces. The judicial branch explains the laws. The Supreme Court is the highest court in the country. The head of the Supreme Court is called the chief justice.

The people of the United States can change the Constitution. These changes are called amendments. There are 27 amendments to the Constitution. The first ten amendments are called the Bill of Rights. These were added to the Constitution in 1791. The Bill of Rights gives rights and freedoms to all people in the United States. The 1st Amendment guarantees freedom of speech, freedom of the press, freedom of religion, and freedom of assembly. Other amendments in the Bill of Rights guarantee the rights of people who are accused of crimes. They have the right to go to court, have a lawyer, and have a fair and quick trial. The Bill of Rights also protects people in their homes. The police need a special document from the courts before they can go into a person's home.

Other amendments to the Constitution are also very important. The 13th Amendment ended slavery. The 14th Amendment made all African-Americans citizens of the United States. The 15th Amendment gave African-Americans the right to vote. The 19th Amendment gave women the right to vote. The 26th Amendment gave citizens eighteen years old and older the right to vote. Eighteen is now the minimum voting age in the United States.

1. *We the People* are the first three words of ____.
   a. the Bill of Rights
   b. the 1st Amendment
   c. the Supreme Court
   d. the Preamble to the Constitution

2. The Bill of Rights is ____.
   a. the introduction to the Constitution
   b. the first ten amendments
   c. the first amendment
   d. 27 amendments

3. The President ISN'T ____.
   a. the chief justice
   b. the Commander-in-Chief
   c. the chief of the executive branch
   d. the head of the armed forces

4. The Supreme Court ____.
   a. enforces the laws
   b. explains the laws
   c. makes the laws
   d. writes the laws

5. People who are accused of crimes DON'T have the right to ____.
   a. have a lawyer
   b. have a fair and quick trial
   c. go into a person's home with a special document
   d. go to court

6. An amendment that DIDN'T give voting rights to more people is ____.
   a. the 13th Amendment
   b. the 15th Amendment
   c. the 19th Amendment
   d. the 26th Amendment

ANSWER KEY

WORKBOOK PAGES 1–2

A. SENDING A LETTER
1. Richard   4. 33140
2. Turner   5. 4F
3. M.   6. 76 Sunset Street

C. WHAT'S MISSING?
apartment number
state
street number
last name
zip code

D. A REGISTRATION FORM
(See page 171.)

F. FIX THE FORM!
1st line: LAST, FIRST
2nd line: SOCIAL SECURITY
3rd line: DATE
4th line: PLACE
5th line: E-MAIL

WORKBOOK PAGES 3–4

A. MALE OR FEMALE?

Male	Female
husband	wife
father	mother
son	daughter
brother	sister
grandfather	grandmother
grandson	granddaughter

Male and Female
parents
children
baby
siblings
grandparents
grandchildren

B. FAMILY ALBUMS
1. brother   9. husband
2. sister   10. wife
3. siblings   11. children
4. mother   12. son
5. father   13. daughter
6. grandparents
7. grandfather
8. grandmother

C. YOUR FAMILY
1. g   5. f
2. h   6. d
3. a   7. e
4. b   8. c

D. A FAMILY TREE
1. n   8. g
2. j   9. e
3. i   10. h
4. d   11. a
5. l   12. k
6. c   13. m
7. f   14. b

WORKBOOK PAGE 5

A. WHO ARE THEY GOING TO INVITE?
her aunt
her niece
her mother
her sister-in-law
her new mother-in-law

B. ANN'S NEW FAMILY
1. mother-in-law   6. nephew
2. father-in-law   7. niece
3. daughter-in-law   8. cousins
4. sisters-in-law   9. uncle
5. brothers-in-law   10. aunt

C. WHO ARE THEY?
1. aunt   4. niece
2. nephew   5. uncle
3. son-in-law   6. cousin

WORKBOOK PAGE 6

UNIT 1 READING
1. d   4. d   7. c
2. c   5. a   8. c
3. b   6. b

WORKBOOK PAGE 7

A. WHERE ARE THEY?

On the Wall	On the Floor
bulletin board	bookcase
chalkboard	chairs
clock	desks
map	teacher's desk
P.A. system	tables
screen	wastebasket
whiteboard	

On the Table	On the Bookcase
computer	globe
keyboard	pencil sharpener
monitor	
mouse	
overhead projector	

B. THE SUPPLY CLOSET
pencil sharpeners   erasers
rulers   calculators
spiral notebooks   chalk
thumbtacks   markers
textbooks   notebook paper
pencils

C. WHICH IS DIFFERENT?
1. b (The others are things you write with.)
2. d (The others are people.)
3. b (The others are related to a computer.)
4. a (The others are things that go on the wall.)
5. c (The others are books or notebooks.)
6. c (The others are pieces of furniture.)

WORKBOOK PAGE 8

A. Match the words.
1. your book.   4. each other.
2. your name.   5. your hand.
3. the lights.

B. Circle the correct answer.
6. the board   9. the dictionary
7. Say   10. Check
8. Take

C. Underline the correct answer.
11. book   13. homework
12. answers   14. word

D. Cross out the words.
15. your seat   18. blanks
16. your dictionary   19. Ask
17. Turn on

E. Put the words in order.
20. Mark the answer sheet.
21. Do your own work.
22. Take out a piece of paper.
23. Break up into small groups.
24. Write on a separate sheet of paper.

F. Unscramble the words.
25. partner   28. Discuss
26. mistakes   29. away
27. Repeat

G. Put the actions in order.
2
4
1
3

WORKBOOK PAGE 9

A. A PICTURE
1. next to   4. in front of
2. between   5. to the right of
3. behind   6. to the left of

B. LABEL THE BOXES
Top shelf:
Calculators   Notebooks   Workbooks   Erasers

Bottom shelf:
Rulers   Pens   Markers   Pencils

C. WHERE IS IT?
1. e   4. f
2. c   5. a
3. d   6. b

WORKBOOK PAGE 10

C. WHICH COMES FIRST?
1. b   4. b
2. a   5. b
3. b   6. a

WORKBOOK PAGE 11

A. COMPLETE THE NOTES
1. take   6. walk
2. come   7. feed
3. wash   8. Study
4. do   9. clean
5. go   10. iron

WORKBOOK PAGES 12–13

D. MARIO'S FREE TIME
1. He watches TV.
2. He plays basketball.
3. He writes letters.
4. He listens to music.
5. He listens to the radio.
6. He plays the guitar.
7. He reads the newspaper.
8. He plays cards.
9. He swims.

WORKBOOK PAGE 14

A. WHAT'S THE ANSWER?
1. c   5. f
2. e   6. d
3. a   7. b
4. g

B. A TELEPHONE CALL
1. May I please speak to Rose
2. Hold on a moment
3. Hi
4. What's new
5. Fine
6. May I ask you a question
7. Can you please say that again
8. Thanks
9. You're welcome
10. See you soon

C. CORRECT THE MISTAKES!
1. Nice to meet you.
2. Hi. I'm Susan./My name is Susan.
3. Sorry. I don't understand.
4. May I ask a question?
5. What's new with you?
6. Can you please repeat that?
7. Robert isn't here right now.

8. Can you please say that again?
9. I'd like to introduce my sister.
10. Hi. How are you doing?

WORKBOOK PAGE 15

A. TODAY'S WEATHER
1. d		7. cold	
2. a		8. hot	
3. f		9. cool	
4. e		10. warm	
5. c			
6. b			

C. WHICH IS DIFFERENT?
1. b (The others are temperature scales.)
2. c (The others are forms of precipitation.)
3. a (The others are types of unclear air.)
4. d (The others are related to rainstorms.)
5. b (The others describe temperature.)
6. c (The others are related to hot weather.)

WORKBOOK PAGE 16

UNIT 2 READING
1. b	4. c
2. c	5. c
3. a	6. d

WORKBOOK PAGE 17

A. NUMBERS AND NUMBER WORDS
Cardinal Numbers
12	twelve
80	eighty
19	nineteen
27	twenty-seven
38	thirty-eight
290	two hundred ninety

Ordinal Numbers
5th	fifth
10th	tenth
40th	fortieth
30th	thirtieth
71st	seventy-first
11th	eleventh

B. NUMBERS IN MY LIFE
1. fourteen
2. seventeen
3. three three one five six
4. three zero five – four seven eight – two nine three one
5. seven four nine – two six – one eight nine five

C. WHICH FLOOR?
1. ninth	5. sixteenth
2. first	6. second
3. third	7. fourth
4. fourteenth	

WORKBOOK PAGE 18

A. WHAT'S THE TIME?
(See page 171.)

B. WHICH TIME IS CORRECT?
1. a	5. b
2. a	6. a
3. b	7. b
4. a	8. a

C. MATCH THE TIMES
1. one ten.
2. two fifteen.
3. half past two.
4. one forty.
5. a quarter to three.
6. five to two.
7. two oh five.

WORKBOOK PAGE 19

A. WHAT'S THE AMOUNT?
1. $2.50	2. $6.30	3. $1.76
4. $25.42	5. $2.05	6. $10.71

B. HOW MUCH?
1. 10¢...........................a dime
2. 4 quarters...................one dollar
3. $100.........................a hundred-dollar bill
4. 2 dimes and a nickel....$.25
5. 5 pennies...................5¢
6. 2 five-dollar bills........$10.00

C. BACK-TO-SCHOOL SALE
55¢	$4.33	$2.67
$700	10¢	$1.75
89¢	$125	$15

WORKBOOK PAGE 20

A. WHICH DAY?
1. Friday	4. 1/31/12
2. Monday	5. Wednesday
3. weekend	6. Thursday

B. MONTHS OF THE YEAR
Month	Abbreviation	Number
October	OCT	10
February	FEB	2
August	AUG	8
December	DEC	12
May	MAY	5
July	JUL	7
April	APR	4
March	MAR	3
September	SEP	9
January	JAN	1

C. DATES
Month/Day/Year	Month/Day/Year
August 25, 2007	8/25/07
February 29, 2004	2/29/04
June 11, 1994	6/11/94
March 1, 2000	3/1/00
April 21, 2009	4/21/09
February 3, 2001	2/3/01
July 7, 1977	7/7/77
January 5, 2005	1/5/05
May 31, 2006	5/31/06
October 8, 2008	10/8/08

WORKBOOK PAGE 21

A. TIME LINE
Above time line:

1st row:
yesterday evening, this evening, tomorrow evening

2nd row:
yesterday morning, this morning, tomorrow morning

Below time line:
3rd row:
yesterday afternoon, this afternoon, tomorrow afternoon

4th row:
last night, tonight, tomorrow night

B. SEASONS
February	Winter	January
October	Fall	November
July	Summer	August
April	Spring	May

C. MARIA'S CALENDAR
1. twice a week
2. three times a week
3. once a week
4. every day
5. twice a week
6. three times a week
7. once a week
8. twice a week

WORKBOOK PAGE 22

UNIT 3 READING
1. c	4. d	7. d
2. b	5. a	8. c
3. c	6. b	

WORKBOOK PAGE 23

A. JOE'S TAXI
duplex
house
farm
townhouse
houseboat
apartment building

B. WHERE DO THEY LIVE?
1. d	4. e
2. a	5. c
3. b	

C. HOUSING IN COMMUNITIES
Name of Community	Type of Community	Number of Houses	Number of Condominiums
Fulton	town	3,000	1,000
Parsons	country	1,000	0
Riverdale	suburb	8,000	4,000
Springfield	city	10,000	12,000

WORKBOOK PAGE 24

A. TRUE OR NOT TRUE?
	True	Not True
1.		✓
2.	✓	
3.		✓
4.	✓	
5.		✓
6.	✓	
7.		✓
8.	✓	
9.		✓

B. WHICH IS DIFFERENT?
1. b (The others are furniture items.)
2. d (The others are part of the structure of the room.)
3. c (The others are furniture items.)
4. d (The others are associated with light.)
5. a (The others are electrical.)

C. GOING SHOPPING!
1. 3rd floor
2. 1st floor
3. 2nd floor
4. 4th floor
5. 3rd floor

WORKBOOK PAGE 25

A. IN THE DINING ROOM
1. candlestick	5. saucer
2. spoon	6. china
3. tray	7. table
4. serving bowl	8. mug

B. THE YARD SALE
teapot
sugar bowl
pitcher
buffet
salt shaker
pepper shaker
napkins

C. HOW MUCH IS IT?

glass	$1
coffee pot	$7
platter	$1.50
china cabinet	$35
mug	50¢
teapot	$5
buffet	$40
sugar bowl	75¢

D. FROM MOST TO LEAST

buffet
china cabinet
coffee pot
teapot
platter
glass
sugar bowl
mug

WORKBOOK PAGE 26

B. WHERE ARE THEY?

	On the Nightstand	On the Dresser	On the Bed	On the Window
blinds				✓
pillow			✓	
alarm clock	✓			
jewelry box		✓		
curtains				✓
bed frame			✓	
headboard			✓	
lamp	✓			

C. TWO FURNISHED APARTMENTS

Bedroom 1
curtains
nightstand
clock radio
pillow
quilt

Bedrooms 1 & 2
mattress
dresser
blinds
lamp

Bedroom 2
box spring
headboard
blanket
bed frame
mirror
carpet

WORKBOOK PAGE 27

A. WHERE IN THE KITCHEN?

Floor
kitchen chair
refrigerator
garbage pail
dishwasher

Counter
dish rack
canister
dishwasher detergent
toaster oven

Wall
cabinet
potholder
spice rack
microwave

Kitchen Table
food processor
cookbook
placemat
cutting board

B. BARGAIN HUNTING

```
        SHOPPING LIST
      The Kitchen Store
          toaster
         coffeemaker
         can opener
       dishwashing liquid

          Home-Mart
         tea kettle
           blender
        electric mixer
          potholder
```

WORKBOOK PAGE 28

A. WHICH IS DIFFERENT?

1. c (The others are pieces of furniture.)
2. d (The others are things a baby plays with.)
3. b (The others are things a baby sits in.)
4. c (The others are things a baby sits in.)
5. a (The others are things a baby sits in.)

B. THE BABY REGISTRY

1. True
2. False
3. False
4. True
5. False
6. True
7. False
8. True

WORKBOOK PAGE 29

B. WHAT IS IT?

1. k
2. h
3. a
4. f
5. c
6. i
7. b
8. l
9. e
10. d
11. g
12. j

WORKBOOK PAGE 30

A. REPAIR TIME!

deck
drainpipe
fence
lawn chair
screen door
tool shed

B. WHICH HOUSE IS FOR SALE?

___ ___ ✓ ___

WORKBOOK PAGE 31

A. HOW MANY?

mailboxes	15
vacancy signs	1
intercoms	1
sprinklers in the sprinkler system	2
buzzers	15
balconies	4

B. A NEW APARTMENT

4 Give a security deposit.
2 Meet the landlord.
6 Open the lock with the key.
1 See a vacancy sign.
3 Sign a lease.
5 Rent a moving truck.

C. PEOPLE, PLACES, AND THINGS

People
building manager
doorman
neighbor
superintendent
tenant

Places
balcony
basement
hallway
lobby
storage room

Safety Items
door chain
fire alarm
fire escape
fire exit
smoke detector

D. THE BEST APARTMENT

Ellen   #4
Tom   #1
Jerry   #3
Ann   #2

WORKBOOK PAGE 32

A. THIS HOUSE HAS PROBLEMS!

The roof is leaking.
There are mice.
A sink is clogged.
The hot water heater is broken.
A wall is cracked.
The front steps are broken.
There are cockroaches.

B. THESE PEOPLE REPAIR THINGS

1. chimneysweep......chimney.......dirty
2. plumber...............sink............clogged
3. roofer..................roof...........leaking
4. painter.................paint..........peeling
5. locksmith.............lock............broken
6. cable TV..............cable TV.....isn't working company

C. LOOK IN THE YELLOW PAGES!

1. 555-254-4963
2. 555-257-6983
3. 555-258-1879
4. 555-258-3176
5. 555-254-8278
6. 555-258-8836

WORKBOOK PAGE 33

A. MATCHING SUPPLIES

1. d
2. e
3. b
4. f
5. a
6. c

D. TIME SPENT ON CHORES

	Carl	Jane	Lily	Ron
vacuum	4	1	3	4
mop	2	3	1	2
dust	1	2	4	3
sweep	3	4	2	1

WORKBOOK PAGE 34

A. THE SUPPLY CABINET

1. fly swatter
2. paint pan
3. glue
4. fuses
5. step ladder
6. masking tape

B. WHO USES THEM?

1. lightbulbs
2. a mousetrap, roach killer
3. a plunger
4. a tape measure
5. duct tape
6. paint, a spray gun

C. THIS WEEK'S SPECIALS!

	True	Not True
1.	✓	
2.		✓
3.		✓
4.		✓
5.	✓	
6.	✓	
7.	✓	
8.		✓
9.		✓
10.	✓	

WORKBOOK PAGE 35

A. GREG'S TOOLBOX

Tool/Hardware	✓	How Many?
bolt		
chisel	✓	1
drill bit	✓	1
hammer	✓	2
hand drill		
level	✓	1
machine screw		
mallet		
nail	✓	5
nut	✓	3
Phillips screwdriver	✓	2
pliers	✓	2
scraper		
screwdriver	✓	1
washer	✓	2
wire	✓	1
wire stripper		
wood screw		
wrench	✓	1

C. TOOLS IN THEIR TOOLBOXES

(See page 171.)

WORKBOOK PAGE 36

A. THREE KINDS OF TOOLS

Tools for Digging
hoe
shovel
trowel
weeder

Tools for Cutting
clippers
hedge trimmer
lawnmower
line trimmer
pruning shears

Tools for Watering
hose
nozzle
sprinkler
watering can

B. WHAT ARE THEY USING?

1. rake
2. shovel
3. shears
4. watering can
5. hose
6. fertilizer
7. clippers
8. line trimmer

C. GARDEN TOOLS FOR SALE

Item	Price
shovel	$25.00
rake	$15.00
wheelbarrow	$60.00
lawnmower	$150.00
weeder	$14.00
hoe	$19.00
pruning shears	$27.00
hose	$33.00
line trimmer	$30.00
nozzle	$12.00

WORKBOOK PAGE 37

UNIT 4 READING

1. c
2. d
3. b
4. a
5. b
6. c
7. a
8. d

WORKBOOK PAGE 38

A. WHERE CAN HE GO?

1. card store, drug store, book store
2. bakery
3. bakery, convenience store, delicatessen, grocery store
4. flower shop
5. barber shop
6. cleaners
7. clothing store, department store, discount store
8. computer store, department store, discount store, electronics store

B. SHOPPING IN GLENDALE

1. Midtown Bank
2. Phil's Furniture Store
3. Sam's Service Station
4. Star's Coffee Shop
5. Main Street Clinic
6. Glendale Bus Station
7. Central Opticians
8. Bill's Book Store
9. Blake's Pharmacy
10. Classy Copy Center
11. Busy Bee Day-Care Center

WORKBOOK PAGES 39–40

A. WHERE IS IT?

1. shoe store
2. nail salon
3. pet shop
4. music store
5. ice cream shop
6. video store

B. SHOPPING AT THE MALL

1. 4
2. 1
3. 11
4. 9
5. 12
6. 14
7. 1
8. 15
9. 3
10. 5
11. 7
12. 17
13. 13
14. 16
15. 6
16. 10
17. 8

WORKBOOK PAGES 41–42

A. CAN YOU FIND THEM?

People
bus driver
meter maid
pedestrian
police officer
street vendor
taxi driver/cab driver

Vehicles
bus
garbage truck
ice cream truck
motorcycle
subway
taxi/cab/taxicab

Buildings
city hall
courthouse
fire station
jail
office building
parking garage
police station

B. WHERE IS IT?

1. police station
2. parking lot
3. fire alarm box
4. bus
5. public telephone

C. SPRINGFIELD'S BUDGET

- 7 fire hydrants
- 3 parking meters
- 2 traffic lights
- 1 sewers
- 4 sidewalks
- 6 street lights
- 5 street signs

Money Spent in 2005

sidewalks	$40,000
fire hydrants	$100,000
parking meters	$30,000
traffic lights	$25,000
sewers	$15,000
street lights	$90,000
street signs	$55,000

Money Spent in 2006

parking meters	$34,000
sewers	$13,000
sidewalks	$45,000
fire hydrants	$100,000
traffic lights	$20,000
street signs	$60,000
street lights	$93,000

D. WHICH IS DIFFERENT?

1. c (The others are on the sidewalk.)
2. b (The others are places where people wait for transportation.)
3. d (The others are people.)
4. a (The others are paid employees.)
5. a (The others are types of transportation.)
6. b (The others are related to the law.)
7. b (The others are types of vehicles.)
8. c (The others are buildings.)
9. d (The others are underground.)

WORKBOOK PAGE 43

UNIT 5 READING

1. d
2. c
3. b
4. d
5. a
6. b
7. c
8. a

WORKBOOK PAGE 44

A. FROM YOUNG TO OLD

4 3 6 1 5 2

B. WHAT DO THEY LOOK LIKE?

1. Not True
2. True
3. Not True
4. True
5. True
6. True

C. A MISSING PERSON

1. teenager
2. short
3. thin
4. long
5. curly
6. blond

D. FATHER AND SON

Father	Both	Son
short hair	straight hair	long hair
thin		heavy
tall		short
beard		mustache

WORKBOOK PAGE 45

A. SYNONYMS

1. wealthy
2. loud
3. skinny
4. hard
5. little

B. OPPOSITES

1. light
2. dull
3. straight
4. short
5. ugly

C. WHICH WORD DOESN'T BELONG?

1. c
2. d
3. a
4. c
5. d
6. a

E. ANGELA'S ENGLISH CLASS

Class Evaluation	Yes	No
1. The class is very large.	✓	
2. The teacher speaks very fast.	✓	
3. I feel comfortable in class.		✓
4. The class is very noisy.	✓	
5. The classroom is neat and clean.		✓
6. The classroom is very hot.	✓	
7. The homework is very difficult.		✓
8. The class is very long.		✓

WORKBOOK PAGE 46

A. DEAR JANE

Hungry
Lonely
Confused
Worried
Exhausted
Embarrassed
Homesick
Jealous
Bored

WORKBOOK PAGE 47

UNIT 6 READING

1. c
2. c
3. b
4. d
5. a
6. d

WORKBOOK PAGE 48

A. ERIC'S SHOPPING LIST

Number	Fruit	Unit Price	Total Price
3	apples	$.40	$1.20
2	pears	$.50	$1.00
3	bananas	$.60	$1.80
2	oranges	$.55	$1.10
2	watermelons	$4.00	$8.00
2	lemons	$.70	$1.40
1	grapefruit	$.65	$.65
2	pineapples	$3.50	$7.00

B. THEY GO TOGETHER

1. c
2. a
3. b
4. e
5. f
6. d

C. LINDA'S FRUIT SALAD

My Shopping List
1 banana
1 coconut
2 pears
3 apricots
1 honeydew melon
2 mangoes

A. HOW LONG CAN YOU KEEP THEM?
1. True
2. Not True
3. True
4. True
5. Not True
6. Not True
7. True
8. Not True
9. True

B. FIND THE RECEIPT
___ ___ _✓_

A. WHICH IS DIFFERENT?
1. c (The others are types of poultry.)
2. b (The others are parts of a chicken or turkey.)
3. d (The others are types of meat.)
4. b (The others are types of fish.)
5. a (The others are types of shellfish.)
6. d (The others are types of meat.)
7. a (The others are types of beef.)
8. b (The others are types of fish.)

B. LOOK AT THE RECEIPTS
1. Save More, $13, $50, trout
2. Price Cutter, $16, $15, $24
3. Super Shopper, $35, $16
4. Grocery Basket, $15, $22, $6

B. DAIRY PRODUCTS AND FAT

4	2	8	10	3
5	1	9	6	7

C. BEVERAGES AND CALORIES

4	6	10	9	8
2	3	5	7	1

(Answers will vary.)

A. FIX THE SIGNS!
Packaged Goods: mayonnaise
Baking Products: pickles
Canned Goods: mustard
Condiments: cookies
Baked Goods: salt

B. SAM'S SUPERMARKET
(See page 171.)

C. SHOPPING WITH COUPONS

Food	Aisle	Save
cereal	C	25¢
flour	B	50¢
ketchup	D	40¢
bread	A	30¢
peanut butter	E	75¢
soup	F	35¢

A. WHICH IS DIFFERENT?
1. c (The others are paper products.)
2. b (The others are paper products.)
3. d (The others are for babies.)
4. a (The others are types of food wraps.)
5. c (The others are types of food.)

B. JUDY CHEN'S PANTRY

Item	Has	Needs
baby cereal		✓
baby food	✓	
cat food		✓
diapers	✓	
dog food		✓
formula		✓
liquid soap	✓	
napkins		✓
paper cups	✓	
paper towels	✓	
sandwich bags	✓	
soap		✓
straws		✓
tissues	✓	
trash bags	✓	

A. HOW MANY?

2	4	3
3	3	8

B. GROUPING WORDS

People
bagger
cashier
clerk
manager
shopper

Things You Can Buy
candy
gum
magazine
produce
tabloid newspaper

Parts of a Store
aisle
can-return machine
checkout line
scale

A. WHAT'S THE CONTAINER?

Can
coffee
soup
tuna fish

Box
cereal
cookies
tissues

Jar
baby food
mayonnaise
pickles

Roll
paper towels
plastic wrap
toilet paper

Bunch
bananas
carrots
grapes

Half-Gallon
ice cream
milk
orange juice

Package
pita bread
rolls
tortillas

Pound
cheese
ground beef
potato salad

Container
cottage cheese
sour cream
yogurt

B. RECYCLING IN EASTON
C   P   C
C   P   X (Dirty Can)
P   X (No plastic) C

A. ABBREVIATIONS
1. c
2. a
3. d
4. e
5. b

B. MATCHING MEASUREMENTS
1. c
2. a
3. f
4. e
5. b
6. d

C. ADD IT UP!
1. 1 pint
2. 1 ounce
3. 1 gal.
4. 3/4 lb.
5. 1 quart
6. 1/2 gallon
7. 2 fl. ozs.
8. 1 tsp.

D. COMPARE THE RECIPES

Who Uses More?	Amy	Rick
black beans		✓
carrots		✓
cheese		✓
garlic	✓	
ground beef	✓	
jalapeño peppers	✓	
kidney beans		✓
olive oil	✓	
onions		✓
pepper	✓	
salt		✓
spices	✓	
tomatoes	✓	
vinegar		✓

A. PREPARING THE CHILI

3	7	4
5	9	1
2	6	8

C. PREPARING CHICKEN
bake
grill
broil
fry
roast

A. ACTIONS IN THE KITCHEN
1. c
2. d
3. f
4. a
5. g
6. e
7. b

B. WHERE ARE THEY?
1. T
2. F
3. T
4. T
5. F
6. F

C. JULIE AND DAN'S GIFT REGISTRY

ITEM	NEED?		QUANTITY
saucepan	yes	**no**	
skillet	**yes**	no	1
pot	**yes**	no	2
lid	**yes**	no	2
steamer	**yes**	no	1
roasting pan	**yes**	no	1
roasting rack	**yes**	no	1
casserole dish	**yes**	no	2
cake pan	**yes**	no	3
rolling pin	**yes**	no	1
spatula	yes	**no**	
colander	yes	**no**	
measuring cup	yes	**no**	
measuring spoon	**yes**	no	1
kitchen timer	**yes**	no	1
bottle opener	**yes**	no	1
can opener	yes	**no**	
ice cream scoop	yes	**no**	
paring knife	**yes**	no	2
carving knife	**yes**	no	1

A. INGREDIENTS

1. c	5. h
2. g	6. e
3. d	7. b
4. f	8. a

B. CATEGORIES

1. F	7. P
2. C	8. C
3. P	9. F
4. C	10. P
5. F	11. P
6. P	12. C

C. NUTRITIONAL INFORMATION

MOST CALORIES
french fries
cheeseburger
fried chicken
fish sandwich
salad dressing
salad
FEWEST CALORIES

MOST FAT
cheeseburger
french fries
fried chicken
fish sandwich
salad dressing
salad
LEAST FAT

MOST SALT
cheeseburger
fried chicken
fish sandwich
salad dressing
french fries
salad
LEAST SALT

A. THE SUNSHINE CAFE

waffles	$3.50
coffee	$1.25
donut	85¢
toast	99¢
croissant	75¢
muffin	$1.50
milk	$1.25
egg salad sandwich	$2.75
danish	$1.75
ham and cheese sandwich	$4.00

B. DO THEY SELL IT?

danish
muffin
sandwiches
waffles
toast

A. WHICH IS DIFFERENT?

1. c (The others are people.)
2. b (The others are places to sit.)
3. d (The others are containers for liquids.)
4. b (The others are places in a restaurant.)
5. d (The others are silverware items.)
6. a (The others are dishware items.)

B. WHAT DO THEY DO?

1. seats the customers
2. leaves a tip, pays the check
3. serves the meal, takes the order
4. clears the table, pours the water, sets the table

D. CUSTOMER SATISFACTION

MARISSA'S KITCHEN CUSTOMER SATISFACTION

Did you like it?	YES	NO
1. Host	✓	
2. Server	✓	
3. Dining Room	✓	
4. Menu	✓	
5. Salad Bar		✓
6. Food		✓
7. Dessert Tray	✓	

A. FRED'S FAMILY RESTAURANT

Left Side:
Salads
Side dishes

Right Side:
Appetizers
Entrees
Desserts

B. ON THE MENU

antipasto	
apple pie	✓
baked chicken	✓
baked potato	✓
broiled fish	✓
chicken wings	
chocolate cake	
fruit cup	✓
Greek salad	✓
ice cream	✓
jello	✓
mashed potatoes	
meatloaf	✓
mixed vegetables	✓
nachos	
noodles	
potato skins	✓
pudding	✓
rice	✓
roast beef	✓
shrimp cocktail	
spinach salad	
tomato juice	✓
tossed salad	✓

C. THE RESTAURANT BILL

Fred's Family Restaurant	
tomato juice	$2.00
potato skins	$4.95
meatloaf	$6.25
roast beef	$8.25
mixed vegetables	$3.25
ice cream	$2.25
jello	$2.75
Total:	$29.70

Fred's Family Restaurant	
fruit cup	$3.50
tossed salad	$3.00
broiled fish	$6.50
rice	$1.95
pudding	$2.95
Total:	$17.90

Fred's Family Restaurant	
Greek salad	$4.00
Caesar salad	$4.25
baked potato	$1.75
french fries	$2.50
baked chicken	$7.95
broiled fish	$6.50
apple pie	$3.95
Total:	$30.90

UNIT 7 READING

1. a	4. d
2. c	5. b
3. b	6. c

C. COLORS AND FLAGS

From left to right under bar graph:
red, white, blue, green, yellow, black, orange

A. WHAT ARE THEY WEARING?

1. skirt	4. a uniform
2. sport jacket	5. jumper
3. suit	

B. TWO CLOTHING SALES

Clothing	Price
dresses	$65
skirts	$45
blazers	$80
shorts	$25
blouses	$35
T-shirts	$16
three-piece suits	$250
sweaters	$50
overalls	$65
shirts	$40
turtlenecks	$20
ties	$30
jeans	$29
jerseys	$18

1. Martin's Department Store $320
2. The Casual Shop $79
3. Martin's Department Store $145
4. The Casual Shop $63

A. WHAT ARE THEY WEARING?

1. coat	4. cap
2. a muffler	5. trench coat
3. tights	6. down jacket

B. CLOTHING FOR DIFFERENT PLACES

Mr. Garcia

H	baseball cap	C	overcoat
C	down vest	H	rain hat
C	ear muffs	C	ski hat
C	gloves	C	ski jacket
C	leather jacket	H	raincoat

C	down jacket	H	rain boots
C	hat	C	scarf
C	mittens	C	ski mask
C	parka	C	sweater jacket
H	poncho	H	windbreaker

C. OUTERWEAR SALE

Clothing Item	Regular Price	Sale Price
caps	$14	$7
rain hats	$40	$20
umbrellas	$12	$6
mittens	$18	$9
rain boots	$30	$15
ear muffs	$8	$4
gloves	$22	$11
ski masks	$20	$10

WORKBOOK PAGE 68

A. WHICH DEPARTMENT?

Sleepwear: nightgown, nightshirt, pajamas, robe

Men's Underwear: boxers, jockey shorts, jockstrap, undershirt

Women's Underwear: bikini panties, bra, camisole, pantyhose, slip

B. WHICH IS DIFFERENT?

1. b (The others are men's underwear.)
2. d (The others are underwear items.)
3. b (The others are types of socks.)
4. c (The others are sleepwear items.)
5. a (The others are worn on the legs.)

C. HOW MUCH WILL THEY SPEND?

1. $30
2. $27
3. $35
4. $54
5. $70
6. $70

WORKBOOK PAGE 69

A. WHAT ARE THEY WEARING?

1. tank top
2. lycra shorts
3. leotard
4. bathing suit
5. sweatband
6. high-tops
7. sandals
8. running shoes
9. cowboy boots

WORKBOOK PAGE 70

A. WHICH ITEM?

1. necklace
2. wallet
3. ring
4. briefcase
5. change purse
6. backpack
7. locket

B. WHAT'S IN THE BAG?

1. c
2. d
3. a
4. f
5. b
6. e

C. MRS. NELSON'S JEWELRY

Items Stolen	Value
diamond necklace	$1,000
gold cuff links	$350
engagement ring	$700
silver bracelet	$300
earrings	$150
silver brooch	$250
gold chain	$100
beads	$400

The robbers didn't take her locket, watch, or pearl necklace.

WORKBOOK PAGE 71

A. WHICH ONE DOESN'T BELONG?

1. c
2. d
3. a
4. c
5. d

B. COMPLETE THE STORE SIGNS

1. striped short-sleeved cotton
2. Solid white wool turtleneck sweaters
3. large print cotton
4. sleeveless floral, linen

WORKBOOK PAGE 72

A. FIND THE OPPOSITE

1. too plain
2. too baggy
3. too light
4. too narrow
5. too low

B. HOW CAN I FIX IT?

1. Shorten it.
2. Lengthen it.
3. Clean it.
4. Take it in.
5. Let it out.

C. SAM'S BARGAIN BASEMENT

1. ripped pocket
2. stained lapel
3. missing button
4. zipper, broken
5. buttonholes, sleeve, large

D. RETURNING CLOTHES

Item	Reason for Return
shoes	The heels are too high.
shirt	The collar is ripped.
jacket	The sleeve is stained.
tie	It's too wide and too fancy.
sweater	The sleeves are too long.
pants	They're too baggy.

WORKBOOK PAGE 73

A. LAUNDRY INSTRUCTIONS

1. sort
2. dark
3. laundry detergent
4. bleach
5. fabric softener
6. unload
7. clothesline
8. clothespins
9. wet
10. lint trap
11. static cling remover
12. iron
13. wrinkled
14. spray starch
15. closet
16. fold
17. put away
18. drawer

B. CLOTHING CARE

1. jersey, jacket, sweater
2. jersey, jacket, sweater
3. blouse, jacket, pants, sweater
4. pants
5. jacket

WORKBOOK PAGE 74

UNIT 8 READING

1. c
2. d
3. b
4. a
5. d
6. c

WORKBOOK PAGE 75

A. WHICH DEPARTMENT?

Electronics Department: stereo system, television
Jewelry Counter: earrings, necklace
Furniture Department: end table, sofa
Women's Clothing Department: evening gown, skirt

Household Appliances Department: refrigerator, stove
Snack Bar: hamburger, nachos
Men's Clothing Department: boxer shorts, necktie
Housewares Department: food processor, iron

C. THE STORE DIRECTORY

1. 1
2. 4
3. 5
4. 3
5. 5
6. 1
7. 5
8. 3
9. 1
10. 2
11. 4

WORKBOOK PAGE 76

A. WHICH IS FIRST?

1. b
2. b
3. a
4. a
5. b
6. b

B. WHERE CAN YOU FIND THEM?

1. sale sign: discount
2. price tag: regular price, sale price
3. labels: care instructions, material, size
4. receipt: price, sales tax, total price

C. COMPARING RECEIPTS

The Dress:

Whose Was More?	Nina	Jackie
discount		✓
original price		✓
sales tax		✓
sale price	✓	
total price	✓	

The Jeans:

Whose Was More?	Nina	Jackie
discount	✓	
original price		✓
sales tax		✓
sale price		✓
total price		✓

WORKBOOK PAGE 77

A. VIDEO OR AUDIO?

	Video	Audio
1. tape deck	✓	✓
2. DVD player	✓	—
3. headphones	—	✓
4. radio	—	✓
5. boombox	—	✓
6. VCR	✓	—
7. speakers	—	✓
8. camcorder	✓	✓
9. shortwave radio	—	✓

B. MATCHING EQUIPMENT

1. DVD player
2. VCR
3. video game
4. record
5. tape recorder
6. remote control
7. speakers
8. audiotape
9. TV
10. compact disc

C. CONSUMER RATINGS

1. T
2. F
3. T
4. T
5. F
6. T
7. F
8. F

WORKBOOK PAGE 78

A. MATCHING

1. d
2. c
3. a
4. e
5. b

C. A BIG SALE!

Camera Equipment
digital camera
zoom lens
slide projector
flash
camera case
film

Telephone Equipment
fax machine
cell phone
pager
cordless phone
answering machine
telephone

WORKBOOK PAGE 79

A. WHICH COMPUTER ITEMS?
1. CD-ROM drive
2. cable
3. track ball
4. spreadsheet program
5. joystick
6. educational software program
7. modem
8. word-processing program

B. SHOPPING AT TECH-CITY COMPUTERS

Item	Angela	Mario	Sarah
central processing unit	✓		
mouse			✓
modem	✓		
LCD screen			✓
monitor	✓		
scanner		✓	
printer		✓	
word-processing program	✓		
notebook computer		✓	

WORKBOOK PAGE 80

A. TYPES OF TOYS
Toys You Usually Use Outside
bicycle
hula hoop
jump rope
pail and shovel
play house
skateboard
swing set
toy truck
tricycle
wagon

Toy Versions of Real Things
construction set
matchbox car
model kit
play house
racing car set
science kit
stuffed animal
toy truck
train set

Toys for Drawing, Painting, and Coloring
coloring book
construction paper
crayons
markers
paint set

B. RECOMMENDED AGES
walkie-talkie set
doll
bubble soap
action figure
beach ball

WORKBOOK PAGE 81

UNIT 9 READING
1. d
2. b
3. c
4. a
5. d
6. c

WORKBOOK PAGE 82

A. WHICH ITEMS?
1. check
2. deposit
3. withdrawal
4. bank officer
5. credit card
6. traveler's check

B. GETTING HELP AT A BANK
1. T
2. B
3. T/ATM
4. T
5. B
6. T/ATM
7. T

C. CHOOSING A BANK

Which Has More?	Best Bank	Star Bank
vaults		✓
security guards		✓
bank officers	✓	
ATMs	✓	
tellers		✓

WORKBOOK PAGE 83

A. TAKING CARE OF FINANCES
1. checkbook
2. PIN
3. monthly statement
4. mortgage payment
5. transfer funds
6. cash

B. FORMS OF PAYMENT
— traveler's checks
✓ credit cards
— online banking
✓ checks
✓ cash
✓ money orders

C. HOUSEHOLD BILLS
Allison   5   1   4   2   3
Charlie   3   2   5   4   1

WORKBOOK PAGE 84

A. POSTAL RATES

book of stamps	$8.40
sheet of stamps	$4.20
postcard	27¢
air letter	65¢
stamp	42¢
roll of stamps	$42

B. ADDRESSING A LETTER
postmark   stamp
return address
mailing address
zip code

C. SENDING MAIL AT THE POST OFFICE
These Items Don't Belong:

Ways to Send Mail	Things You Mail
change-of-address form	mail slot
mail carrier	stamp machine
money order	letter carrier

WORKBOOK PAGE 85

A. BORROWING FROM THE WESTFORD LIBRARY
1. T
2. F
3. T
4. F
5. T
6. F
7. F
8. F

B. WHAT FLOOR?

WESTFORD PUBLIC LIBRARY	
	Floor
Card Catalog	1
Checkout Desk	1
Children's Section	2
Foreign Language Section	3
Media Section	2
Microfilm	3
Periodical Section	1
Photocopier	3
Reference Section	3

C. WHAT'S ON THE CARD?
1. b
2. Buddy Finds a Friend
3. Mary Susan Welles
4. children's

WORKBOOK PAGE 86

A. WHICH IS DIFFERENT?
1. b (The others are places.)
2. c (The others are vehicles.)
3. d (The others are places of worship.)
4. d (The others are people.)
5. c (The others are for play or recreation.)
6. d (The others are people.)
7. c (The others are buildings.)

B. WHAT DOES WATERVILLE NEED?
1. police officers, police cars
2. sanitation workers
3. gym
4. nursery
5. ambulances, paramedics
6. fire engines
7. emergency room
8. eldercare workers

WORKBOOK PAGE 87

A. WHAT'S THE HEADLINE?
1. ROBBERY
2. EXPLOSION
3. VANDALISM
4. TRAIN DERAILMENT
5. CHEMICAL SPILL
6. DOWNED POWER LINE
7. FIRE

B. CRIME IN FIVE CITIES

Robbery	Burglary
Riverton	Riverton
Paxton	Bradbury
Greenbrier	Paxton
Yorkville	Greenbrier
Bradbury	Yorkville

Assault	Murder
Greenbrier	Paxton
Paxton	Riverton
Riverton	Greenbrier
Yorkville	Bradbury
Bradbury	Yorkville

WORKBOOK PAGE 88

UNIT 10 READING
1. c
2. a
3. d
4. b
5. d
6. c

WORKBOOK PAGE 89

A. WHICH IS DIFFERENT?
1. b (The others are part of the face.)
2. c (The others are part of the mouth.)
3. b (The others are part of the face.)
4. d (The others are part of the skeletal system.)
5. b (The others are types of hair.)

6. b (The others are part of the hand.)
7. d (The others are internal organs.)
8. a (The others are part of the eye.)
9. c (The others are part of the leg.)

B. WHAT IS IT?

1. i	7. a
2. e	8. g
3. l	9. j
4. d	10. c
5. k	11. h
6. f	12. b

C. FIND THE EXERCISE

1. C	4. A
2. B	5. D
3. E	

WORKBOOK PAGES 90–91

A. TRUE OR FALSE?

1. F	5. F
2. T	6. F
3. F	7. T
4. T	8. F

B. FIND THE AILMENTS

1. d	6. g
2. f	7. i
3. e	8. a
4. h	9. c
5. b	

C. TIME TO CALL THE DOCTOR

1. itchy   _____
2. scrapes   bleeding
3. _____   cough, breath
4. _____   fever, stiff
5. sore throat   _____
6. _____   blisters, infection
7. vomiting   dizzy
8. sprains

E. WHY ACME'S EMPLOYEES ARE MISSING WORK

(See page 171.)

WORKBOOK PAGE 92

A. THE WHITMAN SCHOOL

adhesive tape
antihistamine cream
antibiotic ointment
Band-Aids
elastic bandage
gauze
hydrogen peroxide
pain reliever
tweezers

B. WHAT CAN THEY USE?

1. antibiotic ointment, Band-Aids
2. hydrogen peroxide, tweezers
3. antibiotic ointment, gauze
4. adhesive tape, elastic bandage, pain reliever
5. antihistamine cream

C. WHAT DO THEY NEED?

antiseptic wipes
first-aid manual
splint

D. WHAT'S THE REMEDY?

1. d	4. c
2. e	5. b
3. a	

WORKBOOK PAGE 93

A. HOW DID IT HAPPEN?

1. d	5. g
2. a	6. c
3. h	7. e
4. b	8. f

C. ARE THEY CONTAGIOUS?

Contagious: measles, mumps, chicken pox, TB, AIDS
Not Contagious: asthma, cancer, depression, diabetes, heart disease, high blood pressure

WORKBOOK PAGE 94

A. THEY GO TOGETHER

1. scale	5. eye chart
2. thermometer	6. X-ray machine
3. syringe	7. blood pressure gauge
4. stethoscope	

C. WHAT ARE THEY DOING?

1. e	5. a
2. f	6. g
3. d	7. c
4. b	

E. THE DOCTOR'S BAG

These items don't belong:
scale
examination table
X-ray machine

WORKBOOK PAGE 95

A. WHICH IS DIFFERENT?

1. c (The others are medical personnel.)
2. a (The others are medical devices.)
3. b (The others are paper forms or cards.)
4. c (The others are types of needles.)
5. a (The others are things you do to a wound.)
6. d (The others are related to a dental procedure.)

B. DOCTOR, DENTIST, OR BOTH?

1. B	7. B
2. DE	8. DO
3. B	9. B
4. DO	10. DE
5. B	11. DE
6. DE	12. B

C. WHEN DOES IT HAPPEN?

7	4
10	2
1	5
9	3
6	8

WORKBOOK PAGE 96

A. BAD ADVICE

1. b	4. b
2. a	5. c
3. b	6. a

WORKBOOK PAGE 97

A. AILMENTS AND MEDICINE

1. e	6. h
2. c	7. b
3. g	8. f
4. a	9. d
5. i	

B. WHAT'S THE DOSAGE?

1. B	4. C
2. F	5. E
3. A	6. D

C. FOLLOW THE INSTRUCTIONS

1. c	4. b
2. a	5. d
3. e	

WORKBOOK PAGE 98

A. SPECIALISTS AND WHAT THEY TREAT

1. f	6. a
2. d	7. h
3. i	8. e
4. b	9. c
5. g	

C. INSURANCE COVERAGE OF SPECIALISTS

Medical Specialist	Referral?	% paid
orthopedist	Yes	100%
chiropractor	No	60%
therapist	No	80%
ENT specialist	Yes	100%
acupuncturist	No	0%
gynecologist	No	100%

WORKBOOK PAGE 99

A. IN A PATIENT'S ROOM

bed control
bed table
doctor
hospital bed
hospital gown
I.V.
medical chart
patient

B. PERSON, PLACE, OR THING?

PER	T	T	PL	PER
PL	PER	PER	T	T

C. WHERE IN THE HOSPITAL?

Person	Floor
anesthesiologist	4
X-ray technician	5
nurse	6
lab technician	2
surgical nurse	4
EMT	1
obstetrician	3

WORKBOOK PAGE 100

A. WHICH PRODUCT?

1. a shower cap	6. hand lotion
2. mouthwash	7. barrette
3. bubble bath	8. eyeliner
4. curling iron	9. shoe polish
5. emery board	10. dental floss

B. WHICH IS DIFFERENT?

1. c (The others are for cleaning.)
2. d (The others are for teeth.)
3. b (The others are for nails.)
4. d (The others are related to shaving.)
5. a (The others are for cutting.)
6. c (The other are makeup.)

C. PERSONAL HYGIENE SURVEY

(See page 171.)

WORKBOOK PAGE 101

A. WHAT DO YOU USE?

Feed the Baby	Change the Baby
bib	baby powder
bottle	diaper pins
formula	ointment
nipple	training pants
	wipes

Bathe the Baby
baby lotion
baby shampoo
cotton swabs

B. BABYSITTING

1. c   4. a
2. e   5. f
3. b   6. d

C. NEWBORN BABY INVENTORY

Items Julie has:	Shopping List:
baby lotion	baby shampoo
baby powder	diapers
bottle	ointment
cotton swabs	wipes
diaper pins	
pacifier	

WORKBOOK PAGE 102

UNIT 11 READING

1. b   4. d
2. c   5. a
3. d   6. b

WORKBOOK PAGE 103

A. WHAT'S THE ORDER?

__4__ high school
__1__ preschool
__6__ graduate school
__5__ college
__3__ middle school
__2__ elementary school

C. AVERAGE NUMBER OF YEARS IN SCHOOL

elementary school
medical school
college
law school
vocational school

WORKBOOK PAGE 104

A. WHERE DO THEY WORK?

1. principal   6. secretary
2. coach   7. P.E. teacher
3. counselor   8. teacher
4. science teacher   9. librarian
5. lunchroom monitor   10. nurse

C. BUILDING AN ADDITION

Room	Old	New
auditorium		✓
cafeteria	✓	
classrooms	✓	
library		✓
main office	✓	
track		✓
science lab		✓
principal's office	✓	

WORKBOOK PAGE 105

A. WHICH SUBJECT?

1. chemistry   5. art
2. Spanish   6. geography
3. health   7. computer science
4. home economics

B. CLASS SCHEDULES

1. chemistry   7. 12th
2. government   8. biology
3. 10th   9. 12th
4. physics   10. 10th
5. 11th   11. 11th
6. geography

WORKBOOK PAGE 106

A. WHICH ACTIVITY?

1. school newspaper   5. international
2. chorus   6. student government
3. orchestra   7. community service
4. yearbook

B. THE WEBSTER HIGH SCHOOL YEARBOOK

Activity	Amy	Jenny
student government	X	2
band	X	4
international club	4	1
drama	2	3
pep squad	2	X
debate club	X	3
choir	3	X
computer club	X	3
yearbook	1	X

WORKBOOK PAGE 107

A. ARITHMETIC MATCHING

50 plus 50..............100.......10 times 10
40 divided by 2.......20.........30 minus 10
1 times 1..................one......2 minus 1
10 minus 5..............FIVE.....4 plus 1
5 plus 5....................ten......100 divided by 10
9 times 2.................18........36 divided by 2

B. MAKING 100

200 divided by 2
10 times 10
108 minus 8
500 divided by 5
40 plus 60
100 minus 0
99 plus 1

C. ON SALE!

1. 1/2   3. 1/4   5. 1/10
2. 2/3   4. 1/3   6. 3/4

D. HIGH SCHOOL MATH

__2__   __1__   __4__   __5__   __3__

WORKBOOK PAGE 108

A. WHICH ONE DOESN'T BELONG?

1. c   4. c
2. b   5. a
3. d   6. b

B. WHICH SHAPES?

1. A, B   6. A, B   11. E
2. C, D   7. A   12. A, B
3. B*   8. A   13. D
4. C, D   9. C   14. E
5. D   10. E   15. C

(*A, B is also correct, since a square is a type of rectangle.)

C. JENNY'S LIVING ROOM

1. 14 feet   7. 39 inches
2. 18 feet   8. 36 inches
3. 7 feet   9. depth
4. 4 feet   10. 37 inches
5. 3 feet   11. length
6. 57 inches   12. height

WORKBOOK PAGE 109

A. CAN YOU FIND IT?

__2__ paragraph
__1__ title
__4__ interrogative sentence
__6__ imperative sentence
__5__ exclamatory sentence
__3__ declarative sentence

B. WHAT'S WRONG?

1. d   7. f
2. g   8. i
3. j   9. e
4. b   10. a
5. c   11. l
6. k   12. h

C. I WROTE TODAY

1. composition   6. feedback
2. brainstormed   7. mistakes
3. organized   8. sentences
4. draft   9. corrections
5. revised   10. final

WORKBOOK PAGE 110

A. MATCHING

1. c   4. f
2. e   5. b
3. a   6. d

WORKBOOK PAGE 111

A. LAND OR WATER?

Land		Water	
canyon	meadow	bay	pond
desert	peninsula	lake	river
island	plains	ocean	stream

B. WHAT ARE THEY?

1. d   5. g
2. f   6. h
3. b   7. a
4. e   8. c

D. WHAT'S ON THE MAP?

ocean   island
lake   seashore
bay   peninsula
river   mountain peak

WORKBOOK PAGE 112

A. NEW SCIENCE EQUIPMENT

Equipment to Order	
24 funnels	$40
12 flasks	$21.50
12 beakers	$22
24 graduated cylinders	$90
48 test tubes	$28
12 Petri dishes	$20

B. WHAT ARE THEY USING?

1. Bunsen burner   5. dropper
2. microscope   6. funnel
3. a prism   7. Petri dish
4. crucible tongs   8. balance

C. A SCIENCE EXPERIMENT

1. c   4. f
2. e   5. d
3. b   6. a

WORKBOOK PAGE 113

A. TRUE OR FALSE?

1. T   5. T
2. F   6. T
3. T   7. F
4. F   8. T

B. FROM SMALL TO LARGE

__3__ planet
__7__ universe
__1__ meteor
__5__ solar system
__4__ Sun
__6__ galaxy
__2__ asteroid

C. WHICH PLANET?
1. Venus
2. Mars
3. Neptune
4. Mercury
5. Mercury, Venus
6. Pluto
7. Saturn, Jupiter

D. WHAT KIND OF MOON?
crescent moon: 3/29/09
full moon: 4/9/09
new moon: 3/26/09
first quarter moon: 4/2/09
last quarter moon: 4/17/09

WORKBOOK PAGE 114

UNIT 12 READING
1. c
2. d
3. a
4. b
5. c
6. b

WORKBOOK PAGE 115

A. WHICH IS DIFFERENT?
1. c (The others prepare food.)
2. d (The others clean buildings.)
3. a (The others are factory workers.)
4. d (The others build things.)
5. b (The others care for people.)

B. WHAT CAN THEY DO?
(Answers will vary. Discuss as a class.)

C. HOW MUCH DO THEY MAKE?
1 accountant
3 actor
2 architect
4 artist
10 barber
6 carpenter
12 cashier
8 construction worker
7 cook
9 farmer
5 firefighter
11 janitor

WORKBOOK PAGE 116

A. WHICH IS DIFFERENT?
1. b (The others work in stores.)
2. c (The others work for the postal service.)
3. c (The others work in a restaurant.)
4. a (The others deliver things.)
5. d (The others wear uniforms.)

B. THE WRONG JOB
1. painter
2. medical assistant
3. machine operator
4. tailor
5. sanitation worker
6. stock clerk
7. welder
8. repairperson

C. GETTING A LICENSE
3 5 1 2
4 8 6 7

WORKBOOK PAGE 117

A. WHAT DO THEY DO?
1. draw.
2. sew.
3. grow vegetables.
4. design buildings.
5. clean.
6. take inventory.
7. sell things.
8. fly airplanes.
9. supervise people.
10. type.
11. translate.
12. build things.
13. deliver things.
14. cook.

C. WHAT ARE THEIR SKILLS?
10 students can paint.
9 students can repair things.
8 students can build things.
7 students can draw and bake.
5 students can sing.
4 students can sew.
3 students can type.
2 students can play the piano.
Only 1 student can drive a truck.

WORKBOOK PAGE 118

A. JOB SEARCH ADVICE
1. d
2. h
3. i
4. g
5. f
6. b
7. e
8. c
9. a

B. WANT ADS
Dishwashers Wanted
FT   hr.
prev.
eves.

Receptionist
avail.   F
exper.   req.
Excel.

1. T
2. T
3. F
4. F
5. F
6. T
7. F
8. T

WORKBOOK PAGE 119

A. WHERE ARE THEY?
R   C   E   M
R   W   W   C
E   W   W   E
W   M   M   E

B. WHAT ARE THEY DOING?
1. sorting
2. paper shredder
3. message board
4. vending machine
5. an adding machine

C. THE FIRST DAY AT WORK
1. rack
2. closet
3. office
4. assistant
5. cubicles
6. swivel chair
7. supply
8. photocopier
9. make
10. type
11. cabinet
12. conference
13. lounge
14. vending
15. cooler
16. message

WORKBOOK PAGE 120

A. THESE SUPPLIES ARE IMPORTANT
1. appointment book
2. paper clips
3. file folder
4. stationery
5. correction fluid
6. pushpin
7. memo pad

B. WHAT SHOULD HE BUY?
1. memo pad, legal pad, Post-It note pad, index cards
2. letter tray, clipboard, paper clips, file folders
3. appointment book, desk calendar, personal planner
4. rotary card file, personal planner
5. letter tray, paper clips, staples, file folders, clear tape
6. letter tray, clipboard, Post-It note pad

C. TAKE INVENTORY!
cellophane tape
correction fluid
envelopes
file folders
index cards
glue sticks
paper clips
pushpins
rubber stamps
staplers

WORKBOOK PAGE 121

A. HOW MANY?
2   14   2
3   4   3

B. WHERE IN THE FACTORY?
1. warehouse.
2. union notices.
3. assembly line.
4. loading dock.
5. work stations.
6. warehouse.

C. PERSON, PLACE, OR THING?
Places in the Factory
loading dock
locker room
payroll office
personnel office
shipping department
warehouse

Things in the Factory
conveyor belt
freight elevator
hand truck
suggestion box
time clock

People in the Factory
factory worker
line supervisor
packer
quality control supervisor
shipping clerk

WORKBOOK PAGE 122

A. AT THE CONSTRUCTION SITE
1. scaffolding
2. blueprints
3. concrete mixer
4. wheelbarrow
5. backhoe
6. toolbelt
7. pneumatic drill
8. ladder
9. tape measure

B. COMPARING CONSTRUCTION SITES
Site 1
blueprints
front-end loader
ladder
lumber

Site 2
cherry picker
jackhammer
tape measure
wheelbarrow

Sites 1 & 2
bricks
dump truck
pipes
sledgehammer

WORKBOOK PAGE 123

A. WHAT DOES IT PROTECT?
1. eyes
2. hands
3. ears
4. back, body
5. mouth
6. head
7. eyes, mouth
8. eyes
9. feet
10. body
11. feet

B. WARNING SIGNS
D   A   B   C
H   E   F   G

C. WHICH WORKPLACE IS SAFER?
The Ajax Company   __ __ __ ✓
The Bay Company   ✓ ✓ ✓ __

WORKBOOK PAGE 124

UNIT 13 READING
1. c
2. d
3. b
4. b
5. a
6. c

WORKBOOK PAGE 125

A. WHICH GROUP?
Forms of Transportation
bus
cab
subway
train

People
bus driver
conductor
passenger
taxi driver

Places to Wait
bus stop
platform
taxi stand

Things That Cost Money
fare card
ticket
token

Things That Give Information
arrival and departure board
bus route
timetable

B. GOING PLACES
1. bus stop
2. fare card
3. conductor
4. platform
5. transfer
6. bus route

C. GETTING TO THE MID-CITY MALL
1. T
2. F
3. T
4. F
5. F
6. T

WORKBOOK PAGE 126

A. PUT THEM IN ORDER
4 6 1 5 3 2
4 2 1 3
2 1 5 3 4

B. WHICH VEHICLE?
1. minivan
2. station wagon
3. convertible
4. tow truck
5. R.V.
6. sedan

C. TOP 10 BEST-SELLING VEHICLES
1. T
2. F
3. T
4. F
5. F

WORKBOOK PAGE 127

A. WHERE IN THE CAR?
H I H O I
I O O H H
O I O H O
H O I H I

B. TYPES OF CAR PARTS
Necessary to Operate a Car
fan belt
battery
brake pedal
transmission
gas pedal
engine

Safety Items
air bag
rearview mirror
seat belt
shoulder harness
brake light
door lock

Luxury Items
radio
air conditioning
CD player
navigation system
sunroof
roof rack

C. THE STATE INSPECTION
In picture on left, circle the following:
taillights, side mirror

In picture on right, circle the following:
windshield wipers, parking lights, headlights,
side mirrors

WORKBOOK PAGE 128

A. ON THE STREETS
1. b
2. a
3. b
4. c
5. c
6. a

B. INTERSTATE HIGHWAYS AND CITY STREETS
Interstates Only
entrance ramp
exit ramp
exit sign
median
shoulder
tollbooth

Interstates & Streets
bridge
route sign
speed limit sign

Streets Only
block
corner
crosswalk
double yellow line
intersection
traffic light

WORKBOOK PAGE 129

A. OPPOSITE PREPOSITIONS
1. c
2. e
3. b
4. a
5. d

C. TRAVELING
1. through
2. onto
3. over
4. down
5. around
6. into
7. past

D. HOW JULIA GETS TO WORK
1. F
2. T
3. F
4. T
5. T
6. F
7. F

WORKBOOK PAGE 130

A. GETTING A DRIVER'S LICENSE
D A G B
H C E F

C. DRIVING DIRECTIONS
(See page 171.)

WORKBOOK PAGE 131

A. AT THE AIRPORT
1. g
2. a
3. d
4. c
5. b
6. e
7. f

B. AIRPORT SIGNS AND MONITORS

Ticket Counter	Gate	Time	Arrival Gate	Arrival Time	Baggage Carousel
3	72	2:15	36	6:10	D
2	18	1:25	78	5:35	C
3	32	2:45	14	6:45	A

WORKBOOK PAGE 132

A. WHERE DO YOU HEAR THESE?

	At the Gate	At Security	On the Airplane
1.		✓	
2.	✓		
3.		✓	
4.			✓
5.		✓	
6.		✓	
7.			✓
8.	✓		
9.			✓
10.		✓	

B. ON THE AIRPLANE
1. cockpit
2. aisle seat
3. call button
4. runway
5. air sickness bag
6. overhead compartment

C. WHICH DON'T BELONG?
These Items Don't Belong:

For Safety
air sickness bag
tray table

Parts of the Plane
terminal
control tower

WORKBOOK PAGE 133

A. TRUE OR FALSE?
1. T
2. F
3. F
4. T
5. F
6. T
7. T
8. F

B. THEY DON'T WORK WITH THEM
1. housekeeping carts
2. ice machines
3. computers
4. room service
5. pools
6. restaurants

C. HOTEL SERVICES
The Drake Hotel
exercise room
pool

The Drake Hotel & The Bedford Inn
restaurant
elevator

The Bedford Inn
meeting room
gift shop

WORKBOOK PAGE 134

UNIT 14 READING
1. d
2. c
3. c
4. b
5. a
6. d

WORKBOOK PAGE 135

A. CRAFT, HOBBY, OR GAME?
C G H G
H C C C
G H C G

B. WHAT DO YOU USE?
1. a thimble.
2. a canvas.
3. a sketch pad.
4. clay.
5. yarn.
6. glue.
7. binoculars.

C. WHICH IS DIFFERENT?

1. b (The others are related to painting.)
2. c (The others enlarge images.)
3. b (The others are hobby equipment.)
4. d (The others are related to sewing.)
5. a (The others are related to painting.)

D. COURSES AT EASTVILLE

Bird-watching
Needlepoint
Photography
Pottery
Origami
Astronomy
Woodworking

WORKBOOK PAGE 136

A. THE WRONG PLACE!

1. planetarium
2. flea market
3. yard sale
4. movies
5. play
6. carnival

C. TRUE OR FALSE?

1. T
2. F
3. F
4. T
5. T
6. F
7. T

D. CROSS OUT TWO!

1. boogie board, swimmer
2. cooler, life preserver
3. lifeguard, surfboard
4. wave, lifeguard stand

WORKBOOK PAGES 137–138

A. THEY GO TOGETHER

1. g
2. o
3. e
4. k
5. i
6. p
7. m
8. n
9. d
10. c
11. b
12. q
13. f
14. l
15. h
16. a
17. j

B. HOW ARE THEY THE SAME?

1. b
2. a
3. b
4. a
5. b
6. b
7. a
8. b
9. b
10. a
11. b
12. a

C. WHICH IS DIFFERENT?

1. b (The others are playing areas.)
2. c (The others are exercise activities that use the legs.)
3. b (The others are types of boats.)
4. c (The others are for winter sports.)
5. c (The others are things you throw.)
6. d (The others are for the feet.)
7. a (The others are things you hit.)
8. d (The others are things you do with a ball.)
9. b (The others are related to basketball.)
10. c (The others are exercise room equipment.)

D. SAFETY FIRST!

1. cycling, mountain biking, rock climbing, inline skating, snowmobiling, bobsledding, horseback riding
2. baseball, hockey, softball, boxing
3. canoeing, kayaking, rafting, sailing, windsurfing
4. inline skating, skateboarding
5. racquetball

WORKBOOK PAGE 139

A. FIND THE TICKETS

$30 $50
$40 $60

B. ENTERTAINMENT REVIEWS

1. Comedy Club
2. comedian
3. opera
4. opera singer
5. concert
6. Concert Hall
7. musicians
8. orchestra
9. conductor
10. screen
11. actor
12. theater
13. ballet
14. ballerina
15. band

WORKBOOK PAGE 140

A. TONIGHT'S TV PROGRAMS

7:00 (2) children's program
     (5) game show
     (7) foreign film
7:30 (4) talk show
8:00 (2) documentary
     (5) western
9:00 (2) nature program
     (4) horror movie
     (7) sports program

WORKBOOK PAGE 141

A. INSTRUMENTS OF THE ORCHESTRA

1. brass
2. percussion
3. strings
4. woodwinds

B. FIND THE INSTRUMENTS

1. G
2. H
3. N
4. F
5. O
6. C
7. I
8. D
9. E
10. B
11. J
12. M
13. L
14. K
15. A

C. WHICH INSTRUMENTS?

Answers will vary and may include the following:
1. bass, flute, clarinet, saxophone, trumpet, trombone, drums
2. electric guitar, drums, electric keyboard
3. violin, guitar, banjo, accordion, harmonica

WORKBOOK PAGE 142

UNIT 15 READING

1. c
2. d
3. b
4. a
5. d
6. c

WORKBOOK PAGES 143–144

A. THEY GO TOGETHER: Places

1. c
2. e
3. g
4. b
5. h
6. a
7. d
8. f

B. THEY GO TOGETHER: Animals

1. d
2. f
3. h
4. g
5. b
6. e
7. a
8. c

C. WHICH GROUP?

Animals	Birds
bear	blue jay
camel	cardinal
dog	crow
elephant	eagle
giraffe	hawk
horse	owl
kangaroo	parrot
lion	pigeon
tiger	robin
wolf	sparrow

Insects	Fish
bee	bass
butterfly	cod
caterpillar	eel
cricket	flounder
fly	sea horse
grasshopper	shark
mosquito	stingray
moth	swordfish
spider	trout
wasp	tuna

D. CROSS OUT TWO!

1. scarecrow, farmer
2. tractor, barnyard
3. twig, koala
4. panda, hyena
5. slug, prairie dog
6. squid, stingray
7. chipmunk, bison

E. HOW ARE THEY THE SAME?

1. a
2. a
3. a
4. b
5. b
6. b
7. b
8. a
9. a

F. WHICH ONE?

1. lambs
2. goldfish
3. beetle
4. sheep
5. bears
6. whales
7. cotton
8. robins
9. porpoises

G. THE SAN BERNADINO ZOO

3	1	3	5	2
4	2	4	3	1
1	5	2	1	1
3	3	1	2	2
4	1	5	5	5

WORKBOOK PAGE 145

A. GOOD OR BAD?

B	G	B	B	G
B	G	B	G	B

B. ENERGY AND ENVIRONMENT CHOICES

1. solar energy
2. water
3. carpool
4. Oil
5. conserve
6. hydroelectric power
7. air pollution
8. global warming
9. hazardous waste

C. ENERGY FOR ELECTRICITY

State A:	3	2	1	4	5
State B:	2	1	4	3	5

WORKBOOK PAGE 146

A. WHAT'S THE HEADLINE?

1. HURRICANE
2. EARTHQUAKE
3. BLIZZARD
4. TORNADO
5. AVALANCHE
6. FLOOD
7. MUDSLIDES
8. TYPHOON
9. TSUNAMI
10. DROUGHT

B. NATURAL DISASTERS IN THE UNITED STATES

	1	2	3	4	5
Tornadoes		✓	✓		
Hurricanes				✓	✓
Forest Fires	✓				
Blizzards			✓		
Volcanic Eruptions		✓			
Floods				✓	
Earthquakes	✓				

WORKBOOK PAGE 147

UNIT 16 READING
1. c   4. d
2. b   5. b
3. a   6. c

WORKBOOK PAGE 148

A. WHICH FORM?
1. proof of residence   4. driver's license
2. passport   5. student I.D.
3. an employee I.D. badge   card

C. THE I-9 FORM
1. Yes   5. Yes
2. No   6. Yes
3. Yes   7. No
4. No

WORKBOOK PAGE 149

A. WHO, WHAT, WHERE?

Who?	Which branch?
senators and representatives	legislative
Supreme Court justices	judicial
president and vice-president	executive

Which building?	What do they do?
Capitol Building	make the laws
Supreme Court Building	explain the laws
White House	enforce the laws

B. TRUE OR FALSE?
1. T   6. T
2. T   7. T
3. F   8. T
4. T   9. F
5. F   10. T

WORKBOOK PAGE 150

A. WHICH IS CORRECT?
1. law   6. Constitution
2. Preamble   7. 13th
3. had to   8. couldn't
4. ten   9. 1st
5. guarantees   10. women

B. WHICH AMENDMENT?
1. 13th   4. 16th
2. 1st   5. 15th
3. 26th   6. 19th

C. THE 1ST AMENDMENT
1. b   3. c
2. d   4. a

WORKBOOK PAGE 151

A. MATCH THE DATE AND THE EVENT
1. b   5. f
2. d   6. c
3. a   7. h
4. g   8. e

B. WHICH CAME FIRST?
1. a   5. b
2. a   6. a
3. b   7. a
4. a   8. b

C. TIMELINE
From left to right on the timeline:
The Revolutionary War
The Civil War
World War I
World War II
The Korean War
The Vietnam War

WORKBOOK PAGE 152

A. WHEN ARE THEY?
1. c   6. d
2. g   7. b
3. a   8. e
4. f   9. h
5. i

B. HOLIDAY TRADITIONS
1. New Year's   7. Ramadan
2. Halloween   8. Memorial
3. Valentine's   9. Martin Luther King, Jr.
4. Kwanzaa   10. Christmas
5. Thanksgiving   11. Veterans
6. Independence   12. Hanukkah

C. HOLIDAYS AND THE CALENDAR
1. fourth
2. last
3. January

WORKBOOK PAGE 153

A. WHICH HAPPENS FIRST?
1. b   4. b
2. a   5. b
3. a   6. a

B. GOING THROUGH THE LEGAL SYSTEM
1. suspect, police officer
2. handcuffs, Miranda rights
3. mug shot, fingerprints
4. suspect, lawyer
5. defendant, judge, bail
6. prosecuting attorney, witness
7. defense attorney, innocent, evidence
8. jury, verdict, guilty
9. fine, jail
10. convict, released

WORKBOOK PAGE 154

A. CITIZENSHIP ACTIONS
1. c   6. b
2. e   7. d
3. f   8. j
4. a   9. h
5. g   10. i

B. WHAT DO THEY HAVE TO DO?
1. laws   4. register
2. a jury   5. naturalization
3. events   6. Allegiance

C. MR. SNYDER'S CITIZENSHIP CLASS
1. F   4. F
2. T   5. T
3. T

WORKBOOK PAGE 155

UNIT 17 READING
1. d   4. b
2. b   5. c
3. a   6. a

WORKBOOK PAGE 2

D. A REGISTRATION FORM

REGISTRATION FORM		
NAME FIRST Fred		MIDDLE INITIAL T.
LAST Simpson		
MAILING ADDRESS		
STREET 26 Main Street		APT. # 3D
CITY Los Angeles	STATE CA	ZIP CODE 90036
TELEPHONE NUMBER (323) 524-9612	E-MAIL ADDRESS fsimpson@ail.com	
DATE OF BIRTH 4/26/81 Month/Day/Year	SEX ☒ Male ☐ Female	SOCIAL SECURITY NUMBER 914-33-6237

WORKBOOK PAGE 18

A. WHAT'S THE TIME?

1. 9:00 2. ⏰ 3. ⏰ 4. 11:30
5. 2:45 6. ⏰ 7. ⏰ 8. 8:50

WORKBOOK PAGE 35

C. TOOLS IN THEIR TOOLBOXES

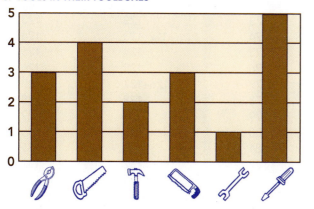

WORKBOOK PAGE 53

B. SAM'S SUPERMARKET

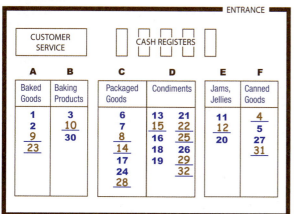

ENTRANCE

CUSTOMER SERVICE		CASH REGISTERS			
A	**B**	**C**	**D**	**E**	**F**
Baked Goods	Baking Products	Packaged Goods	Condiments	Jams, Jellies	Canned Goods
1	3	6	13 21	11	4
2	10	7	15 22	12	5
9	30	8	16 25	20	27
23		14	18 26		31
		17	19 29		
		24	32		
		28			

WORKBOOK PAGE 91

E. WHY ACME'S EMPLOYEES ARE MISSING WORK

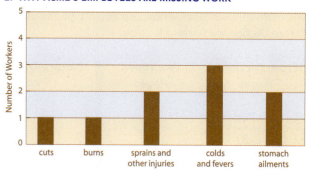

WORKBOOK PAGE 100

C. PERSONAL HYGIENE SURVEY

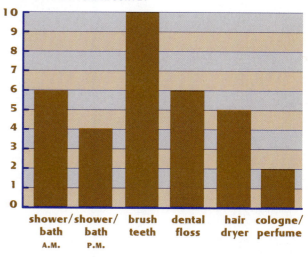

WORKBOOK PAGE 130

C. DRIVING DIRECTIONS

171

PICTURE DICTIONARY/WORKBOOK CORRELATION

This correlation indicates how the activity pages in this workbook coordinate with the lessons in the *Word by Word Picture Dictionary* Second Edition.

Picture Dictionary Pages	Workbook Pages	Picture Dictionary Pages	Workbook Pages	Picture Dictionary Pages	Workbook Pages
1	1–2	55	55	103	105
2	3–4	56	56	104	106
3	5	57	57	105	107
1–3	6	58	58	106	108
4–5	7	59	59	107	109
6–7	8	60	60	108	110
8	9	61	61	109	111
9	10	62–63	62	110	112
10	11	64	63	111	113
11	12–13	48–64	64	101–111	114
12–13	14	65	65	112–113	115
14	15	66	66	114–115	116
4–14	16	67	67	116–117	117
15	17	68	68	118	118
16	18	69	69	119	119
17	19	70	70	120	120
18	20	71	71	121	121
19	21	72	72	122	122
15–19	22	73	73	123	123
20	23	65–73	74	112–123	124
21	24	74	75	124	125
22	25	75	76	125	126
23	26	76	77	126–127	127
24	27	77	78	128	128
25	28	78	79	129	129
26	29	79	80	130	130
27	30	74–79	81	131	131
28–29	31	80	82	132	132
30–31	32	81	83	133	133
32	33	82	84	124–133	134
33	34	83	85	134–135	135
34	35	84	86	136–138	136
35	36	85	87	139–146	137–138
20–35	37	80–85	88	147	139
36–37	38	86–87	89	148–149	140
38–39	39–40	88–89	90–91	150	141
40–41	41–42	90	92	134–150	142
36–41	43	91	93	151–157	143–144
42–43	44	92	94	158	145
44–45	45	93	95	159	146
46–47	46	94	96	151–159	147
42–47	47	95	97	160	148
48	48	96	98	161	149
49	49	97	99	162	150
50	50	98–99	100	163	151
51	51	100	101	164	152
52	52	86–100	102	165	153
53	53	101	103	166	154
54	54	102	104	160–166	155